AF757500

Competition Policies and Consumer Welfare

Corporate Strategies and Consumer Prices in Developing Countries

Edited by

Lahcen Achy

National Institute of Statistics and Applied Economics (INSEA), Morocco

Susan Joekes

Visiting Senior Fellow, Gender Institute, London School of Economics, UK

Edward Elgar
PUBLISHING

Cheltenham, UK • Northampton, MA, USA

© Lahcen Achy and Susan Joekes 2016

All rights reserved. No part of this publication may be reproduced, stored in a retrieval system or transmitted in any form or by any means, electronic, mechanical or photocopying, recording, or otherwise without the prior permission of the publisher.

Published by
Edward Elgar Publishing Limited
The Lypiatts
15 Lansdown Road
Cheltenham
Glos GL50 2JA
UK

Edward Elgar Publishing, Inc.
William Pratt House
9 Dewey Court
Northampton
Massachusetts 01060
USA

A catalogue record for this book
is available from the British Library

Library of Congress Control Number: 2016938596

This book is available electronically in the **Elgar**online
Economics subject collection
DOI 10.4337/9781784717230

MIX
Paper from
responsible sources
FSC® C013604
FSC
www.fsc.org

ISBN 978 1 78471 722 3 (cased)
ISBN 978 1 78471 723 0 (eBook)

Typeset by Servis Filmsetting Ltd, Stockport, Cheshire
Printed and bound by CPI Group (UK) Ltd, Croydon, CR0 4YY

Contents

List of contributors vii
Acknowledgements ix

1. Introduction 1
Lahcen Achy and Susan Joekes

PART I THE DISTRIBUTION OF FOODSTUFFS

2. An assessment of anticompetitive conduct in the supermarkets sector in Costa Rica 29
Randall Arce Alvarado, Donald Miranda Montes and Guillermo Zúñiga Arias
3. The consumer goods distribution sector in Armenia 54
Karine Poladyan
4. The market in cereals in Mali 75
Oumar Idriss Berthe, Massa Coulibaly, Salifou B. Diarra and Martin Sidibe
5. Production and distribution in the beef, poultry and milk sectors in Zambia 94
Thulasoni Kaira, Samuel Bwalya, Wesley S. Kalapula and Florence Banda Muleya

PART II THE DISTRIBUTION OF PHARMACEUTICALS

6. The distribution of pharmaceuticals in Jamaica 123
Kevin Harriott
7. The pharmaceuticals sector in Vietnam 142
Que Anh Pham and Tran Phuong Lan

PART III THE DISTRIBUTION OF SERVICES: INTERNATIONAL MONEY TRANSFERS AND TV PROGRAMMES

8. International money transfer services in Uzbekistan 163
Golib Kholjigitov

9. TV distribution services in Argentina 191
Germán Coloma, Federico Bekerman, Cecilia Castets and Marcelo D'Amore

PART IV PUBLIC PROCUREMENT

10. Public procurement in India 221
Nitya Nanda, M.V. Shiju and Gaurang Meher Diljun

11. Public procurement in Morocco 254
Lahcen Achy and Susan Joekes

Index 283

Contributors

Lahcen Achy, Professor of Economics, National Institute of Statistics and Applied Economics (INSEA), Rabat, Morocco.

Randall Arce Alvarado, Centro Internacional de Política Económica (CINPE), Universidad Nacional, Costa Rica.

Federico Bekerman, Autoridad Federal de Tecnologías de la Información y de las Comunicaciones (AFTIC), formerly National Commission of Competition Defense, Argentina.

Oumar Idriss Berthe, Independent Consultant to the Direction Nationale du Contrôle Financier, formerly Direction Nationale du Commerce et de la Concurrence, Mali.

Samuel Bwalya, UNDP Ethiopia, formerly University of Zambia, Zambia.

Cecilia Castets, Organismo Regulador del Sistema Nacional de Aeropuertos (ORSNA), formerly National Commission of Competition Defense, Argentina.

Germán Coloma, CEMA University, Argentina.

Massa Coulibaly, L'Université de Bamako and Groupe de Recherche en Economie Appliquée et Théorique (GREAT), Mali.

Marcelo D'Amore, Centro de Estudios Interdisciplinarios de Derecho Industrial y Económico (CEIDIE), University of Buenos Aires, Argentina.

Salifou B. Diarra, L'Office des Produits Agricoles (OPAM), Mali.

Gaurang Meher Diljun, Deloitte India, formerly The Energy and Resources Institute (TERI), India.

Kevin Harriott, Jamaica Fair Trade Commission, Jamaica.

Susan Joekes, Visiting Senior Fellow, LSE Gender Institute, London School of Economics, UK, formerly International Development Research Centre, Canada.

Thulasoni Kaira, Botswana Competition Authority, Botswana, formerly Competition and Consumer Protection Commission, Zambia.

Wesley S. Kalapula, Competition and Consumer Protection Commission, Zambia.

Golib Kholjigitov, Kazakh British Technical University, Kazakhstan, formerly the Antimonopoly Policy Improvement Center (APIC) of the State Committee of the Republic of Uzbekistan on Demonopolization, Support of Competition and Entrepreneurship, Uzbekistan.

Tran Phuong Lan, Department for Competition Management and Supervision (VCA), Vietnam.

Donald Miranda Montes, Centro Internacional de Política Económica (CINPE), Universidad Nacional, Costa Rica.

Florence Banda Muleya, Zambia Institute for Policy Analysis and Research, formerly University of Zambia, Zambia.

Nitya Nanda, The Energy and Resources Institute (TERI), India.

Que Anh Pham, Independent Consultant, formerly Consumer Unity & Trust Society (CUTS), Hanoi Resource Centre, Vietnam.

Karine Poladyan, State Commission for the Protection of Economic Competition of the Republic of Armenia (SCPEC), Armenia.

M.V. Shiju, TERI University, India.

Martin Sidibe, formerly Direction Nationale du Commerce et de la Concurrence, Mali.

Guillermo Zúñiga Arias, Instituto Interamericano de Cooperación para la Agricultura (IICA), formerly with Centro Internacional de Política Económica (CINPE), Universidad Nacional, Costa Rica.

Acknowledgements

This book emerges from a longstanding programme of research by Canada's International Development Research Centre into competition policy as an underappreciated yet very important instrument of economic development. Research funded through the IDRC programme was the basis for this book. Susan Joekes was the manager of the programme and Lahcen Achy a principal consultant and advisor. Rohinton Medhora, Brent Herbert-Copley, Andrès Rius and Arjan de Haan were particularly strong supporters of the programme and Julian Clarke and Miriam Ruscio helped greatly in programme delivery. The financial grants provided by IDRC were modest: its greater contribution may have been its ability to mobilise support for the researchers from international experts and to enable the researchers to engage with each other in a spirit of enquiry and in pursuit of good policies for development.

Our first acknowledgement is to the very many competition authorities around the world, too many to mention individually, which participated in the IDRC programme. They include but are not limited to those represented in this book. We appreciate that they all seized the opportunity to enhance understanding of their markets and to fine tune the drafting or the enforcement of their national competition laws.

Our second acknowledgement is to all those who generously facilitated and supported the implementation of the programme as trainers, expert advisers and proposal assessors. Among them we would like to mention Luis Abugattas, Allan Asher, Izak Atiyas, Nigel Caesar, Philip Evans, Simon Evenett, Elizabeth Farina, James Hodge, Peter Holmes, Frédéric Jenny, Eugenio Rivera, Khalid Sekkat and Taimoon Stewart.

1. Introduction

Lahcen Achy and Susan Joekes

OVERVIEW

The fundamental goal of competition law is to support productivity and innovativeness, but in fact the short-term effect of enforcement actions is very commonly to reduce product prices. Consumer welfare gains are a by-product of competitive markets and effective competition policy enforcement. This book presents market studies of a range of goods and services markets in ten developing countries, focusing on the effects on consumers. The markets cover foodstuffs, pharmaceuticals, items purchased to support publically financed activities, TV distribution and international money transfer services. The countries include three in Africa (Mali, Morocco and Zambia) four in Asia (Armenia, Uzbekistan, India and Vietnam), and three in Central and South America (Argentina, Costa Rica and Jamaica).

The studies find a pervasive – although not total – lack of competition in those markets, with identifiable harm to final consumers. Conversely, it may be possible to use the tools of competition policy to bring about gains for consumer welfare. The studies describe the types of investigations undertaken by national competition authorities to understand competition problems within their jurisdictions, the scope of their actions and the influence that competition policy interventions can have on economic outcomes and policy.

PURPOSE OF THE BOOK

The purpose of this book is to give an international profile to the work done by staff and academic associates of young competition authorities, to provide material for discussion in national and international forums and to add to the evidence base for more informed economic policymaking in developing countries.

Studies of competition policy in developing countries have traditionally focused on the effects on producers, that is to say the value of the competitive process to production efficiency, innovation and competitiveness (Hoekman and Holmes 1999). Relatively few studies up to now have addressed competition policy from the consumer perspective, even though competition is not, in the view of some practitioners, an end in itself but an instrument designed to achieve a certain public interest objective, namely consumer welfare (Cseres 2007). Some recent empirical studies (notably by the World Bank, see Licetti 2015 and Kitzmuller and Licetti 2013) have begun to emphasize the impact on consumers. Even so, there is a missing element. Competition rules and enforcement agencies consider that the welfare of consumers comprises a broad pool of intermediate sellers and customers of firms; only occasionally do they consider the impact on the economic interests of final consumers.

Economists traditionally favour a total (production plus consumption) welfare standard on the basis that it generates the most for society as a whole and promotes the maximization of efficiency. Economists consider the consumer welfare standard as arbitrarily favouring one group over another, and possibly impeding the maximization of efficiency, innovation, competitiveness and economic growth. Still, efficiency should not be absolute. It should not be the end but the means to achieve social goals. Consumers usually have a weaker position in the process of bargaining, lobbying and litigation, such that a pro-consumer policy objective seems justified. Therefore, a consumer welfare standard can be seen as a kind of 'rebalancing' measure.

Welfare analysis tends to use a simple framework wherein firms sell products to final consumers; but producers' outputs are most commonly inputs for intermediate actors who then sell on the products to the retail market. When intermediate firms have some market power they may not pass on production efficiencies (or lower producer prices gained as a result of their buyer power) in lower retail prices but keep the savings as rents (Cseres 2007).

This book therefore seeks to understand the characteristics and causes and the consequences for consumers of lack of competition, with interest not only in final retail prices but also in activities within the distribution sector, that is to say in all the businesses involved in transmitting products from the producer to the final consumers. The analysis is based on empirical studies whose authors are thoroughly familiar with the structural and political economy dimensions of the countries concerned.

The book covers the following topics. It reviews the *state of competition* in different economic settings in selected product markets and the distribution activities that lie behind them and identifies the effects on consumers. It describes the *investigations* undertaken by the competition authorities and reveals the kinds of difficulties they faced in so doing.

The studies were based on the assumption, common to all advocates of competition policy, that a workably competitive marketplace is achievable where private impediments to competition are removed and that government intervention to that end may both be necessary and possible. The book thus also discusses the *types of intervention and representation that the competition authorities could make* in each case, including both direct interventions aimed at correcting market failings and other measures intended to empower the authorities within their respective national governance systems.

MAIN FINDINGS ON THE STATE OF COMPETITION

The main general finding of this book is that lack of competition, often attributable to corporate strategies, is a key factor in the failure of markets to function well.

There are two apparently exceptional cases. First, Chapter 8 on the international money transfers market in Uzbekistan describes a spectacular success of the competitive market mechanism. Nevertheless it took several years to reach a non-exploitative market structure and consumers bore the cost in the interim.

Uzbekistan is a low-income country from which many members of the labour force leave each year to work abroad. The stock of workers abroad in 2010 was approximately 2 million people, which amounted to 7 per cent of the population (Ajwad et al. 2014). Remittances sent home by these workers to their households amounted to around US$3.5 billion, equal to nearly 7 per cent of GDP, approximately 30 per cent of exports in 2012 (IMF 2013). At the time of the study, remittances were equivalent to four times the value of foreign direct investment into Uzbekistan.

The tariffs charged on remittance transfers are highly significant to migrant households; they have remained stubbornly high worldwide (World Bank 2013). In Uzbekistan, when the money transfer market opened in the early 1990s and the 'first-mover' company arrived, standard charges were 12 per cent of the amount remitted; some years later, after several other actors had entered the market, the average tariff had come down to 2 per cent. The competitive process was effective in this case despite the first-mover company's attempt to try and exclude other providers from entering the market. However, its tactics proved ineffective in a rapidly growing market. No competition regime was in place in the financial services sector at that time. If it had been, and if action been taken from the outset against the attempted abuse of dominance, the costs to consumers could have been greatly reduced.

The exclusionary tactics of the first-mover company were simply ignored by the agents whose behaviour it tried to restrain and against whom it had no form of redress. The money transfer market displayed some distinctive features that undermined the corporation's exclusionary tactics. The market was expanding on the back of rapid, low-cost technological change and it offered those agents good prospects of providing their services profitably to the new entrants as well. (Such transactions were additional to those carried out for the first-mover.) The money transfer technology was widely shared and agents did not risk forfeiting access to this 'input' by side selling to other providers. These conditions do not apply in all contexts, for example, in the vertical agreements found in agricultural supply chains (Swinnen and Vandenplas, n.d.).

Another apparently competitive case is that of Zambia, discussed in Chapter 5. The study concerns a set of adjacent markets in protein foods (beef, chicken, eggs and dairy). These markets seemed quite well-functioning and competitive, even though the large beef segment was dominated by one very large market actor. The company's position in that segment was due to its superior operational efficiency and the high quality of its products, for which consumers were prepared to pay a premium. The company's marketing strategies included a franchise arrangement for fresh beef meat with the nationally dominant, large-format retailer. The study finds no evidence that the beef company had abused this arrangement. Nor could it be shown, as suspected, that it leveraged its resources into markets for other protein foods where it was also a large actor. However, the company enjoyed major scale economies. These may have served as a barrier to potential rivals if access to land and finance for investment was locally constrained. The study suggests that barriers to entry of any kind that render monopoly more durable may need continuing scrutiny from the competition authority. The authority may also have to urge government to take measures in other domains, in this instance the finance sector, to facilitate market entry and promote the competitive process.

Apart from those two country cases, the chapters all describe markets that are not functioning well, exhibiting a pervasive lack of competition. The main cause is a range of anticompetitive acts by market actors. Two main types of conduct are concerned: exclusionary unilateral conduct by dominant firms and collusion between two or more firms, acting together to generate or seek to acquire greater market power. The ten country studies in this book itemize various instances of corporate conduct of this kind and describe the effects on markets and the outcomes for consumers. Competition policy regimes generally have a third concern, mergers that may have a detrimental effect on competition, but mergers do not emerge as a factor in these studies.

The country chapters are grouped into four sections dealing with groups of related product markets. The themes and findings of anticompetitive acts in the countries in each group are discussed later in this introduction.

In examining the causes of ill-functioning markets, many of the studies also identify factors beyond features internal to, and activities within, the market which contribute to failures of the competitive process. Each country case illustrates the presence of one or more of these external factors. Some relate to the ways in which economic transactions are governed by the state, while others are related to a country's physical characteristics, the level of prosperity and the existence or absence of institutional structures needed to support market functioning. To that extent, the book points to wider problems than corporate strategy in the functioning of markets. It suggests that ambitions to improve market outcomes need to be tempered with a sense of realism and openness to the need to create or strengthen 'market making' institutions or arrangements. The book therefore also illustrates the power of competition analysis as a tool to the understanding of how markets function, or fail to do so, in real world conditions, well beyond the specific provisions and sanctions of competition law.

The toolkit for governance of economic transactions relies heavily on sector regulation, which is normally understood to fall into two categories: economic and social. Economic regulation generally involves a government-directed alteration of or derogation from the unconstrained operation of the market in a particular sector, typically undertaken in order to address market failure. Social regulation pursues predominantly 'social' aims such as personal health, product and service quality standards or environmental protection, without attention to the particular product markets concerned (Dunne 2015). Both types of regulation can have competition effects. The material in this book suggests that a third type, 'procedural' regulation, which does not obviously fall into either the economic or social category, can also put important constraints on competition. Four of the country studies (Morocco, India, Jamaica and Vietnam) exemplify the competition consequences of social and procedural regulation combined. Social regulations may serve as the basis for exclusion of new players into the market to a greater extent than is warranted, either for products, by means of health and safety standards or, for services, by means of accreditation requirements.

On the evidence of the studies in this book, procedural regulations may often play out to impede competition by fragmenting markets into a proliferation of niches. Market niches are insulated from each other in ways which may or may not have a basis in the real economy, but which jeopardize the contestability of the product market on the national plane.

For example, in Morocco, regional and local government administrations have their own procurement agencies. Each delineates a limited geographic market, each with its own familiar market actors. Few of these actors try to be active in more than one geographic market. Companies located in the central business axis of the country manage it better than others but they also tend to be nationally dominant in their line of business. Licensing restrictions set by sector regulatory authorities in the TV industry in Argentina and in pharmaceuticals in Vietnam and Jamaica also serve to limit the number of players in relevant product markets. Within niches, actors attain and can exercise dominance and exploit consumers. The small size of such niches does not make them irrelevant. Those consumers who are located within the scope of each niche are harmed, and the replication of niches throughout the country aggregates into consumer harm on a large scale.

The interesting question from a political economy perspective is the extent to which the market actors that benefit from social and procedural regulations are instrumental in designing and sustaining such regulations. The same question can be raised in relation to competition law itself, as a form of economic regulation. Among the country studies, Armenia's competition law, and the powers of the competition authority, stands out as having been particularly limited in the mid-2000s. Similarly, very weak consideration is given to competition effects in the regulatory instruments affecting public procurement in India. The consequence has included great wastage of public funds, and tarnished public perception of the integrity and competence of government. The situation is now slowly being rectified by the strengthening of the national competition policy regime and better understanding of the need for coordination between pillars of the regulatory framework.

Other instruments of economic governance are price controls and subsidies. These are designed to overcome failures of the market to generate socially equitable outcomes. They are directed at the operation of particular markets, with the intention of protecting particular population groups from their ill effects. Sometimes these interventions may be poorly designed and the negative impact on competition is unintentional. In such cases the competition authority might be able, on the basis of its evidence, to persuade the government to reverse or modify the intervention. Sometimes an intervention may be undertaken because it advances other social goals or because they are based on a more dynamic view of economic development than is promoted through the market mechanism. Mali provides an example of how subsidies can produce the desired effect in the short term, of protecting food security in this case, but at the cost of undermining the competition process on which the evolution of the economy depends.

The challenge is again to distinguish when policy measures legitimately embody – and in practice succeed in promoting – collective measures in pursuit of some non-market goal, from situations where the corporate beneficiaries of the policy exercises leverage, directly (on government, by providing material support) or indirectly (by manipulating public opinion), in order to sustain such distortive measures. A detailed competition analysis can help to assess the outcome of such interventions, reveal whether they do succeed in their social aims, and show the impact on market dynamics.

Finally, poor physical or institutional market infrastructure can also impede the competitive process. Mali, Uzbekistan, Argentina and Costa Rica illustrate this feature. Mali, and perhaps Zambia, has poor financial services. Uzbekistan's transition to a fully competitive money transfer market would have been faster if the national financial institutions had been integrated into international financial payments structures. Morocco's procurement regime would be improved if the governing framework had the status of law and if there were a public institution to monitor public procurements.

Development of physical infrastructure may be impeded by a country's unfavourable geography or by a pattern of widely dispersed settlement. Argentina, Mali and to a lesser extent Costa Rica also illustrate the influence of geography on competition. Investment in physical infrastructure is slow to yield results and may not be financially feasible without technological innovation. In the interim, poor infrastructure leads to market fragmentation. As in Costa Rica, a given product market may look competitive, but is in fact formed of many small, insulated and highly concentrated local markets. In such situations, it may fall to the competition authority to find imaginative ways of promoting competition and enforcing the competition law at the local level. This might be done by cooperating with local authorities responsible for social and procedural regulations. Having consumer protection within the operational scope of the competition authority can also be useful in this connection. In Peru, for example, the competition authority not only saw the possibility of scaling up its pro-competitive interventions through local authority structures, for example as regards the regulation of taxi services (done at local level), but it also learned that consumer complaints were correlated with competition problems in the relevant market (Joekes and Evans 2008). Another implication is that market studies and research into problems may need to be undertaken outside the capital cities, where competition authority staff may otherwise be forced to concentrate their efforts because of pressures on the operational budget.

NATURE OF THE INVESTIGATIONS

This book also reveals the barriers to research and the many sorts of practical difficulties that young competition authorities have to overcome in carrying out market studies. The book complements other volumes, such as by Lewis (2013), which examines the institution building challenges facing new competition regimes in developing countries. It may also be useful to the work of the community of international scholars and practitioners affiliated to the UN, OECD and the International Competition Network (among others), that are building up knowledge of competition law rulings in different jurisdictions and supply technical assistance for enforcement work on that basis.

First, the studies were carried out by the provision of an external research grant to supplement the authorities' normal operational budgets. All the studies were made possible by grants from Canada's International Development Research Centre,[1] with the exception of the Moroccan one.[2] The Centre developed a competition research grant-giving facility on the understanding that new authorities could be worthy beneficiaries of extra support. Most 'mature' competition authorities routinely carry out a number of market studies, which do not need to be triggered by a complaint or by an intention to prosecute a legal case. Young authorities in developing countries – whose need to increase their technical capacity and build up their knowledge of the economy is so much greater – could benefit from having the resources to do the same.

The IDRC granting mechanism also encouraged authorities to carry out the studies in collaboration with external researchers, of whom most were drawn from local universities. The balance of effort between the staff of the authority and external researchers varied from case to case: from a large role for the external researchers (in Argentina, India and Morocco), to cases where the work was almost completely carried out by authority staff members themselves (in Zambia and Jamaica). A variety of other arrangements were in place in the remaining countries. Although not strictly a condition, the grants were intended to enable working relationships of this kind to develop, partly to lever the authorities' own in-house capacity, and partly to broaden interest within the local research community in competition policy. Dissemination activities were also encouraged in the expectation that they could provoke discussion of the types of policy interventions that might be used to correct the harm to consumers caused by competition failures.

Second, the chapters reveal a range of practical problems that the research teams encountered in carrying out their market studies. In Armenia, the study arose from an attempt to overcome the lack of information gathering powers given to the authority under the law, as well as uncertainty about which elements of a weak competition law could have traction in a setting where a relatively large number of product markets are monopolistic or heavily concentrated and the incumbents are believed to have political connections (World Bank 2013). In Zambia, the authority had limited in-house capacity and was not able to look into the technical issue of cross-subsidization. In Argentina, the fast moving nature of the TV industry reflected the rapidity of technological and economic change.

Several of the investigations required coordination with sector regulators both to enable evidence gathering and to define the type of recommendations that could feasibly be made to policymakers for promoting competition. The researchers in Mali, India, Jamaica, Uzbekistan and Vietnam all managed very well the need to instil a sense of confidence and common purpose with the respective sector regulators in order to facilitate their analysis and make feasible policy recommendations.

PRODUCT MARKET GROUPINGS

The country studies in this book are grouped into four sections examining markets in different parts of the economy. Three of the sections deal with the delivery of goods and services directly to the consumer: foodstuffs and household goods in Armenia, Costa Rica, Mali and Zambia, pharmaceuticals in Jamaica and Vietnam and TV and money transfer services in Argentina and Uzbekistan respectively. The fourth section deals with markets where the delivery to the consumer is indirect, through public procurement in India and Morocco.

The Distribution of Foodstuffs in Armenia, Costa Rica, Mali and Zambia

The four chapters in this section are all concerned with the distribution of foodstuffs. They examine the production, distribution and retail sale of food products in fixed location stores including hypermarkets, supermarkets, department stores, convenience stores, and traditional small corner shops. Despite its often traditional appearance on the street, the distribution services industry has been highly dynamic in recent decades and subject to considerable upheaval. The chapters on Armenia and Costa Rica deal with the structure and functioning of the groceries distribution market in general. Of the other two, the chapter on Mali examines the production and distribution of cereals and the chapter on Zambia deals with the production and distribution of animal protein foods.

The food distribution sector has been greatly affected by the two main aspects of the market liberalization agenda over recent decades. Liberalization of trade reduced the prices of imports and incentivized distributors to seek out international sources of supply. In some countries, the trend towards liberalization of services and capital flows facilitated the relocation of distribution sector service companies. More importantly, the industry has also experienced rapid and extensive technological change, largely ICT based, that has improved inventory control and transportation, leading to scale economies that have supported a universal trend towards increasing size of retail outlets (WTO 2010).

These innovations were very disruptive of existing industry structure and inter-firm arrangements. An extensive literature has examined the employment and income effects of the entry of large international supermarket chains activities into developing countries and the distributional aspects of changes in the relationships between retailers and local suppliers of foodstuffs (for example, Reardon et al. 2003). Local supply chains for fresh produce became concentrated as supermarkets sought to deal with larger scale, reliable producers of homogeneous, quality products. The distributional consequences of these changes were frequently considered to be negative. The most vulnerable, i.e., the smallest producers and lowest income consumers, were often marginalized by these changes. The associated redistribution of profit margins along actors in supply chains was often also a cause for alarm.

The four chapters in this section explore the incidence of horizontal restraints and the characteristics of vertical agreements in the respective countries. Horizontal restraints cover price fixing or agreements to restrict output among economic actors that would otherwise be rivals, producing the same good or service. Vertical agreements involve arrangements between actors in a supply chain, carrying out complementary activities. Vertical arrangements may be anticompetitive if they involve abuse of market power – downstream or upstream – by an actor that is dominant at its stage of the supply chain or if they create barriers to entry. Practices that have attracted attention for their possible anticompetitive effect in this regard include resale price maintenance, selective distribution, exclusive dealing arrangements, delineation of exclusive territories, predatory pricing, bundling, and listing, shelf and advertising fees. Some of these practices were found to be present in Costa Rica and Armenia, but they did not impact on the final consumer in ways that allowed for prosecution under the competition law.

The competition effects of vertical arrangements are complex and not treated in the same way across jurisdictions. Franchises, such as those studied in Zambia, are exempted from scrutiny under the competition law in some jurisdictions, such as the EU, on condition that they do not include anticompetitive price setting provisions or territorial and resale prohibitions. Some countries do not rely on competition law provisions to regulate the distribution sector. Instead they have developed codes of good practice – often non-binding or a mix of self-regulatory and legal-regulatory approaches – to govern buyer–supplier relationships and to help prevent and resolve conflicts (WTO 2010). Chapter 3 on Armenia is concerned with market power and the behaviour of market actors in the retail distribution sector in general. First it is concerned to understand the features of the modern fast-evolving distribution sector, which does not in this case include foreign investors. The study focuses on vertical arrangements and examines whether dominant distributors (and suppliers) impose coercive provisions in their transactions in the market that may deter competition. In general, it finds that they do not.

The situation in Armenia is coloured by two special features that are of as much interest as the empirical findings. One is that a relatively large number of food product markets are supplied almost entirely by imports through importing channels that are heavily concentrated. Yet the competition authority had not been able to investigate possible abuse by these importers, partly for political reasons, given that the dominant companies are believed to flourish on the basis of close relations between the business owners and the political authorities. Second, the provisions of the competition law – although modelled on the EU's competition framework – reflected some key elements of the previous central planning regime. During that period, large-scale production was carried out almost entirely by state-owned enterprises, which priced their products on a cost plus basis and were not subject to public scrutiny. Few state-owned enterprises remain, but even so anticompetitive conduct was defined under the Armenian competition law as price rises (whether concerted or not) that are unjustified by underlying changes in costs. This definition had been a significant limitation on possibilities of competition law enforcement.

The Costa Rica chapter (Chapter 2) focuses on retail distribution in three cities. It explores the negotiations and the nature of the contracts struck between supermarkets and suppliers and their agents. It examines how the dominance of one, internationally connected supermarket plays out in the sector. In supermarkets in Costa Rica, market dominance and supermarkets' own-brand products can enable some retailers to reduce the profits and impose stringent conditions on their suppliers. The chapter also bears out the importance of spatial analysis, by showing the different competition status of markets in the three cities. In particular, the lower level of concentration of the market in one locality is associated with the formation of supplier associations. There, cooperation among suppliers significantly increases their bargaining power in negotiations with the supermarket that has a dominant position at national level. This carries clear strategic and perhaps policy implications for redressing what might otherwise seem the overwhelming dominance of a large, internationally connected business in the supermarket segment.

In the study of the production and distribution of cereals in Mali (Chapter 4), the findings point to an external factor – access to finance – having a controlling influence in the cereal distribution market in Mali. The competitive process is also undermined by the government's subsidization of imports and ban on exports. Like the Costa Rican study, this chapter also points out that the presence of supplier associations and trader networks can increase bargaining power and influence the distribution of market power and the associated distribution of economic actors' margins along the supply chain.

Chapter 5 on Zambia examines the impact of the dominance of one 'industrial' beef producer in a country where meat is traditionally produced by small-scale herders and farmers. This is an international but not a foreign enterprise; it is locally owned and the company is expanding into other regional markets. The company is also active in chicken meat, eggs and milk production. The main element of its distribution strategy has been to operate franchised fresh butchery counters in the overwhelmingly dominant supermarket chain, a foreign-owned company. Beef meat prices are set above its rivals thanks to this arrangement. The company's market dominance is undisputed in the beef segment. The competition issue is to understand the extent to which its dominance of the beef market may be sustained by the barriers to entry set by the franchise arrangement, and whether it uses its market power to amass resources and cross-subsidize the other lines of business. The study concludes that insufficient evidence is available to open an official investigation into anticompetitive conduct in any of these markets. It is clear that the enterprise has vastly superior efficiency in beef production but it is not clear whether this producer surplus outweighs harm to traditional producers and consumers. On the one hand, the supermarket requires high product quality standards from which the consumer benefits. On the other, the producer does provide sales opportunities to traditional beef producers and gives them technical assistance to improve the efficiency of their operations. The findings of this study should not be seen as disappointing. It shows the competition authority was able to examine enterprise conduct in all its complexity and that it was ready to acknowledge efficiency improvements where they are found. Moreover, its analysis supported an important 'market making' recommendation that could lead to wider productivity gains without any costs to consumer welfare.

The Distribution of Pharmaceuticals in Jamaica and Vietnam

Almost everyone needs medicines at some point in their life; everyone needs the reassurance of knowing that pharmaceutical products are widely available and accessibly priced.

Almost one-third of the world population, mostly in poor countries, does not have access to the medicines they need to heal their disease or alleviate their suffering (WHO 2004). The World Bank estimated that chronic diseases would be the leading cause of death in the developing world by 2015 (Adeyi et al. 2007). Medicines to treat such diseases exist, but their prices tend to be far beyond the means of developing country governments and populations.

The affordability of medicines can be seen as having three components: national health policies; patent protection; and competition in the supply of pharmaceuticals.

National healthcare policies cover, among other things, the extent of health insurance coverage and a generic drugs substitution policy by the government. Together these determine which drugs are covered by health insurance schemes. In Vietnam (Chapter 7), the list of drugs that are reimbursed by health insurance has not been sufficiently developed on the basis of evidence of cost-effectiveness. The literature on access to essential medicines in developing countries has paid most attention to the role of patents, specifically the relationship between patent protection and high drug prices. The rationale for the patent system rests on the assumption that granting temporary monopolies to an inventor encourages innovation and allows the inventor to recover research and development costs. By the same token, however, patents allow monopolistic pricing and prevent competition for the limited period of patent protection.

The third issue, the structure of the pharmaceutical market, and the associated extent and misuse of market power, may contribute to the extent of competition in pharmaceuticals among drugs, including those with and without patent protection. Most of the literature has overlooked the fact that access to medicines might be restricted by anticompetitive conduct on the part of distributors in developing countries. In both Jamaica and Vietnam, researchers have reported excessive mark-ups among distributors. There are suspicions of abuse of monopoly rights by patent-holders in Vietnam and of companies exploiting their informational advantage to extend their market power in Jamaica (Chapter 6).

Generic drugs are the main source of competitive pressure on patented products. Generics are produced by other producers without a licence from the innovator company after expiry of the patent on the molecule that it designed; the patent-holder continues to produce its patented products with their original name and branding. Thenceforth, both the original branded and the cheaper, generic version of the drug are available to consumers. Greater provision of generics could contribute to greater access to healthcare for all. The evidence shows, however, that in many developing countries this process has not been taking place. Why is this?

First, in most markets, consumers independently determine which product to purchase. By contrast, patients don't themselves make product choices but have to rely on expert prescribers. Furthermore, in general, consumers are able to assess the suitability of products by inspecting them prior to consumption (search goods) or in the course of consumption (experience goods). Medicines are a different case. Drug companies producing branded medicines are able to exploit their informational advantage over other actors to acquire and extend their market power because most patients do not have information or are not in a position to compare the characteristics of generic and branded medications. Asymmetry of information among different market players can be a barrier to the entry of competing products. It limits market competition and denies patients the possibility of purchasing cheaper products. In consequence, producers of patented products enjoy unjustified market power and impose excessive margins.

Second, the pharmaceuticals market is complex in other ways. It is fragmented among different kinds of ailments, for which substitution of products across fragments is not possible. Moreover, imported drugs and overseas companies play a big role in supplying – and limiting supplies to – the market. Both issues complicate analysis and policy recommendations.

There are some striking similarities in the recommendations of Chapters 6 and 7. They highlight two issues. First is the need to create a transparent drug market for consumers and other stakeholders by improving information flows. Information needs to be made available to consumers on medicine choices and prices, and to the public on legal provisions and companies' pricing policies and practices. The second theme is the need to improve drug certification with a view to establishing minimum standards and assessing suitability. Affordability and effectiveness need to be among the criteria in compiling a list of drugs that meet minimum standards.

The Jamaican study calls for reductions in the time needed for drug registration so that generic drugs can be distributed as soon as the counterpart innovator drugs are out of patent. The Vietnamese study emphasizes that governmental procedural regulations can be a source of entry barriers through licensing and other legal or administrative requirements. The business registration process in Vietnam, albeit simplified compared to the past, remains unfriendly, costly and time-consuming, and those factors deter entry. The Vietnamese study also suggests that authorities could increase their room for manoeuvre by more actively exercising their right to list or delist a medicine from the health insurance reimbursement system in order to negotiate medicine prices with suppliers.

The Jamaican study suggests that seminars bringing together pharmacists and policymakers could provide both sides with more balanced and complete views of the market, and ultimately benefit patients. In Vietnam, creating a database on market structure is seen as a way to help create closer cooperation between the competition authority and drug administration and help increase their effectiveness in scrutinizing the conduct of dominant companies.

Overcoming information failures and market fragmentation are challenging problems for competition authorities. A competition authority can detect pricing anomalies but mitigation of information asymmetry of medicines needs knowledge on the bio-equivalence of medicines that is beyond its expertise. It requires a formal cooperation mechanism between the competition and health authorities. In 2007 accordingly, Vietnam issued an inter-ministerial circular between the Ministry of Health, the Ministry of Finance and the Ministry of Industry and Trade laying out a foundation for such a mechanism and detailing a procedure for cooperation among the sector regulator, the competition authority and the price regulator under the Ministry of Finance.

Selected Services: TV Distribution in Argentina and Money Transfers in Uzbekistan

Service industries take many forms. The two country studies in this section concern the TV broadcasting industry in Argentina (Chapter 9) and the international money transfer market in Uzbekistan (Chapter 8). These are not intended to be representative of the whole range of service markets but they show that competition analysis is pertinent and has an important part to play in understanding how well consumers are served or exploited in two very different industries.

The two markets are both very important to economic development. Migrant remittances, sent home by money transfers, are a major contributor to livelihoods and an important source of foreign exchange to many low-income countries. TV is a key source of both entertainment and information, and arguably the most important to relatively low-income groups, and TV's information provision function is a key public good in the functioning of effective and accountable systems of government.

The money transfer industry in Uzbekistan has featured intense competition in recent years, with many players now in the market. But the lack of competition provisions in the regulatory framework for the financial services sector may have lengthened the period of time it took for this situation to become established. A standard competition analysis highlights the harm to consumers caused by the marketing advantages enjoyed by the first-mover company. It also documents the anticompetitive acts the company carried out in attempting to continue uphold rent-seeking, mainly by imposing exclusionary deals with retail outlets. A competition ruling would have pointed to the need for the government to act sooner than it actually did to bring other entrants into the market, reduce prices to the consumer and improve service provision.

TV distribution is shown to be a highly complex and wide-ranging market. In Argentina, as elsewhere, it involves multiple products, horizontal and vertical integration, and new opportunities from ever-changing technology. A well-functioning audio-visual market requires appropriate monitoring and sanctioning of collusive behaviour and anticompetitive practices, for example, to monitor the extent and effects of vertical integration. As elsewhere, while it may yield economic efficiencies that benefit consumers, vertical integration can also raise competition concerns. For example, an entity's control of television programming rights and distributor platforms may enable discrimination against competitors in the downstream market, unduly reducing their access to content. Discrimination can also occur when anticompetitive conditions in the downstream market unduly deny access of content producers to distribution platforms (WTO 2012). The dense web of cross-ownership and contractual arrangements in the Argentinean TV industry complicates the assessment. But the study reveals wide price variations in service provision across regions, associated with variations in the state of competition in distinct geographical markets. This indicates the need for scrutiny of the conduct of industry incumbents at the local level.

The key conclusion of both chapters reiterates a point that has emerged from many of the studies: the need for cooperation between the competition authority and sector regulators. In both countries, policy changes along these lines did follow. In Uzbekistan, the competition authority and the financial sector regulator (the Ministry of Finance) agreed that competition law should apply to financial services. The law was amended accordingly. In Argentina, by contrast, the government shifted the competition enforcement burden towards the industry regulator. This may have been because it recognized the competition authority's limited capacity to deal with the rapidly changing technology in the TV industry. But the outcome was also testament to a growing appreciation by the government of the need to institutionalize competition concerns throughout the economic regulatory framework.

Public Procurement in India and Morocco

The scope of this book is significantly widened by inclusion of competition analysis of procurement markets. Public procurement is an important component of domestic demand in developing countries. If the public procurement system is abused it not only involves wastage of scarce public monies, but also restricts the cost and quality of the goods and services that are provided for consumers by public authorities under procurement contracts and constrains access to other public services.

This topic has been gaining increasing attention in the competition community in developing countries, chiefly focused on restrictions to market competition generated by private suppliers through collusion and bid-rigging. The effect of public procurement regulations and administrative procedures and the distortions they can create in the market are underexplored. The aim of the chapters in this section is to address this knowledge gap by analysing the procedural mechanisms that serve to limit or distort competition.

Both country studies highlight the fact that new entrants face difficulties in accessing procurement markets. Barriers to entry are intrinsic to many aspects of procurement because in any type of tender procedure, procurement agents have the right to determine companies' eligibility to have their offers taken into consideration and the assessments made thereafter. The selection and evaluation criteria used by procurement officials are therefore key.

The main anticompetitive practices found by the authors of the two country studies are various barriers to entry that close off the contestability of procurement markets and concerted acts by suppliers undertaken in order to generate excess profits from procurement contracts and to exclude non-colluding rivals from market opportunities. The more concentrated are the product markets in which procurement takes place, the easier it is for incumbents to exclude any potential newcomers.

Public procurement activities are structurally distinct from other markets in that the procurement agency is a monopsony. This facilitates the establishment and perpetuation of collusive practices among suppliers. It does not undermine the strength of standard competition analysis. And where enforcement of competition law is possible, it complements possibilities of redress through administrative complaints and greatly strengthens the possibility of sanctioning abuse of the procurement system.

The Indian study (Chapter 10) mostly takes a legal perspective, focusing on the content of regulations and the rulings in administrative and competition authorities' investigations. The Moroccan study (Chapter 11) examines the competition outcomes of procurement acts drawing on data from a sample of contracts awarded by selected procurement authorities.

In both cases, public procurement is largely decentralized. In neither country does a central procurement authority exist. Furthermore, public procurements are not subjected to legal provisions but to executive decrees. In India, a multiplicity of regulations applies that are not presented anywhere in a consolidated manner (although two states have come out with state-level legislation on public procurement). Investigations carried out by the respective administrative tribunals report many cases of abuse that include failures from the competition perspective and lead to payment of inflated prices in many procurement contracts. The national competition authority also has a role in sanctioning abuses. Chapter 10 examines six main procurement-related cases investigated by the competition authority, which covered possible barriers to entry in the terms and conditions of tenders, abuse of dominance by procurement agencies, and bid-rigging. Detailed evidence was provided in these cases of the alleged abuses. Yet most of the competition cases were dropped because the scope of the competition law is not clearly delineated in this area.

In Morocco, by contrast, the competition authority has not had any formal role in investigating procurement failures. The carrying out of the study can be seen as an attempt to demonstrate that it could usefully do so. In both India and Morocco, procurement procedures require that the price at which bidders offer to execute a contract should be the main determinant of contract awards. In India, price is unequivocally stated to be the main criterion for evaluating bids. In Morocco, the 'lowest bidder rule' plays a critical role in awarding contracts. Thus procurement seems to be driven by 'value for money' considerations. But the studies show that the way in which the regulations are implemented often undermines this objective.

First, the distribution of tenders by degree of openness greatly affects the contestability of procurement markets. Fully open tenders are the most competition promoting. In India, regulations state that open tenders are the preferred type, but in practice they account for a limited – for some procurement agencies, a very limited – share of procurement calls. The issuance of multiple, extremely small orders is often used to bypass open tendering. In Morocco, by contrast, the great majority of tenders are open. In some instances, however, competitive procurements can be transformed into 'calls for quotations'. These are infrequent but of much higher value than other contracts on average. Connections between suppliers and a contracting authority play a substantial role in access to calls for quotations as well as in general contract negotiations. In consequence, while both open tenders and calls seem to present opportunities for new entrants in

Morocco, both are biased against suppliers that have no connection with the contracting authority, however experienced they may be in the relevant line of business.

Even within open tender processes, some selection and evaluation criteria create entry barriers because they are unreasonably restrictive and the complaints and appeal mechanisms available to suppliers are weak. Biased evaluation criteria are shown to play a major role in India.

Finally, the chapters discuss the lack of contestability of procurement markets due to the conduct of suppliers, notably exclusion and bid-rigging by incumbents. The Indian study describes many confirmed cases of bid-rigging. The Moroccan chapter cannot examine the prevalence of the phenomenon directly. It uses two other techniques. First, it assesses the vulnerability of the regulatory framework to bid-rigging, using international good practice guidelines, and finds it to be high. Second, it analyses the bid rate for tender offers. It finds that the average number of suppliers bidding for contracts tends to be very low (less than three per tender) even though in many of the lines of business in which a procurement contract is on offer, the market is not concentrated. A number of reasons for this restrictive self-selection of offers are explored. This includes recognition by suppliers of the importance of connections with the procurement agency. It may also reflect horizontal agreements among potential suppliers seeking a high probability of success for their submission for each procurement contract. In the geographically fragmented markets that follow from the decentralization of procurement, some suppliers expect competitors to respect the special relationship that they have with particular contracting authorities. Conversely, they refrain from bidding in competitors' 'reserved' markets.

The two studies put forward similar policy recommendations. In both countries, it is considered vital to grant the status of law to the rules governing public procurement, to strengthen the appeal system and to protect bidders' rights. Equally important is to better define sanctions – either administrative or, if appropriate, criminal – to punish non-compliance.

Both countries are also thought to need to make better use of modern IT-based means of managing public procurements. Electronic procedures can reach a broader range of suppliers than traditional means of communications, structure and allow for monitoring of exchanges among actors in public procurement and reduce their physical interaction. They ease procedures and reduce opportunities for illicit agreements or favouritism. In India, online advertising requirements are not always followed and in numerous instances tender documents were not being adequately advertised. In Morocco, the shift to e-government has been slow. The public procurement portal needs to be improved to facilitate access to documents and improve search quality. Delays in e-procurement penalize competition and increase vulnerability to harm from collusion. In general, however, there is a need to limit communication among the players in order not to facilitate collusion against the need for full transparency of procurement agents' actions. As in other areas of procurement policy, much international effort has been expended to identify good practice in this respect. Policies for improving public procurement can draw on the shared experiences that have yielded the guidelines.

Procurement systems also need well-trained officials to draft consultation documents and conduct tenders. Procurement officials in Morocco are almost entirely unaware of the risks of bid-rigging and the harms caused by it. It is estimated that nearly two-thirds of the practices that have competition-distorting effects are due to deliberate acts or negligence on the part of officials. Weak controls and the absence of effective sanctions allow these practices to flourish. Setting up an observatory of public procurement or similar institution to identify bid-rigging could overcome a key weakness in the present system, especially since solid approaches for detecting and preventing bid-rigging have been greatly improved worldwide in recent years.

In India, two reforms are currently under consideration that will have competition promoting effects. First, the international Integrity Pact (IP), a quasi-voluntary agreement between a government organization or department and all bidders for a contract, is being rolled out across government. The IP sets out rights and obligations to the effect that neither side will pay, offer, demand or accept bribes or collude with competitors to obtain a contract. Only those bidders that commit themselves to the IP are considered competent to participate in the bidding process, such that signature of the IP becomes a preliminary qualification in the tendering process. The second reform under consideration is the prospective enactment of a comprehensive national law on procurement that takes competition considerations into account in an integral manner.

This leads to the final recommendation in both chapters. Sound implementation of procurement procedures will require a high level of coordination between the various authorities concerned, notably between procurement authorities and the competition authorities. There are strong complementarities between anticompetitive practices and corruption in public procurement. In both countries, enforcement of competition law and investigation of corruption has up to now been conducted separately, to the disadvantage of both.

CROSS-CUTTING ISSUES

This book illuminates six cross-cutting issues.

First, the hinterland of retail goods and services markets involves the distribution sector, which denotes all those economic activities supporting the transmission of products (goods and services) from producer (or importer) to the final consumer. The main economic actors are wholesalers and retailers, with agents, commissioners and other intermediaries in-between. Competition regimes all over the world find it relatively difficult to analyse and provide convincing evidence of the effects of vertical agreements that are likely to be especially evident in the distribution sector.

Horizontal agreements – between firms producing the same goods or services – are presumed to be damaging to competition and innovation and injurious to consumer welfare. They may reduce output and restrain firms from competing for customers in terms of product price and quality or in particular geographical areas. Horizontal agreements are generally considered as the most egregious type of conduct that are necessarily inimical to the process of competition. Accordingly, in most jurisdictions, collusion is taken as a per se offence and demonstrating the amount of harm caused to consumers is not intrinsic to building a case against the perpetrators. This book describes several successful cases of prosecution of horizontal arrangements in Argentina, Armenia and India, among others. The case of vertical agreements is very different. There is no presumption in economics that these are anticompetitive. Any harm that they cause has to be demonstrated and the extent of harm has to be estimated. Even if consumer harm is demonstrated, it has to be shown that it is not outweighed by dynamic efficiency gains supporting the growth of competitiveness in the longer term. In this connection, efficiency gains that rest on scale economies – the most common type – are likely to be particularly important in small economies. There may therefore even be a presumption in such situations that, on balance, vertical agreements are beneficial, generating economic benefit outweighing any potential harm that they may cause to competition or to consumers. Proof of the harm caused by vertical agreements is very demanding of data and technical analysis (UNCTAD 2010).

The material in this book provides illustration of these difficulties. The difficulty is unfortunate because consumers who make their purchases in retail outlets are very exposed to market structures and corporate conduct in the distribution sector. To gain broad public acceptance, competition policy needs to be able to demonstrate that enforcement of the competition law can immediately provide substantial protection and redress to consumers. The task would be easier if competition issues in the distribution sector could more easily be dealt with. Several of the studies suggest that clearer definitions of anticompetitive conduct in vertical agreements are needed. This could include better understanding of coercive behaviour by dominant distributors vis-à-vis their suppliers. On the other hand, the complexity of the economic assessment of vertical agreements in the distribution sector points to the mixed nature of the outcome. Debates on retail distribution, especially as regards the entry of foreign supermarkets into developing countries, have been very contentious in countries such as India and Egypt (Franz 2010; Sebora et al. 2014). Awareness of the efficiencies and consumer welfare benefits brought about by improvements in supermarket logistics need to be part of the picture. Competition analysis adds some rigour to the debate by better defining the nature of the problem and suggesting appropriate policy responses.

By extension, a second cross-cutting theme is that several of the country studies argue for modification or revision of the national competition law, either to be able to address particular competition problems more satisfactorily or to guide investigations and enforcement actions. This approach is quite consistent with the fact that significant, rolling revisions to competition laws have been taking place in many countries.[3] Thus in Armenia, the authors note the need for clarification in the competition law of exclusive provisions and better definition of unfair trading practices. Recent amendments have brought improvement in the enforceability of the law in some respects. In Costa Rica, better guidance on defining relevant product markets is needed. In Uzbekistan, the author argues that the competition law needed to be extended to cover financial services. And in India, revision of procurement regulations has more firmly integrated competition concerns. In some cases, these changes to the competition law were indeed enacted, either initiated by the findings of the studies (as in Uzbekistan) or reinforced by them (as in Zambia, and in Argentina where the balance of investigative authority was shifted to the industry regulator, in line with other countries).

Third, six of the studies have an international dimension. Argentina, Costa Rica, Zambia and Uzbekistan examine the conduct of foreign-owned market actors in the TV, supermarkets and money transfer services markets. Armenia and Vietnam examine matters of cross-border distribution, since in those cases the relevant product markets are often heavily supplied by imports. The ownership of enterprises is not problematic for competition analysis as such; nor are the respective actors exempt from the scope of the competition law. Had the market studies been part of formal investigations, however, the outcome might have been different. Inter-jurisdictional cooperation for information exchange can fail in such circumstances, especially between a small developing country authority and one in a large advanced economy. Multinational companies have even closed down local operations in a developing country in order to avoid prosecution (Joekes and Evans 2008).

Another cross-cutting concern is the need for joint initiatives between the competition agency and other governmental departments or regulatory authorities in analysis, prescription and policy reform. Distribution activities are not subject to sector regulation in the normal sense of the term (although touched by other bodies of regulation, such as zoning laws). Even so, the studies demonstrate that a competition authority's examination of distribution activities frequently overlaps with the concerns of regulatory authorities. The chapters describe interactions between competition analysis and policy concerns with food security, public procurement, access to medicines, and financial services. One motivation of joint initiatives from the competition perspective is to explore how far promoting competition can strengthen other broad development objectives. This book describes how this process works out in many settings.

The studies also show that much work is often needed to inculcate a 'competition culture'. Most of the countries covered in the book are in a transition from a state-led economy of some type (not necessarily centrally planned) to a market-oriented economic regime. Competition policy is part of a broad set of policy reforms intended to manage that transition. Although there has been a remarkable surge of enactments of competition laws in developing countries under the recommendation of international organizations such as the Organisation for Economic Co-operation and Development (OECD), United Nations Conference on Trade and Development (UNCTAD), the EU and the World Bank, enforcement of the law is rarely perceived as a domestic priority. In many cases, indeed, policymakers perceive promoting competition as a negative factor that constrains sectoral and development policies. For example, national champions – often dominant in the domestic market – are seen to be needed for industrialization, and it is often thought that they do not need to face competitive pressures in their domestic market from foreign companies, such as would follow trade liberalization. More generally, there is lack of understanding and sympathy with the objectives of competition policy and its operation. This is not to say that competition policy should always prevail as an intervention strategy: its imperatives may be trumped by broad social goals or by social regulation. Rather its scope has to be carefully delineated.

A well-resourced competition authority can be appreciated for its suprasectoral advisory function as well as its law enforcement role. The competition authority can make recommendations on market 'making', i.e., identifying market failures or defects and pointing to the necessary components of the institutional landscape and market-supporting infrastructure that have a coherent justification in terms of competition (Dunne 2015). Recommendations of this type are not within the analytic or policy frame of – and are unlikely to be forthcoming from – any other body/government department. The competition authority can also help to establish and demonstrate the public accountability of business, which can be a difficult value to instil in transition countries.

Finally, the studies also show that institutional capacity of competition agencies often needs strengthening. In most countries covered by this book, the competition authorities had an inadequate mandate, either overly loose or too narrow, and limited resources; some were subject to political interference or dependent for support from the executive branch. In Mali, for instance, most of the staff work on fraudulent use of weighing and measuring equipment; similarly in Armenia, much of the authority's effort goes into maintaining a register of dominant firms and chasing up firms to provide operational data to keep the register up-to-date, diverting resources and attention away from investigations of anticompetitive acts in the market. Young competition authorities seek to be able to describe market structures, and assess the impact of corporate practices on consumer welfare – perhaps, in certain political contexts, giving it greater weight within the overall welfare calculus. They therefore need to have the technical capacity and the legal authority to investigate and detect harmful behaviour and impose sanctions. The public standing of competition bodies relies on their showing that they can be effective in helping to achieve just outcomes from the market mechanism.

NOTES

1. See www.idrc.ca.
2. It is notable that the Moroccan Competition Council was headed by an academic professor, M. Benamour, who understood the value of market studies and allocated funds in the organization's budget to this end.
3. Revisions to competition law took place in 44 countries between 1997 and 2007, according to Professor Frederic Jenny in his inaugural address to the CUTS conference on Promoting a Healthy Competition Culture in Sub-Saharan Africa, held at Gaborone, Botswana, on 14–15 February 2008; presentation available through the website of CUTS-CCIER.

REFERENCES

Adeyi, O., O. Smith and S. Robles (2007) *Public Policy and the Challenge of Chronic Non-communicable Diseases*, Washington, DC: World Bank.

Ajwad, M.I., I. Abdulloev, R. Audy, S. Hut, J. de Laat, I. Kheyfets, J. Larrison,

Z. Nikoloski and F. Torracchi (2014) *The Skills Road: Skills for Employability in Uzbekistan*, Washington, DC: World Bank.
Cseres, K.J. (2007) The controversies of the consumer welfare standard, *The Competition Law Review*, **3**(2): 121–73.
Dunne, N. (2015) *Competition Law and Economic Regulation: Making and Managing Markets*, Cambridge: Cambridge University Press.
Franz, M. (2010) The role of resistance in a retail production network: Protests against supermarkets in India, *Singapore Journal of Tropical Geography*, **31**: 317–29. doi: 10.1111/j.1467-9493.2010.00406.x
Hoekman, B. and P. Holmes (1999) Competition policy, developing countries and the WTO, *The World Economy*, **22**(6): 875–93.
IMF (2013) *Republic of Uzbekistan 2012 Article IV Consultation*, IMF Country Report no 13/278.
Joekes, S.P. and P. Evans (2008) *Competition and Development: The Power of Competitive Markets*, Ottawa: International Development Research Centre.
Kitzmuller, M. and M.M. Licetti (2012) Competition policy: encouraging thriving markets for development, *Viewpoint*, note number 331, Washington, DC: World Bank Group Financial and Private Sector Development Vice Presidency.
Licetti, M.M. (2015) Bad news for cartels, good news for the poor in Latin America, *Private Sector Development*, https://blogs.worldbank.org/psd.
Reardon, T., C.P. Timmer, C.B. Barrett and J. Berdegué (2003) The rise of supermarkets in Africa, Asia, and Latin America, *American Journal of Agricultural Economics*, **85**(5): 1140–46.
Sebora, T.C., M. Rubach and R. Cantril (2014) Sainsbury's in Egypt, *Emerald Emerging Markets Case Studies*, http://dx.doi.org/10.1108/EEMCS-04-2013-0031
Swinnen, J.F.M. and A. Vandenplas (n.d.) *Contracting, Competition, and Rent Distribution in Commodity Value Chains*, paper prepared for the Third International Conference on Linking Markets and Farmers, 11–15 March, New Delhi, India.
UNCTAD (2010) *Voluntary Peer Review of Competition Policy: Armenia*, Geneva: United Nations.
WHO (2004) *The World Medicines Situation*, Geneva: World Health Organization.
World Bank (2013) *Migration and Remittance Flows: Recent Trends and Outlook*, 2013-201, Migration and Development Brief 21, Migration and Remittances Team, Development Prospects Group.
WTO (2010) *Distribution Services: Background Note by the Secretariat*, World Trade Organization Council for Trade in Services, S/C/W/326.
WTO (2012) *Regulatory Issues in Sectors and Modes of Supply: Note by the Secretariat*, World Trade Organization Working Party on Domestic Regulation, S/WPDR/W/48.

PART I

The distribution of foodstuffs

2. An assessment of anticompetitive conduct in the supermarkets sector in Costa Rica

Randall Arce Alvarado, Donald Miranda Montes and Guillermo Zúñiga Arias

SETTING THE SCENE

Changes in the Supermarket Business Worldwide

In the past 30 years, large supermarkets have changed the retail business landscape around the world. They have introduced larger stores, provided a wider variety of products, lengthened shopping hours and attempted to reach out to a more diverse clientele. This strategy has transformed traditional retailing.

The entry of large-scale supermarkets has been driven by both supply and demand factors. Changes on the demand side are due to a range of economic, sociological and demographic factors. Improvement in standards of living, increased urbanization and higher female participation in the labour force outside the home have all contributed to promote modern distribution. Large supermarkets offer processed food that saves cooking time. Growth in personal incomes and access to consumer credit have prompted more widespread use of large refrigerators, easing the storage of perishable products and changing shopping habits. Affordability of cars by the middle and upper-middle classes favours the expansion of large supermarkets in the cities' outskirts (Lagakos 2009).[1]

On the supply side, since the 1980s trade liberalization has made it easier and cheaper to import food and non-food products (Reardon and Berdegué 2002). New economies of scale made it possible and profitable for supermarkets to hold inventories of many goods, giving them an advantage over small stores. The trend was reinforced by a surge of foreign direct investment into the retailing sector in a number of developing countries.

The emergence of modern distribution has usually been associated with increased competitive pressure on smaller stores, which used to enjoy some monopolistic features within their neighbourhoods. Modern distribution outlets are often blamed for threatening small businesses' survival, destroying jobs and imposing tight conditions in their dealings with small suppliers.

Information Sources and Definitions of Terms

This chapter is a study of market structure, consumers' purchasing behaviour, and buyer–supplier relationships in the groceries and supermarket segment of the food retail distribution market in Costa Rica. To avoid linguistic clumsiness, we refer to this henceforth as the 'supermarket sector' rather than 'supermarket market'.

The chapter draws on four types of evidence relating to the state of the sector in the 2000s. The main, original source is the data from two surveys in Costa Rica carried out especially for this study by COPROCOM, the national competition authority of Costa Rica.

The first of the two special surveys was of a representative sample of households in three municipalities concerning consumers' choice of location for household shopping by type of outlet (supermarkets or small shops) and their purchases by outlet. The second survey was of suppliers to supermarkets including importers, processors, agri-food producers and wholesalers. It covered relatively large suppliers that dealt with at least five supermarket stores. It focused on suppliers' experiences of dealing with the supermarkets, with special reference to the terms and conditions of their sales contracts and the negotiations leading up to the striking of such contracts.

To describe the structure and dynamics of the sector, the chapter uses data in the public domain on company sales by the main supermarket groups and on national and international mergers and acquisitions among businesses active in the sector in Costa Rica.

Finally, discussions with key informants in the sector yielded valuable information, as did a public consultation around the research findings and a private meeting between the suppliers and representatives of the national competition authority, COPROCOM. COPROCOM officials participated in the field study to improve their understanding of market actors' concerns about the purpose and scope of the national competition law and the prospects for enforcement of its provisions relating to anticompetitive conduct.

We employ some common terms to signify particular meanings in this chapter. 'Supermarket', 'supermarket chain' and 'supermarket group' are used synonymously, to refer to a business under the same ownership. The term 'group' relates to the fact that after mergers and acquisitions, large supermarkets often continue to use pre-existing banners on the stores of the business that they now own. 'Banner' is the name on the storefront, by which it is known by the local population. An 'outlet' is any retail business in a specific locality; it can be a store or a shop. A 'store' is an individual supermarket outlet. A 'shop' refers to a small, local enterprise usually family-owned and managed; it may be one of a set of such outlets under the same ownership.

Competition Issues in Retail Distribution

The evolution of the food distribution market worldwide has been characterized by moves towards both horizontal and vertical integration. Horizontal integration among distributors strengthens their negotiating position vis-à-vis suppliers. Horizontal integration can also facilitate economies of scale. This may benefit consumers, but not if the market concentration that it entails allows firms to attain and abuse a dominant position in the relevant market and to raise their profit margins instead of bringing down consumer prices.

Vertical integration in the supermarket sector, nationally and internationally, can also have mixed effects for local producers and consumers. For consumers, integration can lead to improvements in the quality of products and more product branding, partly because of increases in imports. On the production side, it can create barriers to entry, making it difficult for local producers to make sales to supermarkets. One way to improve access for local producers has been to increase transparency by the use of standard terminology for various production processes by all the different actors in the supply chain (Cook and Chaddad 2000; Zúñiga Arias 2007). The complexity of possible outcomes means that internationalization through vertical integration is neither a necessary nor a sufficient condition for improving consumer welfare and reducing inequalities in retail distribution (Reardon and Barrett 2000).

Both market concentration and vertical integration have been taking place very rapidly in the supermarket sector in Costa Rica. Increases in the size of supermarkets and hypermarkets are a global phenomenon (Geuens et al. 2003). The changes have stimulated rapid technological change and greater efficiency in transportation and logistics (Reardon and Barrett 2000). This has led to reduction in direct costs but an increase in the costs of monitoring and controlling the supply chain. Some observers suggest that there is a direct association between population density and the costs of logistical management and hence of product prices (Einarsson 2008).

A countervailing tendency is for the suppliers of manufactured products to seek to integrate vertically in the face of the negotiating power of the supermarkets and the challenges set by rival producers (Wrigley and Lowe 2002; Pitts and Lagnevik 1998).

Some commentators see consumers as the most important agent driving improvements in the location and quality of distribution services. According to this way of thinking, prices, convenience – including, for example, the increase in the amount of fresh produce on offer in supermarkets (Einarsson 2008) and consumers' wish for a more attractive shopping experience – are more important drivers of change. Three other product-related trends have been noted in supermarkets worldwide: consumers' increased concern for product safety; consumers' increased demand for more processed products and ready-to-eat foods; and the emergence and spread of supermarkets' own-brand products (Nielsen 2004).

Summary Findings

Five main competition issues emerge from this chapter.

First, at a national level, market concentration is high in the supermarket sector in Costa Rica. In two of the three municipalities studied it is somewhat below the national level; but in the third area, Liberia, the market is extremely concentrated. There is clear dominance of one supermarket group both in terms of national sales and in all three localities.

The structure and characteristics of the supermarket sector vary markedly across municipalities. In one locality, Ciudad Quesada, smaller supermarkets have formed an association, which has enabled them to compete against larger supermarkets. In another, Guápiles, two major national supermarkets and a local supermarket chain are all present within a relatively circumscribed area and consumers have some choice between them. Finally, by contrast, in Liberia the only market actors are the nationally dominant supermarket and very small local corner shops, offering poor choice to consumers. These findings suggest that local level studies could reveal competition concerns that might not appear using only aggregated market data relating to the country as a whole. Possible anticompetitive practices are revealed on the part of some supermarkets – one stands out in particular as the main buyer from most suppliers. Two of this supermarket's practices give cause for concern: first, it sometimes unilaterally imposes changes in the terms and conditions of suppliers' sales contracts and, second, it requests information from suppliers regarding the terms that they have agreed in sales of their products to other supermarkets. It may only be able to carry out these practices because it has a dominant position in the sector. But it is not clear that this constitutes abuse of that dominance; the competition authority would need to investigate further to decide whether that is the case.

In addition, a possible anticompetitive practice is revealed on the other side of this type of transaction; that is, on the part of suppliers to the supermarkets. Some small shops allege that suppliers demand exclusive deals for supplying certain products. Suppliers' understanding of the purpose and scope of competition law is shown to be weak.

On the other hand, the suppliers appear to have weak bargaining power in their dealings with the largest supermarket chain. This serves to protect its dominant position. Suppliers are concerned that their prospects for doing further business with this group, their main buyer, will be damaged if they bring a complaint to the competition authority, however justified it may seem.

This bodes ill for possibilities of enforcement of the competition law based on the bringing forward of private complaints, even if they are offered in confidence to the competition authority. It also suggests that, paradoxically, the greater the level of market concentration, the more difficult it may prove to be in practice for an action to be brought for abuse of dominance.

THE REGULATORY FRAMEWORK FOR THE PROMOTION OF COMPETITION IN COSTA RICA

The Competition Law

The law (no. 7472) for the promotion of competition and consumer protection was passed on 20 December 1994. It contains a set of principles, rules and regulations grounded in Article 46 of the Constitution. The law filled in a number of gaps in the legislation relating to the regulation of monopolies and restrictive practices, in accordance with the principle of freedom of trade in the Constitution. It was modelled on legislation in various other countries, such as Chile, Argentina, Mexico, Spain, Germany, Brazil, Venezuela and the USA.

Implementation of the law was given effect through Executive Decree no. 25234 MEIC, 25 January 1996, and pre-existing rules such as law no. 6227 of 2 May 1978 (the General Public Administration Law), and law no. 3367 of 12 March 1966 (the Law on the Regulation of Judicial Proceedings). These stand as the legal instruments that govern enforcement of competition and free markets.

The fundamental objectives of the Competition and Consumer Protection Law are to promote and protect competition and rivalry in the market, as well as the rights and interests of consumers, by preventing and prohibiting monopolies and monopolistic practices and other restrictions on the functioning of the market. It also aims to eliminate unnecessary regulation. The rationale for the competition law is that the whole society benefits from greater openness and efficiency in the economy.

The law sets out five areas of intervention: antimonopoly legislation; economic deregulation; price controls, in exceptional circumstances; unfair competition; and consumer protection. To enforce the law, it stipulates the creation of three commissions: the Better Regulation Commission (charged with deregulation); the National Consumer Commission (to enforce consumer protection provisions); and the Commission for the Promotion of Competition (to enforce the antimonopoly provisions and price controls, as necessary). Responsibility for the regulations on unfair competition lies with the Courts of Justice.

The Competition Enforcement Authority

After the enactment of the competition law in January 1995, the Commission of the Promotion of Competition (COPROCOM) began operations in August of that year. COPROCOM is described as an autonomous agency of the Ministry of Economy, Industry and Trade (MEIC), although it depends on the ministry for its budget and its administrative functions. It consists of five permanent and another five supplementary individual members. The permanent members sit for a four-year term and there are no restrictions on reappointment.

A peer review of Costa Rica's competition policy regime by the Organisation for Economic Co-operation and Development (OECD) highlights flaws in these institutional arrangements. It notes that COPROCOM's dependence on the ministry for resources may militate against its operational independence. In addition, it suggests that the way in which commissioners are appointed and the fact that they work part-time may make them open to conflicting interests (OECD and IDB 2014).

In terms of investigations, COPROCOM is able to proceed either on its own initiative or on the basis of complaints to issue opinions and to sanction anticompetitive practices. Article 27 of the competition law gives the commission the power to:

- investigate the possible existence of monopolies, cartels, collusive or other practices that are prohibited in the law, and to issue sanctions accordingly;
- issue sanctions against restrictions of supply, when they have the effect of harming competition in the market;
- establish the means of coordination necessary for sanctioning and preventing monopolies, cartels, concentrations and illegal practices; and

- issue opinions on matters of competition and rivalry in accordance with the law and with administrative circulars and notices, even if such opinions have no legal force.

The commission has a Technical Support Unit comprising lawyers, economists and administrators. It is managed by an Executive Office that functions as a secretariat.

The commission instructs the Technical Support Unit to determine, case by case, whether there are adequate grounds for opening an administrative procedure to investigate practices prohibited under the law. The Technical Support Unit then makes recommendations to assist the commission to reach decisions.

The commission is, in principle, operationally independent in competition matters. It does not have to respect any order to comply and is not subject to any orders, directives, disciplinary measures or other request whether from the MEIC or any other body.

The final rulings of the commission can be challenged within two months of a ruling by application for the motion to be set aside. When an administrative appeal is exhausted, the final ruling can be appealed through the courts. If the appeal is on legal grounds, the case goes before the Administrative Dispute Tribunal. If the appeal is on constitutional grounds, it goes before the Constitutional Chamber of the Supreme Court. In either case, the commission has to appear before the body concerned to give an account of its ruling.

In pursuit of its mandate to raise awareness of the competition law, COPROCOM has had a two-part work programme. The first part entails preventive actions and advocacy, dedicated to instilling a culture of competition and to spreading knowledge about the benefits that the law can bring for consumers and for the market. The second work stream concerns protection of competition and sanctioning of anticompetitive practices. In this area, it seeks to resolve complaints, investigate concerns and to carry out investigations and determine sanctions on its own initiative.

THE SUPERMARKET SECTOR IN COSTA RICA

The Main Market Actors

There are five main actors in the Costa Rican supermarket sector: three main players and two tiny ones (see Figure 2.1).

CSU and Perimercados have stores in all regions of the country. Mega Super has no stores in the northern province of Guanacaste, which may

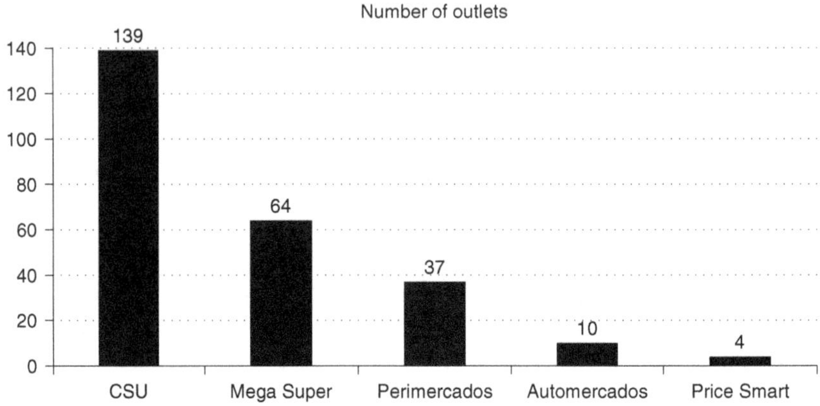

Source: Data supplied by the companies 2007.

Figure 2.1 Costa Rica: number of outlets owned by the main supermarkets

be explained by the strong presence of a local player (Super Compro) in that region; Super Compro was later acquired by Perimercados (see Figure 2.2).

CSU

CSU is the largest player in the supermarket sector. It has more than twice as many stores as the second-largest supermarket (Figure 2.1). It is interesting to examine the evolution of this and other businesses over time. Figure 2.2 shows this evolution. CSU is the sum of four constituent parts: Más X Menos, Palí, Hipermás and Maxibodegas. CSU began operations in 1960 as Más X Menos, and diversified its activities with the introduction of Palí in 1970. Thus it started a process of consolidation in the national market. In 1995, it acquired Rayo Azul, another supermarket that had a relatively large presence at that time. It transformed many of the Rayo Azul outlets into Más X Menos or Palí stores, and closed down the remainder.

Three years later, CSU introduced a new format, Hipermás, which featured larger floor area, greater product diversity and product ranges aimed at middle- and higher-income groups in the population. In 2001, CSU took over Maximercados, changing its name to Maxibodegas in 2005.

Mega Super

This chain made a forceful entrance into the sector in 1999 with the acquisition of SuperSuper, operating since 1983. Later, in 2001, it expanded by opening new outlets that it called Mí Mercado, and one year after

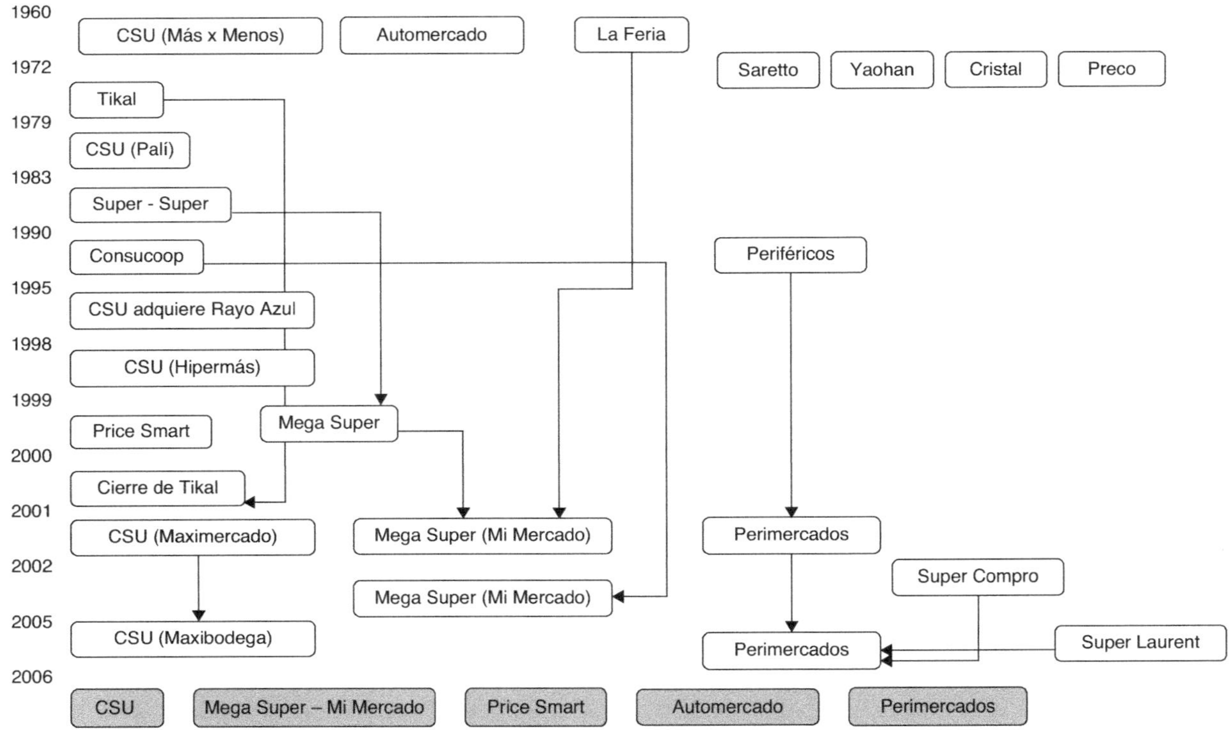

Figure 2.2 *Changes in the configuration of supermarkets in Costa Rica, 1960–2006*

that strengthened its position still further by taking over a chain called CONSUCOOP.

Perimercados

The third largest player, Perimercados, entered the market in 1990 although it did not use its current name until 2000. In its most recent phase, it acquired the two-store Superlaurent group, and in 2005 expanded further by buying out the Super group, which had 17 stores in the northern part of the country. Up to that time, Perimercados had very little presence in that region.

The International Dimension

CSU, the largest national player, also has the greatest number of international links in the Central American region. It has had a regional presence since 1993 when it acquired the Nicaraguan business Cadena La Unión. Later on, in 2000, it expanded its scope by entering Honduras, El Salvador and the Dominican Republic. In 2001, it consolidated its position in the region by allying with La Fraga of Guatemala and Royal Ahold to form the CARHO group. A few years later there was a significant development with the arrival in the region of Walmart Stores, Inc. (USA), the largest company in the world by revenues. In 2005, Walmart acquired a third of the shares of CARHO (raising its stake to 50 per cent soon afterwards) in a move that completed its drive to become a fully multinational business. Through Walmart's investments, CSU is exposed to and shares in the latest international trends in market restructuring and corporate strategy in retail distribution.

Consumers' Shopping Outlet Choices

The household consumer survey

This section examines consumers' shopping location preferences for routine grocery purchases on the basis of data gathered through a special household survey in three municipalities in Costa Rica. The survey generated information not only on consumer behaviour but also on the nature of the retail market in groceries from the consumer perspective. The data is complemented by information on the identity and location of supermarket stores and other outlets in each locality. This approach allows us to analyse the market power of the supermarkets, taking consumer behaviour into account.

A simple random sampling procedure was used that assumed a normal Gaussian distribution of the population parameter. The procedure generated a statistically representative sample of 244 households in the three municipalities (Liberia, Ciudad Quesada and Guápiles), each of which has 40,000–60,000 inhabitants. The sampling procedure took household incomes into account. Consistent with the national household income distribution, more than three-quarters (77.5 per cent) of the households sampled had income of less than 500,000 colones (approximately US$1,000); of those 77.5 per cent, 22.5 percentage points had less than 100,000 colones; 44.3 percentage points had income in the range 100,000–300,000 colones and 10.7 percentage points had income in the range 300,000–500,000 colones.

The identities of the supermarkets are coded (as CO-1, CO-2 etc.) and anonymized in the survey results. The dominance of one particular supermarket in consumer purchases, however, inevitably reveals its actual identity because consumer purchasing habits are consistent with the overwhelming predominance of that supermarket in national sales and with its presence in the respective municipality.

Locational preferences

The survey provided information on consumers' choice of shopping outlet and the reasons for their choices. The itemized shopping locations include the various supermarket chains, including stores that have been acquired by the main chains but still operate under the 'banner' used by the previous owner. The dominant chain has expanded in part through acquisitions and in many cases it continued to operate the newly acquired chain's outlets under their previous banners. The questionnaire also included another category of store, labelled collectively 'small stores'. That category comprises corner grocery stores and specialist food shops such as fresh fruit and vegetable shops, fish shops, butchers, etc.

The main choice of outlet for family purchases proved to be the primary stores of one supermarket chain. It can be inferred that this is the market actor that is dominant in terms of the area of display space, CSU, since, as noted above, it has many more stores than any of its rivals. This chain accounted on average for 37 per cent of all preferences. Its predominance as a shopping destination is strongest in Liberia, where 62 per cent of households do their main shopping there. In that municipality, small/medium-size shops take second place rather than other supermarket chains. By contrast, in Ciudad Quesada and Guápiles, the main supermarket is not the overwhelming choice; instead, fresh food and other small shops combined are very commonly used outlets. The main supermarket chain's outlets attract 50 per cent of shopping visits in Ciudad Quesada and 42 per cent in Guápiles.

Those results do not reflect the real strength of the main supermarket chain in retail sales. Including the shopping preferences expressed for outlets that are part of that business but operate under different names, elevates its aggregate share of locational preferences to 51 per cent, compared to 37 per cent for its own banner stores.

In response to questions about their reasons for choice of shopping outlet, respondents cited three factors. Low prices were by far the main concern, followed by product variety and proximity. There are some variations by geographic area. For example, in Liberia the main reason cited was low prices, whereas in Ciudad Quesada, proximity and product variety also paid a part. In Guápiles, low prices and proximity were cited separately as the two main reasons, whereas the combination of the two only appeared in third place as the reason for choice of shopping outlet.

The predominant supermarket is not only (in aggregate) the first choice of outlet, it also attracts a similar share of the expenditure on food and basic household goods. It accounts for 52 per cent of household shopping in supermarkets in the three localities taken together. It is interesting that the share of expenditure is almost identical to the chain's weight in locational preferences (51 per cent) and not – as one might expect – a higher value. This suggests that the chain's stores are not, on average, relatively larger or do not offer a bigger range of products than their rivals. Alternatively, it may be that their product range is larger but products are lower priced than elsewhere. The latter explanation is consistent with consumers' responses that they are mainly influenced by product prices in choosing their shopping locations; but the data do not allow a full answer to this question.

Another topic is the choice of shopping outlet for 'last-minute' purchases, defined as shopping for products that consumers had forgotten to buy in a previous shopping trip or had run out of at home. In all three geographic areas, small shops or local mini-supermarkets are the most visited for this purpose. In all three areas, the majority (79 per cent) of consumers of last-minute purchases make use of the outlets closest to their homes, almost invariably small stores, for this purpose.

The supermarket sector in three municipalities

The three localities that were selected for the study present distinct configurations of the supermarket and groceries sector.

In Ciudad Quesada, the largest supermarket is used for purchases, but other types of outlet (local supermarkets, small and fresh food shops) are present in the market to a great extent. A special feature is that in this locality 20 medium-sized and small supermarkets have formed a membership organization, the Asociación de Supermercados (ASUM) in order to compete against the large supermarkets. The main activity of ASUM is making bulk purchases of products to be sold; members are invoiced as the products are taken into their respective outlets. This competitive strategy is activated to obtain lower prices from suppliers, both on purchase orders on which economies of scale can be realized and on product lines at which price discounts can be obtained. It has also led to more uniform pricing across their members' outlets. Moreover, some of these outlets are located in the population centre rather than on the outskirts like the larger supermarkets, so they are also convenient for customers.

In Liberia, the main national supermarket has relatively larger presence than in the other localities. Another large chain does not have any outlets in this locality. By contrast, two small regional supermarket chains are represented. There are supermarket outlets in the city centre, whereas small establishments have mostly set up in residential areas on the outskirts of the city.

In Guápiles, the large supermarkets are concentrated on one edge of the city, and the medium-sized and small supermarkets are found largely on the other side. Large supermarkets are located more conveniently for the city centre, have better transportation links, and more people transit through the area on a day-to-day basis. Small shops are mostly located inside the residential areas. A special feature that emerged from field interviews is that in this locality 'mystery shoppers' from the supermarkets go out to check prices and product availability in small stores. Some suppliers are reported to offer rewards to small shops if they refuse to buy their rivals' products. If a complaint about such conduct were placed before COPROCOM, it might well be deemed to be anticompetitive according to Article 12a of the national competition law on monopolistic practices.

In Guápiles and Liberia, small shops get information about market trends and consumer tastes from their main suppliers. The market is therefore quite transparent concerning the products that are of main interest to consumers, current promotions and so on. Nevertheless, small shops are mostly reactive towards market trends. The sector as a whole is quite disorganized. Small shops have little or no negotiating power with their suppliers regarding prices, quantities or promotions or in any other dimension and they imitate the product displays of the large supermarkets. These observations support the idea that the small shops focus on facilitating consumers' last-minute purchases. They offer little or no additional services in their transactions with consumers and sell a limited range of products. This stance may make them vulnerable to problems in the future stemming from the strategic actions of the large supermarkets. If the amount of consumers' last-minute purchases declines over time, the ability of small shops to earn a livelihood will fall away.

Market actors in the supermarket sector have limited knowledge of competition policy and the activities and powers of the enforcement authority, COPROCOM. According to a survey of producers and suppliers,[2] only 15 per cent of businesses had heard of COPROCOM and none of them knew much about its operations. As an adjunct to this study, COPROCOM officials therefore undertook public-awareness activities to correct this ignorance of competition policy in the retail sector. A meeting was held in each of the selected localities of the study with local businesses. Different concerns emerged in each place. In Ciudad Quesada the main topic of interest was price dynamics in pharmaceuticals, in Guápiles the issue was price-checking by external agents and in Liberia the discussions centred on whether, in the carbonated drinks market, suppliers had the right under the competition law to impose exclusive dealing arrangements.

The Relationship between Supermarkets and Suppliers

The supplier survey

The selection of the suppliers sample was made from a 2003 register of 3,000 supermarket suppliers, which was provided by COPROCOM. The sample included 145 suppliers, selected on the basis of scale and the importance of the product. The majority fit the size criterion, having five or more supermarket clients; the rest were smaller suppliers handling key consumer products, such as basic goods.

The larger the number of supermarkets that a supplier does business with, the greater its familiarity with the negotiation process and the greater its bargaining power with the supermarket buyers. Any weakness that they experienced in negotiating with the supermarkets would certainly be found to a greater degree among smaller suppliers. Thus small suppliers' situation is reflected within the survey indirectly.[3]

Ninety-three out of the 145 suppliers responded to the questionnaire. Of those, 44 per cent were producers/manufacturers, 19 per cent were importers, 16 per cent were processors, 10 per cent were wholesalers and 10 per cent were unclassified. There were no significant differences in the reported results by type of supplier, hence this issue is not pursued. The great majority of suppliers (85 per cent) supplied the national market and the rest sold only at regional level. Sixty-five per cent of the suppliers made annual sales of at least 1,000 million colones (approximately $US2 million).

Membership of a producer or supplier association may be significant to a supplier's bargaining power. Almost four out of five (78 per cent) of the respondents are members of such an organization. The main associations are CACIA (to which 23 suppliers belong), the Business Chamber (23 members) and the Merchants' Chamber (19 members). Does membership of a producer or supplier association influence the level of exclusivity

Table 2.1 Exclusivity of distribution and supplier membership of industry associations

		Member of an industry association		
		Yes	No	Total
Exclusive supplier of a product	Yes	29	9	38
	No	36	9	45
	Total	65	18	83

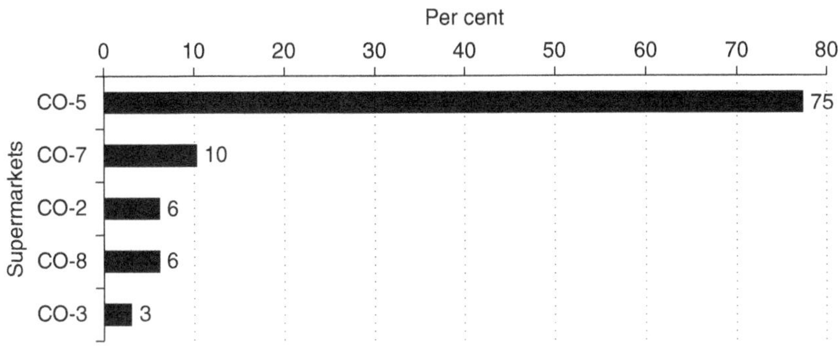

Source: Based on the survey conducted by the authors.

Figure 2.3 Main supermarket buyers of suppliers' products

that a supplier enjoys in the distribution of its products? Exclusivity grants a greater power of negotiation in the terms of a distribution agreement; membership of an association may strengthen a supplier's ability to demand exclusivity in a product, and perhaps to maintain it by for example accepting another supplier's exclusivity in a different product. Table 2.1 shows, however, that there is no such association in practice. Slightly less than half of all suppliers (29 out of 65 suppliers) enjoying exclusive deals; but similar, very high proportions (between 75 and 80 per cent) of association members are found in both cases.

Transactions between Suppliers and Supermarkets

Next we consider the share of suppliers' sales to different supermarkets.

The largest supermarket for retail sales is also, unsurprisingly, the largest single buyer of suppliers' products. In Figure 2.3, 76 per cent of suppliers sell to this retailer, which is marked CO-5 in the graphic. (We can infer

Table 2.2 Suppliers' sales to selected supermarkets, per cent

	10–20	21–35	36–60	Over 60
CO-5	33	36	28	3
CO-7	71	25	4	0
CO-8	82	15	3	0

Table 2.3 Types of sales transaction, by supermarket

	Verbal contract (%)	Written contract (%)	Verbal agreement (%)	Written agreement (%)	Other (%)
CO-1	15.2	10.9	32.6	39.1	2.2
CO-2	10.7	16.0	26.7	46.7	0.0
CO-3	15.1	13.7	28.8	42.5	0.0
CO-4	18.4	10.5	42.1	28.9	0.0
CO-5	9.1	24.7	15.6	50.6	0.0
CO-7	14.7	16.0	22.7	46.7	0.0
CO-8	15.0	15.0	22.5	47.5	0.0
CO-9	5.6	9.3	33.3	51.9	0.0
CO-10	12.9	14.5	27.4	45.2	0.0
CO-11	12.5	0.0	43.8	43.8	0.0

Note: Data are not rounded and not all rows sum exactly to 100.

that this is CSU, but discuss the results in the anonymized form used in the questionnaire.) The other suppliers' principal buyers are CO-7, CO-2, CO-8 and CO-3 in that order. One in five of all suppliers make no sales at all to either CO-5 or CO-1. Nineteen per cent of suppliers make no sales to CO-9 and CO-2, and 11 per cent make no sales to CO-7.

The proportional quantity of suppliers' sales (by value) to the main supermarket is skewed towards higher levels: 31 per cent of sales to CO-5 are 36 per cent or more of their total sales. By contrast, this proportion of suppliers' sales (36 per cent or more) going to rival supermarket chains is only 4 per cent to CO-7 and 3 per cent to CO-8.

Table 2.3 sets out information on the form in which sales to supermarkets are made. Deals are most commonly made by written agreement but the results vary considerably by supermarket. For example, CO-5 uses written contracts and agreements to a much greater extent than other supermarkets. Even so, about a quarter of its transactions with suppliers are done on a verbal basis.

Table 2.4 Suppliers' assessments of the degree of difficulty of sales conditions in transactions with supermarket CO-5

	Price (%)	Delivery (%)	Payment method (%)	Quality specifications (%)	Promotions (%)	Amount of discount (%)
Conditions of sale						
Very demanding	67.5	64.8	27.1	56.9	63.5	64.4
Normal	31.1	33.8	71.4	41.7	36.5	33.7
Light	1.4	1.4	1.4	1.4	0	1.9
Total	100	100	100	100	100	100

The suppliers' survey responses also permit a scoring of supermarkets' perceived ability to influence suppliers' actions, relative to their own power to set their commercial and other terms of transactions. The measure is strongly correlated with the size of the supermarket chain. CO-5 again is perceived to be the buyer with by far the greatest ability to influence the conditions of sale. Along with the four next largest supermarkets (CO-8, CO-7, CO-2 and CO-9), its influence outweighs the suppliers' ability to set terms (in their view). The difference between the scores of the two more 'powerful' supermarkets in this sense is statistically significant.

By contrast, the two smallest, local supermarkets are considered to have much less weight in setting conditions of sale, and suppliers are confident that they have more leeway in those instances.

Suppliers were also asked for their opinion on the toughness of the deals struck by supermarket buyers across a number of dimensions. Table 2.4 relates to deals struck by supermarket CO-5, the dominant supermarket. It shows the proportion of suppliers considering that CO-5 imposes 'very demanding', 'normal' or 'light' conditions of sale. In all respects except for payment conditions, the majority of suppliers consider that CO-5 requires 'very demanding' conditions. Almost none of them consider that CO-5 sets 'light' conditions in any dimension.

In a further elaboration, 32 per cent of suppliers say that at times a supermarket has unilaterally modified the conditions of sale that had previously been agreed. The provision that has most often been modified is exclusivity and the supermarket that has most often taken this step is CO-5 (see Table 2.5).

Despite the supermarkets' greater overall power in negotiating sales conditions, suppliers can and do also change the conditions on their own initiative from time to time. The high value of sales to the national market that nearly two-thirds (65 per cent) of suppliers enjoy (see Figure 2.3), gives them the negotiating power to do this.

Table 2.5 Elements of transactions modified unilaterally by supermarkets: number of cases reported

	Discounts	Quantity	Price	Exclusivity	Payment method	Inventory maintenance	Other
CO-1	0	0	0	1	1	2	1
CO-2	0	1	0	2	1	3	3
CO-3	0	0	0	2	1	2	2
CO-4	0	0	0	1	1	1	1
CO-5	1	7	3	16	2	9	4
CO-7	0	2	1	2	1	6	3
CO-8	1	7	1	7	2	4	2
CO-9	0	1	1	1	0	3	2
CO-10	1	0	0	1	0	1	1
CO-11	0	0	0	0	0	0	0

Table 2.6 Information requests to suppliers about their sales to other outlets, by supermarket

	Prices	Volume	Payment method	Quality specifications	Exclusivity
CO-1	0	0	0	0	0
CO-2	4	0	0	0	0
CO-3	1	1	0	0	0
CO-4	0	0	0	0	0
CO-5	17	3	5	2	3
CO-7	3	0	0	0	0
CO-8	5	1	0	0	1
CO-9	2	0	0	0	1
CO-10	3	1	0	0	0
CO-11	0	0	0	0	0

Suppliers report that supermarkets sometimes ask for sensitive market information relating to their sales to other outlets (see Table 2.6).

CO-5 is the supermarket that has most frequently had recourse to this type of practice. The most common instances are requests for information on the product prices obtained by a supplier to another outlet. Less frequently information was requested about payment methods. Supermarkets vary in the extent to which they ask for information. CO-1, CO-4 and CO-11 have never requested information from a supplier about the terms of its sales to other outlets, and very few instances are recorded

Table 2.7 Proportion of suppliers finding that negotiations with supermarkets are beneficial, by supermarket

	Yes (%)	No (%)
CO-1	93.0	7.0
CO-2	93.5	6.5
CO-3	89.4	10.6
CO-4	91.7	8.3
CO-5	68.6	31.4
CO-7	87.7	12.3
CO-8	88.6	11.4
CO-9	87.5	12.5
CO-10	88.9	11.1

for the remaining supermarkets (CO-2, CO-3, CO-7, CO-8, CO-9 and CO-10).

In an assessment of the benefits of negotiation with supermarkets, the great majority of suppliers (89 per cent or more of respondents) stated that with all supermarkets except one, negotiations had been beneficial for them; that is, had added to their profits (see Table 2.7). The exception was supermarket CO-5. A significantly lower proportion of suppliers (69 per cent) described their dealings with this supermarket as beneficial to them – but nevertheless this implies that more than two-thirds of suppliers acquiesce to the sales conditions set by the monopsonist buyer. The benefit to them is to obtain access to a far greater volume of retail sales.

Finally, for almost one in five (19.5 per cent) of suppliers, at least one of their products had been displaced by a supermarket's 'own-brand' product during the previous seven years. The situation is compounded by the fact that, for supermarkets CO-2, CO-5, CO-7 and CO-8, at least one supplier reported that it had been faced with price or quantity conditions set by the supermarket relating to products that were competing with the buyer's own-brand products. CO-5 was the most difficult case for suppliers; their prices were prescribed in eight out of 58 cases and the quantity supplied was prescribed in seven out of 49 such cases. Even so, this does not amount to a high rate of what might be called coercive conditions for suppliers (see Table 2.8).

Understanding the ways in which supermarkets manage the commercialization of their own-brands is completed with the observation that one-third of suppliers report that they manufacture or supply – or have done so in the past – the products that the supermarkets sell under their own-brand name. The practice is most commonly reported for

Table 2.8 Conditions set on suppliers' prices and quantities of goods sold in competition with supermarkets' own-brand products, by supermarket

	Price condition		Quantity condition	
	Yes	No	Yes	No
CO-1	0	44	0	39
CO-2	1	55	1	49
CO-3	0	54	0	48
CO-4	0	38	1	35
CO-5	8	50	7	42
CO-7	3	52	3	46
CO-8	3	52	2	48
CO-9	0	45	1	40
CO-10	1	46	0	42
CO-11	0	29	0	26

supermarkets CO-5 (37.5 per cent) and CO-7 (16 per cent). In addition, in some cases they indicated that the production of the supermarket's own-brand products had impacted negatively on the sales of their own goods, particularly for supermarkets CO-5 and CO-7. It was sometimes a requirement of their main transaction that they also supply or make the own-brand product.

Market Concentration in the Supermarket Sector in Costa Rica

Measuring the level of competition

In this study we measure the level of competition using one of the most common measures, the Herfindahl–Hirschman Index (HHI). This takes the sum of the squares of the percentage of sales of each of the top 50 businesses in the relevant market (or all, if there are fewer than 50 businesses).[4] The highest possible value of the HHI is 10,000 (when there is a sole business in the market with 100 per cent of total market sales) and the lowest possible value is 100 (when there are 100 or more businesses each with less than 1 per cent of total sales). An HHI value of less than 1,000 signifies a competitive market, a value of 1000–1800 refers to a moderately competitive market and a value of 1,800 indicates a concentrated market.

The HHI is here measured in three ways: (1) using data collected through the supplier survey carried out for this study; (2) using data collected by the COPROCOM, the competition authority, in 2003–4 and (3)

Table 2.9 Level of market concentration in the supermarket sector, HHI for different datasets

HHI – whole country, two different datasets	
HHI – supplier survey data, 2007	High concentration (2,905)
HHI – COPROCOM data, 2003–4	High concentration (2,902)
HHI – three localities, consumer survey data, 2007	
HHI – Ciudad Quesada	High concentration (2,537)
HHI – Guápiles	High concentration (2,053)
HHI – Liberia	Very high concentration (4,394)

using data from the consumer survey carried out for this study in three localities, as above. The calculation is based on the supplier survey and refers to the proportion of suppliers' sales to supermarkets. It is in effect a proxy measure of market structure, using the number of competing supplier businesses in the market as the basis for each one's notional share. This is the methodology used by US Department of Justice in merger cases. In this approach, the midpoint of the percentage of sales reported by each supplier in the sample is weighted by its frequency. This yields a proxy value for the sales of each supplier to the various supermarkets. In the other cases, the index is calculated with reference to the market share of each supermarket as measured in that particular study.

As shown in Table 2.9, the level of concentration in the supermarket sector in Costa Rica is high by all three measures throughout the country. The value of the concentration index is at least 1.6 times the standard threshold level (1,800) that indicates a concentrated market.

As regards the three localities, for two (Ciudad Quesada and Guápiles) the level of concentration is below that of the national market. By contrast, in Liberia the level is 1.5 times the national rate. These results are consistent with our field observations and reflect the differences in market conditions among the localities discussed above. They are also consistent with the spread of consumers' shopping choices as discussed above (and shown by the data in Table 2.1).

The local market in Guápiles is the most competitive. Two major national supermarkets (CO-5 and CO-7) and a local supermarket chain are all present within a relatively circumscribed area and are in more intense competition with each other than elsewhere.

Ciudad Quesada, the next most competitive market, is characterized by the presence of the two largest national supermarkets, CO-5 and CO-7, and an associative grouping of smaller supermarkets, ASUM. The grouping allows the medium-sized regional supermarkets to remain in the market in the face of the larger players. Small shops are also active on the outskirts of the city.

Finally, Liberia, the least competitive and most highly concentrated local market, is characterized by the absence of supermarket CO-7, the second largest actor in the national market. This has allowed the dominant actor, CO-5, to build up a very high proportion of sales. The acquisition of CO-10, a regional supermarket, by CO-8 not long before seems to have had no effect on the level of concentration. Moreover, there are almost no medium-sized supermarkets in this locality, only small shops that are found mostly on outskirts of the town. The dominance of CO-5 forces them into the role of suppliers of last-minute goods to local consumers.

CONCLUSIONS

This chapter has examined consumer preferences for routine household purchases as between supermarkets and other types of outlet (grocery stores, mini-supermarkets, sellers of fresh produce, butchers, etc.). Where the main household shopping trip is concerned, product pricing is the main determinant, along with proximity in some cases. In this respect, there is no significant difference in the shopping habits among residents of the three localities studied. To survive in the market, small shops depend on their strategy of supplying last-minute goods for consumers.

The structure of the supermarket sector in the three localities varies in important ways and the strategies used by local businesses differ accordingly. Nevertheless, CO-5 is the supermarket with the greatest presence in the market in all locations and the majority of consumers choose to make their main purchases in its stores. Another large supermarket, CO-7, has an important presence in two of the three localities, and CO-8 in the third. There is a very high level of market concentration with one clearly dominant actor, through several alternative methods of calculation. High market concentration may be associated with the mergers, acquisitions and buy-outs seen at international (regional) level in this sector, culminating in the recent purchase of the largest Costa Rican supermarket by an international chain. The Costa Rican supermarket sector demonstrates the global tendency to concentration evident in the internationalization of supermarkets and the emergence of supermarket own-brand products.

The study has also provided new information about the relationship between national supermarkets and their larger suppliers. For the majority of suppliers, supermarket CO-5 is the principal buyer; sales transactions are made in a relatively transparent market (66 per cent of suppliers claim to know which suppliers are selling products similar to their own) and sales transactions are mostly carried out by written agreement. For the majority of suppliers, sales are profitable but nearly one-third of suppliers report that their profit margin is reduced in the course of negotiating a deal with the largest supermarket, CO-5. Moreover, this supermarket (CO-5) was the most prone to making unilateral changes to the terms of a proposed transaction, particularly with respect to exclusivity, quantity and inventory replenishment.

Finally, the study examines the role of supermarkets' own-brand products. Some suppliers report that sales of their products to consumers are negatively affected by competing supermarket own-brand sales. In addition, they find that the quantity of their sales, and conditions set by the supermarket buyers are affected by the existence of supermarket own-brand products. However, these effects are not strong.

In consultative meetings with stakeholders held when the provisional results of this study were revealed, the findings were confirmed. Some other interesting points emerged from those discussions in connection with businesses' compliance with the provisions of the competition law and the practicalities of enforcement of the law. Many businesspeople expressed concern about the possible follow-up actions – in terms of penalties and directives – of any competition investigations that the competition authority, COPROCOM, might undertake in pursuance of its mandate. Accordingly, they were uncertain about the economic value to themselves of bringing a complaint. Furthermore, it was believed that a complaint or accusation/allegation could rebound severely on a complainant's operations and even lead to it going out of business. This acts as a break on any supplier's decision to bring a complaint. Even if an action is understood to contravene – or seems inconsistent with – the law, in such a concentrated market, suppliers considering whether to bring a complaint have to take account of the possible impact on their future ability to sell their products to the supermarkets. Suppliers also believed that the results of the study provided sufficient evidence for COPROCOM to carry out its own investigations in the supermarket sector.

The results of this study could be used to help the more precise specification of monopolistic conduct in the supermarket sector within the terms of the competition law. Particularly pertinent are the findings of unilateral changes to sales conditions, imposition of new conditions, and demands for confidential information on the conditions of a supplier's sales to other outlets. These elements are similar to the monopolistic practices that are prohibited according to Article 12 of the competition law. There would seem to be sufficient information in the present study to serve as a basis for the competition authority to undertake a more in-depth examination. The quasi-legal nature of any such examination means that COPROCOM is the appropriate body to carry it forward; and under Article 27 of the competition law, COPROCOM has the power to request information and to issue rulings and impose sanctions against anticompetitive conduct.

NOTES

1. Lagakos (2009) argues that it is only rational for supermarkets to enter a market when the population has reached certain levels of durable goods ownership (most notably, cars to get to the stores and large refrigerators).
2. For this study, COPROCOM surveyed all suppliers and producers in COPROCOM's company database. For legal reasons, the survey had to be carried out by the authority and could not be done by the researchers themselves. The sample is described in more detail in the section below on the 'supplier survey'.
3. Statistical tests showed no significant differences in the responses of suppliers with respect to size.
4. $HHI = \Sigma_{i=1}^{n} CM_i^2$ and $\Sigma_{i=1}^{n} CM_i^2 = CM_1^2 = CM_2^2 = CM_3^2 + \ldots + CM_n^2$ where HHI = Herfindahl–Hirschman Index, CM_i = Market share of business *i* and *n* the number of businesses in the market.

REFERENCES

Cook, M.L. and F.R.R. Chaddad (2000) Agroindustrialization of the global agrifood economy: bridging development economics and agribusiness research, *Agricultural Economics*, **23**(3): 207–18.

Einarsson, Á. (2008) The retail sector in the Nordic countries: a description of the differences, similarities, and uniqueness in the global market, *Journal of Retailing and Consumer Services*, **15**(6): 429–526.

Geuens, M., M. Brengman and R. S'Jegers (2003) Food retailing, now and in the future: a consumer perspective, *Journal of Retailing and Consumer Services*, **10**(4), 241–51.

Lagakos, D. (2009) *Superstores or Mom and Pops? Technology Adoption and Productivity Differences in Retail Trade*, Federal Reserve Bank of Minneapolis Research Department Staff Report 428, June.

Nielsen, A.C. (2004) *What's Hot Around the Globe*, Copenhagen: A.C. Nielsen.

OECD and IDB (2014) *Competition Law and Policy in Costa Rica: A Peer Review*, Paris: Organisation for Economic Co-operation and Development.

Pitts, E. and M. Lagnevik (1998) What determines food industry competitiveness? in W.B. Traill and E. Pitts (eds), *Competitiveness in the Food Industry*, London: Blackie Academic & Professional, pp. 1–34.

Reardon, T. and C. Barrett (2000) Agroindustrialization, globalization, and international development: an overview of issues, patterns, and determinants, *Agricultural Economics*, **23**: 195–205.

Reardon, T. and J.A. Berdegué (2002) The rapid rise of supermarkets in

Latin America: challenges and opportunities for development, *Development Policy Review*, **20**(4): 370–528.
Wrigley, N. and M. Lowe (2002) *Reading Retail*, London: Arnold.
Zúñiga Arias, G. (2007) *Quality Management and Strategic Alliances in the Mango Supply Chain from Costa Rica: An Interdisciplinary Approach for Analysing Coordination, Incentives and Governance*, PhD thesis, Wageningen University.

3. The consumer goods distribution sector in Armenia

Karine Poladyan[1]

SCOPE OF THE CHAPTER AND SUMMARY FINDINGS

The Republic of Armenia is a territorially small, economically open, landlocked country with a population of approximately 3 million.[2] Once the economic shocks of the early 1990s caused by the collapse of the Soviet Union were over, the Armenian economy grew very fast. It recorded annual average rates of growth of 5 per cent from 1994 to 2000 and 11 per cent from 2001 to 2008, although it was then badly hit in 2009 by the global financial crisis. Some observers claim that the economy's ability to recover a sustainable growth path is dependent on the adoption of further reforms, including to competition policy, to improve the functioning of the market economy (World Bank 2006).

The economy is highly trade-dependent. In many basic consumer goods markets there is limited domestic production capacity. Some major products – including final goods such as vegetable oil, butter, sugar and rice and ingredients such as wheat for the making of bread and pasta by local processors – are imported. The difference between world (import) product prices and the cost of living for consumers is determined by the operational efficiency of and by the margins obtained by processors and by market actors (wholesalers and distributors) in the distribution sector.

This chapter examines the market in the distribution of basic consumer goods in a transition country where both private actors and the competition authority are struggling to detach from centrally planned habits and adopt the practices of a market economy. The current national regulatory framework, of which the competition law and the enforcement regime are part, was set up to facilitate the transition to the market economy. However, in three key respects, competition policy in Armenia reflects the former system of administrative control of economic activity. The concept of price formation by enterprises embedded in the competition law is coloured by practices in the former economic system; the scope of anticompetitive practices is not adequate and is not well-defined; and the power of the competition authority to carry out investigations is severely curtailed. As a result of these factors, the Armenian competition authority has been more constrained than many other enforcement agencies in its attempts to intervene in the market when restrictions on competition are suspected. Nevertheless, the competition authority has fined various market actors for anticompetitive practices. In consequence, awareness of the nature of the process of competition and of the activities of the authority is spreading within the business community and market players are adapting their practices accordingly.

This chapter describes the national competition authority's efforts up to the late 2000s to act against anticompetitive practices in the distribution sector. It also reports the results of empirical research that was carried out to see whether new avenues of evidence-gathering, focusing less on prices than on enterprises' actions intended to impede competition, could have traction in application of the competition law.

The chapter concludes with a discussion of what needs to be done to strengthen the promotion of competition in Armenia. Several avenues are explored, including possible modification of the legal framework, strengthening the capabilities of the competition authority, and continued advocacy work within the business community.

UNDERSTANDING THE CONTEXT

In 1992, the Armenian economy, like other former centrally planned economies, embarked on the transition away from central planning towards the market economy. Many state-owned enterprises were privatized. A legal framework was introduced to conform to the operation of market. It recognizes private property rights and exemplifies the norms and includes many of the provisions for regulating commercial activity that are similar to those in jurisdictions with long experience of the market system.

The Law of the Republic of Armenia on the Protection of Economic Competition was enacted in 2000. The competition authority, the State Commission for the Protection of Economic Competition of the Republic of Armenia (SCPEC), was established shortly afterwards.

The legacy of central planning has affected competition enforcement in four main respects. The first factor relates to market structures in the Armenian economy. In the era of central planning, most products and services were provided by state-owned enterprises. After the transition, many of these enterprises were privatized. Nevertheless, change of ownership has not led to the emergence of many actors in the relevant market. In many markets and market segments, successor companies to the state-owned enterprises retain a monopoly position, or else are dominant players in concentrated market structures. No state-owned enterprises are present in the consumer goods distribution sector at either wholesale or retail level, but in several markets for specific foodstuffs the number of economic actors remains very small (World Bank 2013). The most commonly cited cases are sugar and wheat. Sugar was 100 per cent imported and three large companies controlled the import trade. Similarly, although 51 companies were active as importers of wheat, the market, which is completely dependent on imports, was also highly concentrated, with two dominant entities.[3]

Concentration and the presence of dominant companies do not necessarily harm consumers. Indeed, a market with only two firms could be competitive if the two companies were in rivalry rather than in collusion. And insofar as monopoly in the distribution chain represents complete vertical integration, it can be an efficient form of organizing distribution activities. In general, however, the existence of highly concentrated markets should – but in this case cannot – lead a competition authority to pay attention to potential problems of abuse of dominance or monopolistic behaviour, including the holding down of output and supply to the market and the erection of barriers to the entry of rivals.

The second way in which the historical context affects competition policy is that the competition law – and, of necessity, its enforcement – focuses on price setting as the main measure of anticompetitive actions, rather than on issues of abuse of dominance and erection of barriers to entry. The law embeds a conceptual approach to price-setting that was the norm among enterprises under central planning; that is, as an arithmetic cost-plus procedure. In the market economy, competition policy enforcement rests on the understanding that market actors seek primarily to reconcile supply and demand factors and to maximize their profits. They determine their product prices in response to a range of factors, including but not limited to costs. The Armenian competition law, however, proposes that the main measure of anticompetitive acts is rises in prices introduced in parallel by different market actors that are not justified in terms of changes in production costs. Accordingly, presenting evidence of parallel product price rises unjustified by changes in underlying costs was the main way in which the competition authority, SCPEC, had to substantiate allegations of anticompetitive actions.

This emphasis diverts the attention and resources of the competition authority away from an interest in barriers to entry and other anticompetitive acts that are characteristic of abuses of dominance in other jurisdictions. This diversion of effort was reinforced by the third element special to the Armenian competition law, relating to the way in which information is provided to the authority by large enterprises. The authority is required to maintain a register of dominant companies in all the main product markets in the economy. These companies are required to provide information on their market operations to the authority on a six-monthly basis, covering sales volumes, cost structure and prices, with appropriate justification if there are changes. Some observers believe that this provision reflects an attempt to overcome the former lack of accountability of state-owned organizations (Nicholson and Mirzoyan 2006). But it is an ineffective requirement. Many firms do not provide information to SCPEC due to the low penalties and absence of strict administrative regulations. Indeed the provision is counterproductive, in that it absorbs a great deal of effort on the part of the authority's staff and resources, diverting them from other work (UNCTAD 2010).

Another factor is that the Armenian economy suffers a high level of under-reporting of economic activities, in particular to the tax authority. Enterprises under-report the scale of their activity primarily in order to minimize tax liabilities; the process often begins at the border with inducements to the customs service to under-record import flows. Although such practices are pervasive, they are not found throughout the economy (UNCTAD 2010). Nevertheless, the scale of shadow activity in the Armenian economy is extremely large. It was generally estimated at 40–50 per cent of total GDP in 2005 by both the SCPEC in a 2007 internal report and by external observers (Nicholson and Mirzoyan 2006). The practice makes for a severe lack of information about real market conditions in Armenia across all economic sectors. With respect to competition policy in particular, under-reporting creates difficulties for the fundamental procedure of estimating market size and, by extension, for the accurate identification of dominant companies and their real market shares.

A final issue is that the ability of the authority to carry out investigations is severely curtailed compared to other jurisdictions. SCPEC is required to give three days' notice to enterprises of its intention to collect information and documents from them. This gives businesses plenty of time to conceal or destroy incriminating evidence should they need to do so. The provision is in principle offset by the requirement that enterprises provide information to SCPEC on a routine basis. But, as noted, companies do not always abide by it and in any case they would not include any information on concerted practices.

Attempts by the SCPEC to investigate possible anticompetitive acts in the distribution sector have also run up against some other concerns.

Where there is a high proportion of imports in a particular market, it is not easy to identify the primary economic actors that drive particular actions. The manufacturer of the product or the importing company or its representative may determine the conditions of production and sale of a product along the distribution chain depending on the nature of the contractual relationship between the various parties. SCPEC's limited information gathering powers does not give it access to such documentation.

Two further specific features of the competition law are particularly important to the distribution sector. First, the law is neutral, i.e., does not prohibit or suggest that special attention be paid to exclusivity provisions in vertical agreements in the distribution sector. This is a crucial dimension of inter-company relations within the distribution chain because exclusivity deals are a barrier to the entry of new firms. They can serve to maintain the bargaining power exercised by dominant or monopolistic companies in their commercial relations with other entities. Exclusivity provisions may also impede the competition process, to the detriment of consumers, by limiting the selection of items on sale and increasing the price at which they are offered. Finally, the law contains no definition of 'unfair trade', even though the competition law states that this constitutes a type of unacceptable (anticompetitive) behaviour. For example, there is no guidance in the legal framework to guide the authority to address a situation where a distributor – hitherto the sole distributor that has invested in product advertising and other types of promotion – finds itself facing a rival that has entered the market to sell the same product. It profits from the brand enhancement that the distributor has created. The SCPEC has nevertheless come to a determination that such a situation does not constitute unfair trade.

The SCPEC has often been frustrated from taking distribution cases forward by one or more of these factors. For this reason it finds that the concepts and provisions laid down by the national legislation do not currently adequately enable it to interpret and gather evidence on the competition effects of commercial relations in the distribution sector. This is the case even where economic activity is limited to the transfer of imported products along the distribution chain from point of entry into the territory and sale to the final consumer. The SCPEC is powerless, for example, to investigate the rapid growth of enterprises claiming that they have exclusive dealing privileges in their commercial dealings with foreign suppliers, as has been observed in the Armenian distribution system.

However, disagreements in interpreting evidence on anticompetitive actions have arisen between the competition authority and the court of appeal. In one case, the court of appeal issued a determination that implied that SCPEC should not rely purely on economic evidence relating to information on prices and cost structures. The court asked for additional evidence of enterprise behaviour, notably of a conspiracy or 'meeting of minds' on the part of the alleged perpetrators, as is common in other jurisdictions (UNCTAD 2010). These disagreements have a positive side in suggesting that the legal framework could accommodate evidentiary approaches other than the focus on formulaic price determination. In its judgment, the appeal court also revealed its awareness of the potential for concerted actions by enterprises to damage competition and disadvantage consumers other than through direct price increases. They could, for example, agree to limit output and impede the competition process by erecting barriers to entry and blocking any challenges to the incumbents.

This development opens the door for the competition authority to introduce different types of reasoning into its decisions. As well as describing successful cases brought by the SCPEC in the next section, the present study therefore contains an empirical examination of some facets of enterprise behaviour in the distribution sector. The idea is to establish whether behavioural, rather than price-based, evidence could reveal anticompetitive acts in vertical arrangements within the distribution sector.

THE LEGAL TREATMENT OF DISTRIBUTION ARRANGEMENTS

The legal framework that applies to the distribution sector is rudimentary. Such definitions as exist are set out in the Law of the Republic of Armenia on Trade and Services. This distinguishes between distributors and dealers (or agents) in a simple form and does not scrutinise contract conditions freely arrived at between parties within the distribution sector on the understanding that contract variations may often seek to encapsulate the realities of commercial risks and rewards in this line of business.

The law on trade and services does seek to regulate commercial relations between suppliers, distributors and dealers. Distributors, which may make retail sales, are considered as formally and legally independent of the supplier. By contrast, dealers, which may also make retail sales, are included in an organization's sales network and act as its agent. This scheme is more or less equivalent to the status accorded to those actors in distribution arrangements in many other jurisdictions, although it does not reflect the complexities often found in practice.[4] For example, the normal characteristic of a distributor (as opposed to a dealer) is that it mobilizes the funds to acquire ownership of the products that it sells on. But some hybrid arrangements waive this requirement. The distributor may not, in those cases, acquire the products but rather handles them in the manner of an agent. Nevertheless, the SCPEC treats distributors as autonomous actors, even in those circumstances.

Another feature of the legal framework is that interventions by the SCPEC have little deterrent effect on non-resident enterprises. Competition law enforcement respects contracts between economic actors, whatever their legal status, and SCPEC can issue decisions sanctioning any anticompetitive act. But the law does not enable it to impose fines on non-resident entities.

In addition, official recognition through the registration process, of a company that has a monopolistic or dominant position over imports into a particular market may restrict the possibility of open competition from other firms registered as active in the same product market. However, there is a lack of clarity in this respect. As noted, the competition law does not pay any attention to exclusive dealing provisions in distributor agreements. There is therefore no general presumption that such provisions, although apparently intended to restrict competition, have such an effect. The competition authority would have to demonstrate on a case-by-case basis that any such provision in a commercial contract has an anticompetitive effect in practice.

SCPEC DECISIONS IN SELECTED CONSUMER PRODUCT MARKETS

The SCPEC has long been concerned about potentially anticompetitive practices in the distribution sector. Nevertheless, as noted, its ability to take action has been constrained by the impediments set by the legislative framework and the limited prosecution possibilities given to it under the competition law. The authority has succeeded in bringing a small number of such cases to a conclusion and its investigations have brought information to light about organizational arrangements in the distribution sector. In this section, the findings of the investigations and case outcomes are described for five food product markets and two other consumer goods markets (fuel and vehicles) where the analysis sheds light on the realities of competition law enforcement in Armenia.

Information on all the cases brought by the Competition Authority in the 2000s is laid out in Table 3.1. The data shows the number of competition decisions taken categorized by type of allegation rather than by economic sector.

Enterprises' failure to submit information is the predominant offence. As noted, this is probably due to the fact that the competition authority has limited powers and the law specifies low fines for infringement. One hundred and sixty determinations of this type were brought over the nine-year period. All but one of these involved fines. In the remaining case, as column two of Table 3.1 shows, the offending business was issued a 'warning and desist' order.

'Unfair competition' cases formed the second most common type of offence. The SCPEC has responsibility for consumer protection as well

Table 3.1 Decisions in competition cases by SCPEC, 2001–9

Type of decision	Number of decisions taken	Warnings and cease and desist orders, without fines
Abuse of dominance	8	1
Anticompetitive agreements	5	2
Mergers	5	–
Unfair competition	78	23
Failure to submit information	159	1
Submission of false information	8	1
Total	263	28

Source: Based on UNCTAD (2010, p. 32).

as promotion of competition. Most of the unfair competition cases dealt with retail malpractices such as fraudulent and inaccurate product labelling. Cease and desist orders that lead to the end of the practice in question have an important place in protecting consumers in this connection.

In third place, nine cases (eight decisions and one warning) have been pursued by the SCPEC concerning markets where one or more actor had a dominant position and was alleged to have abused its position. Three of these decisions related to the distribution of food products and are discussed below.

In other jurisdictions, the main concerns relating to anticompetitive practices in the distribution sector are abuse of dominance and anticompetitive agreements (which can be horizontal or vertical). In its distribution sector cases, SCPEC has only prosecuted economic entities for unjustified price setting in the context of horizontal agreements, involving a firm or firms holding a dominant market position. No vertical agreement cases have been brought in connection with the distribution sector.

Following its case investigations, SCPEC succeeded in sanctioning economic actors in three food markets: eggs, butter and vegetable oils. Market investigations of the distribution of sugar, beer, meat products, motor vehicles, and petrol and diesel fuel have also taken place, although no sanctions were imposed.

Eggs

In this market, the major actors were fined for coordinated price increases. Three major economic entities operate in the 'chicken eggs with shell' product market: Lusakert Pedigree Poultry Plant (the dominant player), Arzni Pedigree CPS (the second player with biggest sales volume) and

Yerevan Poultry Plant (the third player). As a result of a decision of the SCPEC, these three companies were fined for coordinated price increases in December 2006. It is worth mentioning that the state had previously established tax privileges for egg-producing economic entities, which are exempted from profit tax and VAT.

The SCPEC found that the three dominant companies had increased their profits in varying proportions, even though production volumes exceeded sales volumes and the companies did not export. In other words, they restricted the volume of sales of eggs. Their dominance in the market allowed them to influence general market conditions (volumes and product assortment). The companies uniformly and simultaneously 'artificially' increased their output prices and were able to do so without forfeiting profits. The cost of production was 28–40 AMD per unit, whereas the eggs were priced at 60–80 AMD in retail stores. The dominant company did not submit any evidence in justification of its price and profit increases. All three companies were fined for anticompetitive conduct resulting from a horizontal agreement.

The basis of the SCPEC's decision to fine the companies was that, according to the competition law, a sales price increase is unjustified (artificial), if an economic entity, other factors being equal, gains significantly higher profit (more than 5 per cent, which was proven in this case) from product sales, compared with the period before the price increase came into effect. SCPEC also noted that if, when external and internal factors change, an economic entity maintains the price of a product (or fails to alter the price of the product (up or down) in proportion to those changes), it is also imposing artificial prices. A failure to change the product price can, however, be justified and exonerated from sanction if other economic factors require it, including, for example, loss of consumer confidence, reputational loss of the company, price changes in the international market or the need for the company to generate resources to modernize its production facilities or to cover credit or bankruptcy liabilities and so on.

The SCPEC ruling rested on comparison of the price information submitted by the companies and retail shops. The SCPEC had suspicions regarding the veracity of this information. The sales prices declared by producers differed significantly from the prices that shops stated that they paid to the producers. But the prices should have been identical or very similar because there are no intermediaries in this market. All three egg-producing companies sell their products directly to the shops. The price data therefore suggested that additional profit was being generated for the producers and not declared. The SCPEC was able to estimate the likely scale of the profit increases from the costs, market prices and sales volumes data for the period in question.

Butter and Vegetable Oil

The markets for butter and vegetable oils are linked since these products are highly substitutable. SCPEC fined a large number of actors in this product market for making simultaneous price increases unjustified by changes in costs. SCPEC's decision rested on observation of price increases on butter and vegetable oil during August and September 2007. Nineteen economic entities selling butter and 23 entities selling vegetable oil were fined.

SCPEC investigated the butter product market in 2007 (and had also done so in 2004). Almost all butter sold on the domestic market in Armenia is imported; domestic production accounted for only 0.2 per cent of butter sales in 2006. One company (Fleetfood) had been identified as having a dominant position in 2004, but it subsequently suspended operations and went into liquidation along with a number of other companies. The number of market actors fell from 33 in 2004 to 24 in 2006. In 2007, three main actors were identified: Maranik, with a 35 per cent share; Salex with 24 per cent; and Valetta with 21 per cent.

The vegetable oils market was highly concentrated in 2007. As in the case of butter, the level of concentration had increased over the previous few years. The three largest economic entities had similar market shares and had joint dominance: Vas Group had a market share of 27 per cent, Salex Group had 23 per cent and Enterprenerue F. Karapetyan had 21 per cent.

Although international prices in the broad product categories increased in the period under investigation, the prices of the specific products actually imported into Armenia changed very little. Nevertheless, retail prices charged within Armenia increased significantly. Importing companies, intermediaries and retail outlets all reported marked price increases, even though this did not seem justified on the basis of detailed information on cross-border prices. The investigation was complicated by the poor level of documentation regarding acquisitions and sales by actors in the distribution chain. This made it impossible to determine the extent of price increases at each stage of the distribution chain or to identify any concerted actions on the part of market players. Despite the less-than-exhaustive evidence compiled and presented by the SCPEC in this case, it reached a decision to fine the 23 companies involved.

Sugar

In the mid-2000s, the market for granulated sugar in Armenia was supplied almost entirely from imports.[5] Three large companies effectively controlled the import trade: 21 companies were active but the combined market share of the top three companies by volume was 99.9 per cent. Moreover, two of the top three companies imported sugar solely for use as an input in their own food-processing factories. The market share of the dominant company (Salex Group) was 91.4 per cent.[6] This actor was suspected by SCPEC of abuse of dominance but a case was not brought on these grounds. Instead, SCPEC carried out an investigation, as permitted under Chapter 6, Article 9 of the competition law on the grounds that the company was suspected of submitting unreliable information.

The company made sales of sugar both from its own warehouse and from its own shops. According to data provided by the company, the release price for 1kg sugar was 240 AMD for retail sales and 215 AMD for wholesale transactions. However, the SCPEC's monitoring revealed that the retail price reached 270–370 AMD per kilogram. It is not surprising that the retail price for sugar sold should be higher than the wholesale price from the warehouse. On occasion, however, the selling price of granulated sugar imported by the company was increased significantly. But it was discovered that retail sales also take place in outlets that cannot be controlled by the sugar importer. Hence, no case was brought on price grounds. Furthermore, the SCPEC analysed the data submitted by Salex Group, and found that the margin between retail and whole prices was justified.

Beer

In 2004, most of the beer sold in Armenia (94 per cent) was locally produced. Beer was manufactured by two large companies: Yerevan Beer with 55 per cent of the market (by volume) and Kotayk Brewery with 38 per cent of the market (by value) in 2004. A third market player had recently emerged: Shirak Gyumri Beer-Malt Factory, located in Gyumri, the second-biggest city 120km from Yerevan. According to data submitted to SCPEC by the two main companies, the average final selling price of beer was in the range of 390 AMD per 500ml bottle in 2006–7.

The two dominant companies mostly sell their products to wholesale intermediaries who then deliver the product to traders. Yerevan Beer has a single company outlet store in the Yerevan suburbs but the bulk of its output is sold to driver-distributors at the output (selling) price; driver-distributors then deliver to final sales outlets, adding a surcharge (of 5–10 AMD per 500ml bottle). Kotayk Brewery supplies approximately 62 intermediary businesses, which then sell on the product to retail, wholesale and other publicly trading outlets. In both cases, the intermediaries are separate economic entities, mostly individual entrepreneurs with their own trucks. Beer producers therefore do not have their own distribution system as such, but the intermediary driver-forwarding agents were suspected of maintaining close links with the manufacturer. Beer prices in retail outlets are significantly higher than the release price and the price of beer sold in the firm's own stores. The difference is shared along the distribution chain among the manufacturer, intermediary and final trading outlet in unknown proportions.

The major actors in the beer market were suspected of concerted artificial pricing but SCPEC found no evidence of anticompetitive practices. Information on the major manufacturers' price structures revealed no concerted conduct in their price policy even though monitoring of prices in the retail market showed near simultaneous price increases, which suggested that some concerted action might be happening. The SCPEC decided that the prices charged by these economic entities in 2006 and January 2007 were justified. However, SCPEC provided information to the government of Armenia's Tax State Service and suggested that it should itself examine beer selling prices along the chain of intermediaries.

The emergence of the third market actor, Shirak Gyumri Beer-Malt Factory, made it desirable for SCPEC to continue monitoring or to conduct another survey of this product market in case this arrival provokes changes to the distribution system or to the pricing strategies of the main players.

Meat Products

SCPEC undertook its investigation into this market on the same grounds that were used for the enquiry into the butter and vegetable oils markets, i.e., that prices appeared to be raised without any cost justification.

The product market consists of prepared meats such as cooked and smoked solid meat preparations (excluding any containing previously ground (minced) meat, such as sausages). In 2008, the market included 33 enterprises, of which 25 were producers and eight were importers. Local producers accounted for approximately half the value of final domestic sales of meat products in Armenia at that time. The SCPEC investigation found that one company, Geghard Meat Factory, had had a dominant position in the market since 2004 but that its position had weakened in the following few years. It was removed from the national register of dominant undertakings. In 2008 no dominant undertaking was identified and the market was considered to have a medium level of concentration. In the intervening period, one new entrant came into the market and total market sales volume had increased 2.1 times.

The investigation also showed that the distribution system for meat products contains several different chains with overlapping geographical operational areas. This provides for plentiful competition, even in the presence of a dominant supplier.

The dominant player, Geghard Msamterqi Kombinat, produced a wide range of meat products. It owns so-called 'shops on wheels'. The whole range of company products was sold through these outlets. The vehicles travel widely throughout the country and reach the great majority of consumers. In addition, the company supplies its products to other retail outlets using its own vehicles.

No significant general increase of the company's product prices was revealed but SCPEC observed that price discrimination was common, with the same product being sold to different buyers at different prices.

Other producers also supply retailers of meat products and most retail outlets throughout the country sell the products of all the major producers. It followed that SCPEC found that no concerns were actionable under the law on any aspect of price-setting.

Non-food Consumer Goods: Petrol and Diesel Fuel and Sales of Vehicles

Apart from food product market studies discussed above, the SCPEC also investigated the distribution of two product areas that account for significant shares of consumer budgets: fuel and vehicle sales. In both cases, the products are all imported and the distribution channels and the final market are highly concentrated. The findings of the investigations are discussed here because the cases reveal additional limitations of competition enforcement on the basis of the competition law in Armenia at the time.

All petrol and diesel fuel sold in Armenia is imported. In 2005–6, two major companies – Flesh and the slightly smaller Kagh Petrol Service – each accounted for around 40 per cent of the market in both types of fuel. Therefore together they accounted for more than 80 per cent of petrol and diesel imports and were identified as dominant entities in both fuels by the SCPEC. Around 10–12 other companies are active in the fuel market, but Flesh and Kagh Petrol Service were the only companies registered in this line of business in the government enterprise registry.

The two companies have their own distribution networks in the form of filling stations that they own and through which they conduct retail sale of fuel. They also sell their products from their warehouses either to other filling stations or directly to large-scale consumers.

The SCPEC started a case for unjustified price increases but, in the absence of proof, it did not impose any fines. Furthermore, the investigators concluded that, regardless of the nature of the price increases, the practice could not be qualified as abuse of dominance as prescribed by the competition law. No sanctioning decision was issued. It was not possible to present evidence that any restriction of competition in the market had resulted from its pricing practices.

Second, in the autumn of 2007, SCPEC considered a case pertaining to the distribution of motor vehicles, following a complaint made by a registered enterprise, EMC. The company imported factory-purchased KIA brand cars and was the official representative of KIA Motors in Armenia. Another company, Valensia, had imported KIA brand cars manufactured in 2006 from the United Arab Emirates. These were being sold below the prevailing market price in Armenia. These vehicles had improperly come out of customs clearance registered as 2007 production cars. EMC expressed concern that vehicles imported by Valensia were being sold as new vehicles. This would result in the decline of KIA's brand rating, create impediments to the fulfilment of the company's assumed liabilities with the manufacturer and distort competition.

During investigation of the case, SCPEC recognized that the sales description of the 2006 cars was misleading and fraudulent. This was a matter of consumer protection. As a competition case, the investigation was hampered by the exclusivity provision inherent in EMC's 'sole distributorship' contract with the producer. The Armenian legal framework is neutral in respect of such provisions in inter-company contracts. Thus, SCPEC was not able to pronounce on whether another company had the right to import KIA brand cars into Armenia and, if so, on what conditions, at what prices and from which countries.

INVESTIGATING COERCIVE CONDUCT IN VERTICAL AGREEMENTS

The focus in the competition law on proving anticompetitive conduct largely on the basis of prices that are unjustified on the basis of production costs, and the lack of concern for collusive actions and 'meeting of minds' among economic entities, are important limitations on the scope for the enforcement actions by the competition authority. Its capacity to act is limited even further in the absence of powers for invoking company-level information. These constraints have impelled SCPEC to explore other possible avenues for promoting competition within the confines of the law.

One approach that SCPEC decided to pursue was to examine more carefully the scope for action involved in the concept of 'unfair competition' within the competition law. More precisely, it decided to investigate coercive behaviour among parties to commercial agreements in the distribution sector as an instance of 'unfair competition'. Coercion would seem more likely where the party setting the terms of the transaction had a dominant position, so the investigation focused on distribution segments that seemed to contain a dominant firm (subject to the lack of transparency about real conditions in markets, as discussed above).

In other jurisdictions, a range of such behaviours have been observed on the part of both principals (suppliers/manufacturers) and distributors. Practices described in the literature[7] have included suppliers' insistence on exclusive supply and quantity forcing. On the retailer side, possible practices would be shops' refusal to stock certain products and a requirement that the supplier has carried out a certain amount of advertising of its product. The SCPEC therefore decided to look into coercive behaviour of this type. Moreover, it decided to look at such practices both as embodied within commercial agreements and as activated informally outside such agreements. The objective of the research was therefore to collect data and behavioural evidence that could be grounds for subsequent allegations of 'unfair trading'. The objective was to facilitate greater clarity and consistency in competition law enforcement and to find areas in which behavioural evidence might have traction in case actions.

It was believed that this avenue of enquiry would be valuable for the possibilities of enforcement because, as noted, the court of appeal has occasionally had recourse to behavioural evidence in overturning SCPEC 'economically based' (cost-based) cases (UNCTAD 2010).

Design of the Survey

SCPEC carried out two surveys of retail outlets (hereinafter 'shops') regarding sales conditions of various consumer food products, particularly carbonated, sweetened drinks (soft drinks), beer, eggs and ice cream.

Shops functioning in the Republic of Armenia were classified into three groups:

> *Class A* consists of the largest stores and those created in recent years that are publicly known as 'supermarkets'. They operate in the capital Yerevan (population 1 million) and the next two biggest cities of the republic, Gyumri (population 125,000) and Vanadzor (population 100,000).
> *Class B* consists of traditional, medium and relatively big shops functioning in certain districts of the three biggest cities of the country. They have maintained their clients since Soviet times and are key participants in the distribution system. The shops have several departments and more than three outlets.
> *Class C* consists of small shops and kiosks operated in city districts, sometimes in backyards. They were mostly started in the post-Soviet

period and have been gradually increasing their weight in the distribution sector. These shops usually trade through a single outlet.

Questionnaires were administered to representatives of managers of retail outlets[8] in Yerevan and surrounding area and in the two next biggest cities, Gyumri and Vanadzor.[9] The inquiry covered 99 shops, accounting for approximately 9 per cent of Class A shops, 40 per cent of Class B shops and 50 per cent of Class C shops.

The main purpose of the survey was to probe the incidence of some types of commercial behaviour in the distribution sector that has the potential to restrict competition. The focus was on the existence of commercial conditions beyond the terms of contractual agreements imposed by dominant entities or groups on their commercial partners, with a view to making proposals to improve the interpretation of legal provisions and prospects for competition law enforcement.

Survey Findings: Distributors' Practices

The main results concern the extent to which exclusive dealing and quantity forcing are imposed on distributors by suppliers within the terms of their agreements. Table 3.2 sets out the findings regarding exclusive dealing conditions.

The survey results show that exclusive dealing is very rarely a condition of distributor agreements for consumer goods in the Republic of Armenia. The only exceptions are found among suppliers to medium-sized outlets (Class B), mostly in relation to the sale of soft drinks and one case of ice cream.

Similar findings emerged from the responses regarding quantity forcing, i.e., the practice whereby a supplier's distribution agreement includes a

Table 3.2 Presence of exclusive dealing requirements in distributor agreements, by class of shop and product

Shop category		Product			
		Soft drinks	Beer	Eggs	Ice cream
Large	Yes	0	0	0	0
	No	9	9	9	9
Medium	Yes	5	0	0	3
	No	35	40	40	37
Small	Yes	2	0	0	0
	No	48	50	50	50

clause obliging the retailer to make a minimum quantity of sales. In this case, the majority of respondents reported that no such provision was included in its contract with the supplier. The only exceptions were three small (Class C) shops out of a total of 50 and one medium-sized (Class B) shop out of a total of 40. Opinions of quantity forcing were strongly negative among the respondents. Several went so far as to say that any attempt to impose this condition would be a 'requirement restricting their rights'.

The survey also probed the issue of binding commercial practices in the distribution system beyond the contractual terms laid out in distributor agreements. The Coca-Cola case investigated by the competition authority in 2005 had revolved on this point. In that situation, a supplier had compelled shops not to collaborate with rivals of the Pepsi cola company, under a threat that refrigerators allocated to the distributor by the supplier would be taken back.

The results revealed the following picture: no large (Class A) shop reported any coercive behaviour that surpassed contractual conditions, whereas three medium-sized (Class B) shops (out of 40) and eight small (Class C) shops (out of 50) did so. The conduct was present – in very limited degree – in all product groups but mostly in the soft drinks market. The compulsion was in all cases conveyed orally by the supplier usually requiring the distributor not to place rivals' products in the display refrigerators provided by the supplier, or more generally not to deal at all in rival products.

It is important to keep the scale of such conduct in proportion. The overwhelming majority of respondent shops reported no cases of extra-contractual behavioural abuses by suppliers in the product markets under study. Some respondents reported that such behaviour used to be much more widespread in the past. They believed that the reason was that decisions had been made against such practices by the competition authority and market actors were now largely aware of the regulations.

With regard to business relationships within the distribution sector, the majority of respondents reported that they were satisfied with the quality of cooperation they enjoyed with suppliers. The dissenters included one large (Class A) shop that was dissatisfied with its ice cream supplier and two medium-sized shops that expressed dissatisfaction with their beer and egg suppliers. Three out of the total of 23 medium-sized shops expressed unsatisfactory relationships (with beer and eggs suppliers) and 12 of 31 small (Class C) shops were dissatisfied with their relationships with the suppliers of eggs, beer and ice cream. The results suggest that SCPEC should at least keep monitoring the situation, even if the degree of dissatisfaction is not high enough to warrant a case investigation.

The respondents struggled with their perception of the prevalence of market competition in general and 'fair competition' in particular. The response rate was again lower than on factual questions, indicated by a higher proportion of 'don't know' responses. Negative answers were concentrated among the largest (Class A) stores in this case. By contrast, the smallest shops (Class C) tended to be more at ease, perhaps because they operate in an atomistic market with many players in a competitive process.

Survey Findings: Retailers' Practices

Coercive behaviour may not be limited to downstream pressure on distributors, within or outside the terms of distributor agreements. It may occur in the opposite direction. Certain actions have been observed in Armenia that fit this description, such as 'refusal to stock' when retailers block manufacturer or wholesaler access to their stores, and 'imposition of minimum advertising requirement' when retailers refuse to stock a product that is insufficiently advertised and unknown to consumers.

The research team carried out a second survey in an attempt to investigate how widespread such practices were. The population in this case was businesses entered in the registry of entities that operated as manufacturers or distributors of a wide range (31) of consumer products, mostly foodstuffs and also medicines. Unfortunately, the response rate to this survey was extremely low. But the results – however unscientific – did yield examples of refusals to stock products on grounds that the retailer had insufficient display and storage space. There was no report of a retailer refusing to stock on the grounds the product was not known to consumers because of inadequate advertising. Nor were there any reports of quantity restrictions by the retailers.

CONCLUSIONS

Some conclusions can be drawn on the basis of this research.

First, from the procedural perspective, the research effort demonstrated the need for the competition authority to have more powers and more resources at its command (particularly internet-based resources) to improve its data collection capabilities. In general, the business climate is not encouraging for survey work: respondents were often unwilling to cooperate, sometimes aggressively so. Armenian market actors are highly reluctant to submit information or respond to surveys. When they do, the likelihood of providing misleading or false information can be high. This tendency may be intensified by the presence of certain 'elite' groups of actors in the distribution chain; these are well-known companies or companies owned by nationally famous persons. They include monopolistic or dominant players, and perhaps also the largest shops (Class A, supermarkets), which may be able to dictate conditions to suppliers and perform a 'price-setting' role for the retail consumption system as a whole.

At the time of this study, SCPEC had very limited scope for investigating and intervening in the market. The research sought to explore another angle for possible investigations, by looking into the behaviour of business actors in the distribution sector. The specific objective was to look into coercive aspects of contractual arrangements, using a survey instrument to generate data. However, the survey results did not show that agreements between suppliers and shops in soft drinks or the other selected product markets included many binding provisions of a coercive nature. Nor did the survey results show that business agreements in the distribution sector promote any other behaviours that might be an infringement of the competition law. Finally, no so-called 'extra-contractual' binding behaviour was revealed. Therefore, SCPEC could not open any cases or conduct any further investigations in these areas.

Despite these disappointing findings, SCPEC could continue to examine other forms of inter-firm cooperation that are taken as *prima facie* evidence of anticompetitive acts in other jurisdictions. Alternatively, other ways will need to be found to sanction other acts that give rise to excess profits to the detriment of consumers. Certain provisions of the competition law may need to be modified; for example, giving separate treatment to vertical and horizontal agreements as advocated by the authors of the UNCTAD peer review (UNCTAD 2010). Indeed, the provisions in the competition law that required decisions on the competition effects of horizontally coordinated actions to refer to 'unjustified' changes in prices were amended in 2011, bringing competition enforcement closer to other jurisdictions in recognizing per se anticompetitive conduct. The competition law might also be revised to admit behavioural evidence, as the administrative court of appeal seems to allow.

The research did yield some positive results. It demonstrated to the authority that there has been progress over time in the performance of the distribution system and greater understanding and observance of competition principles on the part of market actors in that sector. The situation could be attributed in part to the transparent style of operations of the SCPEC, whose decisions are elaborated and discussed in the public domain. The advocacy work of the SCPEC therefore needs to continue.

Publicity around the actions of the European Commission (EC) is part of this effort. For example, the EC's Directorate General for Competition had issued a resolution in respect of the Coca-Cola Company case[10] and this had heightened appreciation within the business community of the importance of avoiding anticompetitive practices.

Despite the fact that the empirical evidence that was uncovered by this research was inconclusive, the formulation of the objectives and methodology for the research was a valuable exercise for the competition authority. It showed how a regulatory authority can put research activity to good use to examine other options for law enforcement, attempt to clarify legal regulations and reduce uncertainty for all concerned.

NOTES

1. The views expressed here are personal and do not necessarily reflect those of the SCPEC RA.
2. This information was taken from official website of the President of the Republic of Armenia, www.president.am/en/general-information.
3. This estimate is from a SCPEC investigation of the market carried out in 2010.
4. Distributorships can be 'hard' or 'soft'. Under a hard agreement, the distributor is required to purchase a specified amount of goods from the principal (manufacturer or upstream distributor), whereas in a soft agreement the distributor buys only according to need to supply his business, i.e., in proportion to its retail sales of the product. In practice, a wide array of contractual arrangements are found in the distribution sector. For example, mixed or hybrid distributor–agency contracts include different balances of rights and obligations (regarding, for example, product liability responsibilities) of the parties.
5. Dependence on imports of sugar ended in 2010 when a newly constructed sugar beet plant began operations.
6. SCPEC 2006 Activity report, http://competition.am/uploads/resources/2006Activity reportENG.pdf and SCPEC RA 2010 Activity report www.competition.am/uploads/resources/Report_2010_vo137.pdf (in Armenian).
7. Kenneth Rolnicki *Managing. Channels of Distribution* (in Russian, Кеннет Ролницки 'Управление каналами дистрибуции'); Linda Gorchels Ed Marien, Chuck West *Management of Distribution Channels* (in Russian, Линда Горчелс, Эд Мариен, Чак Уэст 'Управление каналами дистрибуции'); Joanna Goyder, EU Distribution Law.
8. The questionnaire was administered by research teams consisting of students of the Slavonic University of the Republic of Armenia and Yerevan Engineering University under expert supervision. Two employees of SCPEC also participated in the inquiry.
9. Interviewers reported that the atmosphere in the interviews was sometimes tense, to the point that respondents were reluctant to give out information. Some respondents seemed to lack insight and information into the issues that were the subject of inquiry and the accuracy of their answers is doubtful.
10. http://ec.europa.eu/dgs/competition/index_en.htm.

REFERENCES

Nicholson, M. and A.R. Mirzoyan (2006) *Information Needs and Institutional Development*, Armenian International Policy Research Group, Working Paper No. 06/08 SCPEC (n.d.) www.competition.am.

UNCTAD (2010) *Voluntary Peer Review of Competition Policy: Armenia*, Geneva: United Nations.

World Bank (2006) *Armenia: The Caucasian Tiger, Vols 1 and 2*, Poverty Reduction and Economic Management Unit, Europe and Central Asia Region, Washington, DC: World Bank.

World Bank (2013) *Republic of Armenia, Accumulation, Competition and Connectivity, Poverty Reduction and Economic Management Unit, Europe and Central Asia Region*, Washington, DC: World Bank.

4. The market in cereals in Mali

Oumar Idriss Berthe, Massa Coulibaly, Salifou B. Diarra and Martin Sidibe

SETTING THE SCENE

Cereal products play a key role in Mali, not just through their contribution to the agricultural value-added and employment of the population, but also in terms of their share of household expenditure. The challenge of securing a regular supply of grain and ensuring that markets operate in a competitive manner are major concerns for the government. Apart from their economic significance, these issues have an important social and political dimension.

To this end, food security has been historically a main objective of Mali's agricultural policy and a range of approaches have been adopted to achieve this goal. Between the 1960s and the 1980s, the government's policy was interventionist and prices were set by the state through Mali's Agency for Agricultural Produce (OPAM),[1] which was also responsible for trade in cereals. This policy was designed to supply grain to urban areas at low cost while also offering incentivizing prices to farmers. However, the limitations of this approach became apparent from the 1980s onwards, when there was a drop in cereal production, a shortfall in supply for domestic consumption and a surge in OPAM's accumulated deficit.

The country then embarked on a policy of liberalizing the cereal market, chiefly through the Programme to Restructure the Cereal Market (PRMC). Today, this market is fully liberalized. In addition, in 1992, Mali became one of the first sub-Saharan African countries to introduce a law on freedom of pricing and competition. As a consequence, cereal prices have no longer been set by state authorities but determined by supply and demand on different markets.

For several years, imports of subsidized cereals from advanced countries offered a large swathe of the population access to cheap food. This changed, however, when food prices on the world market went up in the late 2000s. The liberalization of the cereal market generated great volatility in prices that in turn had a negative impact on the purchasing power of households, restricting their ability to meet basic food needs. Trade unions and consumer associations expressed their dissatisfaction with the soaring prices by frequent demonstrations, as in 2000 and 2007.

In this context, a comprehensive understanding of the way the cereal market operates in Mali is essential before the design of any economic policy measures, especially when poverty is reaching worrying levels – in 2006 it affected 58 per cent of the population (32 per cent in the cities and 70 per cent in rural areas).[2]

This chapter focuses on the grain market supply conditions and the degree of competition in this market. First, it describes the cereal market with special reference to millet, sorghum and rice, which are the three main cereals consumed by households. The analysis concentrates on the pattern of production and consumption in the different Malian regions. Second, it identifies the main distribution channels for millet, sorghum and rice by taking the entire supply and marketing chains in two important Malian cities: Timbuktu and Bamako. Third, the chapter explains the mechanisms for setting and transmitting prices in the markets for the three main cereals in the two cities selected, together with an evaluation of the intensity of competition in these markets. Finally, the chapter draws out the implications of this operating framework for competition policy and consumers' welfare. Emergency measures to curb upward spikes in prices, which are usually justified on the grounds of achieving domestic food security and social stability, tend to inhibit market mechanisms and generate perverse dynamic effects on both producers and consumers.

METHODOLOGY

The chapter is based on a field study and involves three different questionnaires (one for government officials, one for cereal merchants and a third for cereal transporters), covering the views and perceptions of the key stockholders of the cereal market on the following points:

- Current market organization and operations.
- Influence of the variability of international market prices on the local market.
- Action taken by the government to cushion the effects of the price rise.
- Level of market players' knowledge.
- Level of competition in the market and the role of the competition authority.

A total of 154 people were interviewed:[3] 46 from the government (41 in Bamako and five in Timbuktu), 62 cereal merchants (37 in Bamako and 25 in Timbuktu) and 46 transporters (25 in Bamako and 21 in Timbuktu).

The study focused on millet, sorghum and rice in two different locations: Bamako and Timbuktu. The three cereals were chosen because they are the ones most frequently consumed by Malian families based on previous household expenditure surveys. Bamako was singled out because of the size of its population, which is approximately 2 million. The town of Bamako also has one of the highest rates of poverty in the country. This makes it particularly interesting in terms of the country's social stability. Furthermore, Bamako is the main supply centre for a large number of other places. Timbuktu was selected because it is heavily populated and isolated, factors that lead to concerns about regularity of supply. In addition, Timbuktu as a region is dependent on regions to the south for its millet and sorghum.

We use the term 'intermediary' for any economic actor involved in the process of buying and selling that transfers grain from producer to consumer. We distinguish collectors, wholesalers/semi-wholesalers, importers and retailers.

Collectors sell wholesalers the cereals bought from producers in villages or markets in the areas of cultivation. Wholesalers and semi-wholesalers handle transactions involving large volumes of cereals. They sell to retailers or consumers the cereals acquired from assemblers/aggregators and other wholesalers. Importers buy cereals abroad, generally intending to sell them to domestic semi-wholesalers or retailers. Finally, retailers sell to final consumers, small amounts of cereals bought from wholesalers and semi wholesalers.

CEREAL MARKET DYNAMICS

Cereal Production

Between the 1984/5 and 2008/9 seasons, overall grain production increased substantially from 1.1 million to 4.2 million tonnes. Millet, sorghum and rice accounted for 84.8 per cent of cereal production in 2008/9. Output of the three main cereals reached 3.5 million tonnes in 2008/9, compared to under a million tonnes in 1984/5. Due to the government's investments, rice yields rose from 6.6 quintal (100kg) per hectare in the early 1980s to more than 20 quintal per hectare in 2008/9. However, yields of millet only increased slightly and those of sorghum remained the same over this period, as reported in Table 4.1.

Table 4.1 Yields in quintals

	Rice	Millet	Sorghum	Total
1984/5	6.62	5.69	9.55	6.97
2004/5	24.41	7.14	8.28	12.07
2005/6	22.84	7.80	8.45	10.90
2006/7	25.78	7.55	8.39	11.25
2007/8	27.62	7.41	8.26	10.36
2008/9	21.50	8.31	9.40	11.54

Source: Cereal production statistics, National Institute of Statistics (DNSI), Mali.

Data on gross regional production show that the Ségou region is the main centre for millet, accounting for 37 per cent of total production followed by the regions of Mopti (22.5 per cent), Sikasso (17.3 per cent) and Koulikoro (16.8 per cent).

Sikasso with (34.5 per cent), Koulikoro (27.5 per cent) and Kayes (18.9 per cent) are the main centres of sorghum production. The Ségou region is responsible for 51.7 per cent of total rice production, making it the main rice-growing centre. It is followed by Mopti (18.1 per cent), Sikasso (11.9 per cent) and Timbuktu (10.6 per cent).

No single centre predominates in the production of millet and sorghum. However, Ségou plays a dominant role in the case of rice due to favourable climatic conditions and, more importantly, to government investment, through the Office du Niger, in rice cultivation systems with full water control through irrigation. On the other hand, Timbuktu appears almost totally dependent on other regions in the south for its consumption needs in terms of millet and sorghum.

Cereal Consumption

The share of households' expenditure on food items exceeds 43 per cent and can reach as much as 60 per cent for half of the Malian population.[4] Detailed figures on food consumption confirm that a significant portion of the budget is allocated to rice, millet and sorghum, and thus any variation in their price can generate large effects on households' living standards. Table 4.2 shows that, on average, the three cereals absorb 36.1 per cent of the food budget at the national level (30.2 per cent in the cities and 40.5 in villages). For the poorest 20 per cent of households, the three cereals take up to half of the food budget.

Expenditure on rice tends to dominate in urban consumption. In rural

Table 4.2 Share of the food budget devoted to the three main cereals

	National	Urban	Rural	20 per cent poorest households	Timbuktu	Bamako
Rice	18.6	20.3	17.3	12.3	35.3	18.9
Millet	11.8	6.7	15.6	28.8	10.4	5.3
Sorghum	5.7	3.2	7.6	8.7	2.1	2.8
Total	36.1	30.2	40.5	49.8	47.8	27.0

Source: Based on the integrated household survey undertaken by the Malian National Institute of Statistics in 2006.

Table 4.3 Available production and market needs (in '000 tonnes)

	Available production*			Market needs**			Gap		
	Millet	Sorghum	Rice	Millet	Sorghum	Rice	Millet	Sorghum	Rice
2006/7	146	216	473	428	197	419	−282	19	276
2007/8	25	253	455	500	231	489	−425	22	−34
2008/9	103	322	603	500	231	489	−397	91	114

Notes: *Production – (own consumption + own provision); **Purchase + barter.

Source: Cereal production statistics, National Institute of Statistics (DNSI), Mali.

areas, both rice and millet are important spending items. There are also regional differences in households' consumption patterns. Food expenditure appears much more dominated by cereals in Timbuktu, with a high share allocated to rice. On the other hand, food consumption in Bamako seems more diversified with a lower share of households' budgets spent on cereals. One needs also to account for the difference in budget levels and standard of living between the two cities in interpreting those figures.

In addition, there are several different varieties of millet, sorghum and rice and their prices are not similar. The study assumes that millet and sorghum are homogeneous but differentiates between local rice (Gambiaka) and imported rice which contains itself different varieties. Those most commonly consumed in Mali are RM40, ELB, RM25 and BB.[5]

A comparison of available production and consumption needs, as shown in Table 4.3, indicates that between the 2006/7 and the 2008/9 seasons, the cereal market was marked by a significant domestic supply shortfall for millet and a slight surplus in that of sorghum and rice. In addition, only in the 2006/7 season was the overall market supply for the three cereals

Table 4.4 Cross-border flows of cereals (tonnes/year)

	Imports *– of which imports from West African region*		Exports *– of which exports to West African region*	
	Millet/sorghum	Rice	Millet/sorghum	Rice
2007	74	137,143	3,020	–
	–66	*–36,090*	*–3,013*	
2008	7	165,716	354	–
	–5	*–423*	*–224*	
2009	0.80	278,166	7,048	0.780
	–0	*–245*	*–6,975*	*–0*

Note: The figures in roman indicate the Malian total imports and exports. The figures in italics indicate Malian imports and exports from the West African region.

Source: National Department of Commerce and Competition (DNCC).

greater than demand. The overall deficit amounted to 437,000 tonnes in 2007/8 and 192,000 tonnes in 2008/9.

Meeting domestic demand needs brought about a considerable amount of inter-regional trading and imports, especially of rice, by traders, as shown in Table 4.4. This indicates that all three cereals have been imported and exported over recent years. However, whereas millet and sorghum were exported rather than imported by the West African region as a whole, there were more international imports than exports of rice by this region. Over the period 2007–9, more than 10,000 tonnes of millet/sorghum were exported to the West African region and only 71 tonnes imported from this region. Rice exports were negligible, while imports amounted to 581,025 tonnes of which 36,758 tonnes came from the West African region. These figures report the formal flows that are only part of the picture. Informal trade channels are equally if not more important particularly in years of bad harvests.

Openness to trade means exposure to external price shocks both for producers and consumers. The issue of price-setting and price transmission is examined later in the chapter.

Supply and Distribution Channels

Only part of cereal production reaches markets. The other part, which can be substantial in some regions, is allocated by producers to their own use.

Marketed production goes through the distribution channel before its ends in the basket of consumers. The collectors of cereals constitute the first component in the channel, the wholesalers come in as the second layer, the semi-wholesalers the third and finally the retailers represent the last (Sanogo et al. 2005). In general, collectors/assemblers operate in villages or weekly markets. They travel to production zones and buy cereals from small and medium-sized producers, aggregate them and sell them to itinerant or locally based merchants who then transfer them to wholesalers and semi-wholesalers. Collectors account for 60–80 per cent of cereal transactions in areas with a production surplus. In some cases, collectors can be agents of wholesalers who can furnish them with cash advances.

Wholesalers, semi-wholesalers and retailers operate mostly in urban centres of both production and consumption regions. Wholesalers sell the cereals they have acquired from merchants at wholesale markets. Those active in regions of production sell to those in consumption centres and secure the transportation of cereals. The semi-wholesalers carry out distribution by buying from wholesalers and selling to retailers and consumers on the semi-wholesale market. Retailers carry out distribution by purchasing from semi-wholesalers or wholesalers and selling in the consumer market mostly to limited income consumers. Middle and high-income consumers usually buy from urban outlets and supermarkets.

The government often grants tariff exemptions and/or subsidies to specific market players to import rice in order to ensure the country has a 'sufficient' supply of cereals, especially in periods of increasing international prices as in April to September of 2008. Sometimes, the government intervenes directly with special sales and in extreme cases resorts to free distribution of cereals through Mali's Agency for Agricultural Produce.

Both the length and density of the distribution channel are important for proper understanding of the price formation and the magnitude of margins at different distribution layers. Different factors are crucial in shaping trade channels as examined below.

Bamako and Timbuktu Distribution Channels

The Bamako route appears to be closer to the main production basins and have greater supply potential from most of the regions. Conversely, the Timbuktu route suffers from limited supply due its remoteness. Delivery costs tend to be lower for Bamako route because the road network is better and there are also economies of scale that derive from a larger consumption market. In addition to the considerable demand of Bamako's population, the Bamako route meets demand from large institutional buyers, from other neighbouring regions of Mali and Upper Guinea. In contrast, on the Timbuktu route, the market shrinks as one leaves zones of supply and approaches areas of consumption. Timbuktu is chiefly a place of final consumption where there are no wholesalers. All those factors serve to limit competition in this market.

Millet, sorghum and local and imported rice are transported on both the Bamako and Timbuktu corridors. However, only a tiny amount of imported rice is carried on the Timbuktu route as most local rural inhabitants grow their own rice.

In addition to the business-related costs and storage costs, market players face extra costs arising from illegal practices and obstacles to trade such as roadblocks and corruption.

There seems to be two groups of merchants involved in the cereal trade in Mali. The two groups differ in terms of the scale of their activities, their access to credit and legal system, their managerial capacity and the market served. The first group is made up of small-scale operators with little managerial skill and no access to formal credit or the legal system to ensure contracts are respected. They act locally in the market and serve to store and transport cereals in the local or regional market. The second group is made up of major operators with a degree of managerial capacity and access to credit and the legal system. They serve to connect between regions within the country as well as connecting the domestic market with the international market through imports and exports.

The interviews show that bank credit only accounts for 5 per cent of the funding of activities. This situation strengthens the hand of large wholesalers in areas of consumption (chiefly Bamako) who play a major role in funding players' activities upstream and have the power to negotiate and set prices.

PRICE-SETTING AND PRICE TRANSMISSION

We look now at the mechanisms for setting and channelling prices in the markets for the three cereals (millet, sorghum and rice) with particular reference to Bamako and Timbuktu. We then evaluate the intensity of competition in these markets and examine the international price variations' effects on domestic prices and supply conditions.

Price-setting and Market Competition

The prices of millet, sorghum and rice are, in principle, unregulated throughout the country and set freely by supply and demand forces.[6] In general, prices tend to be low when supply is abundant (post-harvest time) and gradually increase as supply drops and the season advances.

In practice, however, physical constraints due to the remoteness of some regions, poor infrastructure, inadequate public policies and actors' anticompetitive behaviour have distortionary effects on prices and seem to penalize much more the poorest households.

An analysis of time series of prices for dry grain, especially millet, reveals that overall prices tend to be higher in Timbuktu than in Bamako. Other factors accounting for high prices in the north of the country relate to the small number of markets; the high transportation costs and risks of supply interruption often due to inaccessibility and limited supply choices.

The poor state of the roads, long distances between different regions and limited availability of transport vehicles often mean that excess demand in one region (zones of consumption in the north) coexists alongside excess supply in zones of production without genuine spatial arbitrage opportunities. Due to its more developed road network, the proximity of its supply markets and the vast scale of the volumes involved, Bamako's delivery costs are much lower and therefore prices are more competitive.

Cereal prices can be regulated or imposed in some circumstances. For example the wholesale and retail price for imported rice RM40 was set by the authorities in 2005, 2008 and 2009. The decision of institutional buyers such as OPAM, WFP or NGOs to enter the market and make large transactions affects prices. Sudden changes in export and import policies of the government also lead to volatility in market prices. In recent years, authorities imposed taxes on exports and then banned exports of some cereals to neighbouring countries. They have also removed tariffs on imports and offered subsidies to importers.

In addition to the government, private actors tend also in some circumstances to restrict market competition and free price determination. Dominant players in the marketing network fix the prices they pay to dependent collectors (Diarra 2008). However, such imposed prices are only relevant for market price determination where there are no other collectors from competing networks. Similarly, there is a growing tendency for farmers' professional organizations to negotiate a fair price for their members instead of dealing individually with collectors and merchants. Such negotiated prices are observed by all members and usually rise over time.

Although Malian regulations crack down on unfair and anticompetitive practices, 58 per cent of traders interviewed align their prices with those of their competitors and 60 per cent admit that they usually agree with other operators on prices. In the same vein, transporters confirm that they have to respect the prices indicated by their unions. Aware that consumers do not check the weight of cereal bags, some traders cheat over the weighing process and offer prices that are slightly lower than those prevailing in the market. Some transporters also drop the price of transportation and compensate by overloading their lorries.

Few if any traders know there is a law on competition: almost 80 per cent of traders and even a larger proportion of transporters state that they are unaware of the existence of a competition law. Their unfamiliarity with this law is due to lack of information in two cases out of three, and due to non-application of laws on cereal trading in other cases. One out of two interviewed operators did not know that there is an authority that oversees competition. Although they are familiar with the DNCC (National Directorate for Trade and Competition), formerly the DNAE (National Directorate for Economic Affairs), this is only in its role of checking prices and seizing fraudulent or out-of-date stocks. Poor communication and poor enforcement of the competition law are frequently quoted as the main reasons for this. Market players' knowledge gap combined with the strongly interventionist culture of the administrative and political authorities are serious challenges for a proper implementation of competition policy in Mali.

Price Transmission from Producers to Consumers

There are four major markets involved in the trade of grain from producer to consumer: production market, assembly market, wholesale/semi-wholesale market and retail market. At each stage there is a change in the price charged for each cereal, and that accounts for gross margins. The latter could be divided into two components: transportation and other transaction costs and the net margin. Such decomposition, although vital, could not be performed due to lack of information on different costs incurred by cereal dealers from collectors to retailers.

Table 4.5 provides data on average absolute gross margins for each of the three cereals, with a distinction between local and imported rice, associated with each trading stage in Bamako and Timbuktu, over the period 2007–9.

On average from the production market to the retail market, the price of one kilo of millet sold in Bamako increased by 65 FCFA, which is the equivalent of a total gross margin of 62.5 per cent. Out of that margin, 52 per cent was captured by retailers, 40 per cent by collectors and only 8 per cent by wholesalers. For the same cereal, the gross margin in absolute value is 14 per cent higher in Timbuktu. The breakdown of the margin between the various intermediaries seems similar to the one in Bamako with more than 90 per cent of the gross margin shared between collectors and retailers.

As far as sorghum is concerned, the gross absolute margin from the production to the retail markets is quite similar for both Bamako and

Table 4.5 Price changes at different trading stages (in FCFA by kilograms)

		Collecting market		Wholesale market		Retail market		Total gross margin	
		Bamako	Timbuktu	Bamako	Timbuktu	Bamako	Timbuktu	Bamako	Timbuktu
Production market	Millet	26	33	5	6	34	35	65	74
	Sorghum	21	32	5	11	35	16	61	59
	Local rice	45	32	5	11	31	10	81	53
Imports	Imported rice	–	–	80	85	25	25	105	110

Source: Authors' calculations based on OMA data.

Timbuktu. There is, however, a noticeable difference in the way the gross margin is shared among operators. Bamako's retailers earn most of the margin (58 per cent), while Timbuktu's collectors earn most of the margin (54 per cent). A second difference exists in the share of the gross margin that goes to wholesalers (19 per cent in Timbuktu compared to 7 per cent in Bamako).

Conversely, the total gross margin on local rice was much higher in Bamako than in Timbuktu at 81 and 53 FCFA respectively. As indicated earlier, most of the rice traded in Timbuktu is produced locally and thus lower transaction costs would be incurred. Regarding the sharing of the margin, collectors earn most of it in both cities. The difference is striking, however, between the portions of the margin captured by wholesalers and retailers in the two cities. In Bamako, wholesalers only earn 6 per cent of the total gross margin compared to 21 per cent in Timbuktu. On the other hand, retailers earn 38 per cent of the gross margin in Bamako compared to 19 per cent in Timbuktu.

The market structure, for imported rice, tends to be oligopolistic, with a few big players tightly controlling supply in the domestic market. The value of total gross margin is much higher for imported rice compared to other cereals including locally produced rice as it amounted to 105 and 110 FCFA in Bamako and Timbuktu respectively. In addition, unlike other cereals, most of the margin was captured by importers who also operate as wholesalers. They earn roughly three-quarters of the total gross margin. Those who operate in rice imports are usually of large size, well-connected and endowed with more equipment and financial capacity than other actors. The conducted interviews indicate that limited access to finance is an obstacle to competition in the cereal market and particularly in the imported rice market.

Finally, the Observatoire du Marché Agricole's (OMA) agricultural market information system supplies information on prices and volumes traded in and between markets. Informational barriers seem present, however. This is chiefly due to the lack or underutilization of the information needed for decision-making. A large proportion of actors do not make use of this information, despite it being broadcast on radio and TV. This includes producers, retailers and a number of semi-wholesalers. In the same vein, prices for consumers are rarely publicized by producers and traders.

Price Transmission for International Prices to Domestic Markets

We review the state of the international rice market between 2007 and 2009 and examine the effects it may have had on the domestic market,

Table 4.6 Share of the different intermediaries in the margin

Intermediary	Millet		Sorghum		Local rice		Imported rice	
	BKO	TIM	BKO	TIM	BKO	TIM	BKO	TIM
Aggregators/ assemblers	40	45	35	54	56	60	–	–
Wholesalers/ importers	8	8	7	19	6	21	76	77
Retailers	52	47	58	27	38	19	24	23
Total	100	100	100	100	100	100	100	100

Source: Our calculations based on OMA data; BKO refers to Bamako and TIM refers to Timbuktu.

both in terms of prices and supply flows. We also convey the opinions of the consumers' association and other public institutions as to these effects. Particular emphasis is given to the rice markets in Bamako and Timbuktu. Millet and sorghum are not considered here because they are mainly supplied by domestic producers and their imports are insignificant.

Figure 4.1 portrays the trend in world rice prices between 2007 and 2010, according to World Bank data. Prices are expressed in US dollars per metric ton.

Figure 4.1 shows that at the beginning of 2007 (from January to April) the price of rice on the world market was relatively stable. It declined very slightly in May and posted an impressive upward movement that began the last quarter of 2007 and went on till May 2008. Over that short period, rice prices more than doubled and global rice stocks registered their lowest levels for decades. Although rice prices declined starting from July 2008, their levels continued to be above those recorded in previous years.

Several factors explain why rice prices suddenly rocketed on the international market after the second quarter of 2007. The first factor was supply shortages triggered by unfavourable weather conditions in major producing countries and transformation of larger quantities of cereals including rice to meet booming demand for biofuels. The second factor was the change in consumption patterns in some emerging countries that increased their demand for specific food products such as rice. Government policies that restricted food exports in some countries and the global rise in oil prices exacerbated the upward move of prices both for rice and other food products. Oil is an input in the production process and is used in domestic and international transportation of commodities.

Most interviewees, either consumers or administrative staff and private

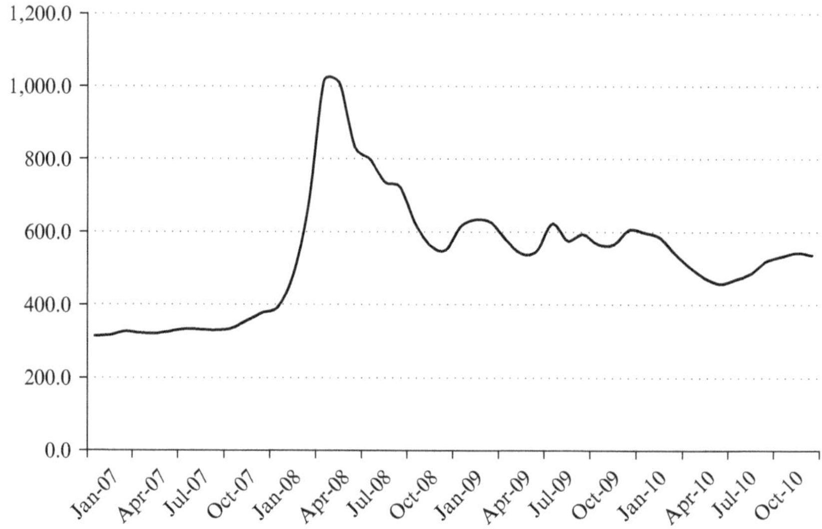

Source: World Bank (http://data.worldbank.org/data-catalog/commodity-price-data).

Figure 4.1 Trend in world rice prices (US dollars per metric ton)

operators, agree that price instability on the international market has strongly impacted domestic prices and supply conditions. Fluctuations in world rice prices had a negative effect on rice imports between 2006 and 2009 as reported in Table 4.7. Imports were lower in 2007 and 2008 compared to 2006, just when global rice prices were shooting up, and increased in 2009 by as much as 54 per cent with respect to 2006, as prices started to move down.

To a large extent, the combination of higher import prices and supply shortage shaped domestic rice prices during the period 2007–9. Figure 4.2 compares the behaviour of world market and domestic prices for imported rice. Both prices are expressed in the domestic currency FCFA by kilogram. Although domestic prices broadly mimic international prices, spells with discrepancies between both prices do exist. For instance, when the world price remained almost stable in the first half of 2007, the domestic price was both higher and more volatile. In 2008, domestic price reproduced the same upward trend as the international price in the first six months of 2008, but the former peaked at levels lower that the latter. While the international price started to decline during the second half of 2008, domestic prices continued to increase and failed to mirror the downward trends of international markets. Thus Malian consumers did not fully reap the benefit of lower international prices.

Table 4.7 Rice imports (by metric ton)

	2006	2007	2008	2009
Quantity	180,208	137,142	165,716	278,165
Percentage variation	–	−23.9	20.8	67.9

Source: National Department of Commerce and Competition (DNCC).

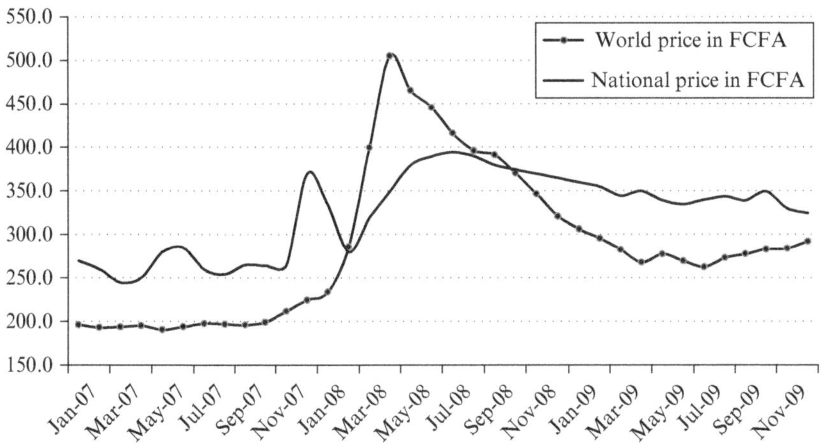

Source: World prices are based on World Bank data converted using end-of-the-month exchange rates and national prices are from the Malian observatory of cereal prices.

Figure 4.2 Comparison of trends in world and domestic rice prices (FCFA/kg)

Rice prices in Bamako and Timbuktu as reported by the Malian observatory of cereal prices, and represented in Figure 4.3, reveal that prices in both locations broadly mimic the national trend with some minor differences and time lags. In particular, when international prices soared, prices in Bamako stayed above those in Timbuktu and later converged following the decline in international prices.

Differences between international and domestic prices are chiefly attributable to the policies on exemptions and price-setting adopted by the Malian government,[7] worried that if rice prices remained high or continue to increase, this would carry serious economic and political risks. To protect the country's rice supply and cushion the effect of the increase in

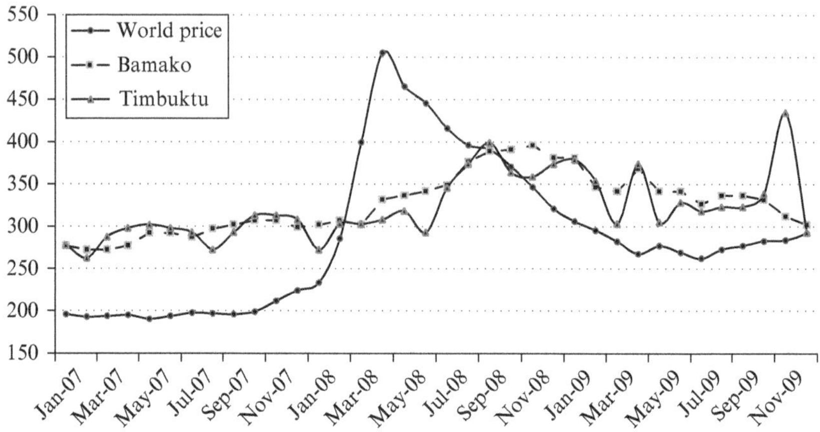

Source: World prices are based on World Bank data converted using end of the month exchange rates. Prices for Bamako and Timbuktu are from the Malian observatory of cereal prices.

Figure 4.3 Comparison of trend of world price and price of imported rice in Bamako and Timbuktu (in FCFA/kg)

international prices on the population's purchasing power, the government decided on certain measures such as exemption of fees and taxes on rice imports, temporary suspension of exports, setting of ceiling prices for this product in 2008 and 2009, as well as the establishment of cereal banks in the 703 communes of the country.

In the specific case of exemptions on rice imports, relatively large-sized actors in the market participated in this operation by signing contracts with the government. Guidelines were drawn up for setting wholesale and retail ceiling sale prices, of 300,000 FCFA per metric ton and 310 FCFA per kilogram respectively. In 2008, the contracted volumes exceeded 370,000 metric tons but only 45 per cent of this amount was actually imported. Despite exemption measures, imports remained lower than expected, mainly due to the non-availability of the product on the international market and its excessive price.

Interviews conducted show that local people were aware of all the measures taken by the government; in particular many knew of the creation of cereal banks (78 per cent of those surveyed), suspension/reduction of customs fees (68 per cent) and the suspension of VAT (51 per cent). Although these measures are held to be appropriate by local people (71 per cent of those interviewed), they are nevertheless thought by 51 per cent of interviewees to be insufficient to preserve the purchasing power of poor households. The suspension of customs fees and VAT as well as the export ban came in for most criticism. They did not necessarily benefit consumers, as part of their expected effect was captured by large importers and wholesalers who earn sizeable margins as previously highlighted. At the same time, the measures were mainly centred on consumers and neglected the negative effects on rural farmers. If domestic production is to be increased, the authorities need to be concerned by the perverse effects of their measures on the incentives of the local producers.

CONCLUSIONS AND IMPLICATIONS FOR COMPETITION POLICY

Cereal products play a key role in Mali, not just through their contribution to the agricultural value-added and employment of the population, but also in terms of their critical role for households' consumption. The challenge of securing a regular supply of grain and ensuring that the market operates in a competitive manner are major concerns for the government. Apart from their economic significance, these issues have an important social and political dimension. This chapter has highlighted several dysfunctional aspects in the cereal market in Mali.

The degree of competition of the domestic market depends on supply and demand adjusting to each other through the price mechanism in all areas of the domestic market. However, the poor state of the roads, long distances and limited availability of transport vehicles often mean that excess demand in one region (zones of consumption in the north) coexists alongside excess supply in zones of production. Due to its more developed road network, the proximity of its supply markets and the vast scale of the volumes involved, Bamako's delivery costs are much lower than on the Timbuktu route. In addition to the high demand from people in the capital, the Bamako route handles demand from the northern part of the country, Upper Guinea and purchases by public institutions. In contrast, on the Timbuktu route, the market is smaller with a limited number of wholesalers and a lesser degree of competition.

Traders who are active in the cereal market are generally organized into networks. The existence of these networks reduces transaction costs by building up trust between members. However, this tends to concentrate market power. Network members have priority in commercial transactions. These are tacit, quasi-exclusive contracts that are implemented between buyers and sellers at all stages of the distribution process.

Traders often get together to fix prices and manage flows in the supply and distribution network. These agreements cover all cereals: millet, sorghum and local rice.

The market information system, which supplies data on the prices and volumes traded in the markets, is underutilized by players. This is due to the ill-adapted nature of the market information system, which does not take into account the coordination of channels of distribution and the level of commercial margins. In addition, although the regulations call for prices to be publicized, this is rarely observed by traders.

To secure a 'sufficient' supply of cereals for the country in critical moments, the government often offers subsidies to specific rice importers. These subsidies, which take the form of import tariff exemptions, generally favour a few wholesalers with the proven capacity to cater to the whole country, and tend to distort the free play of competition. The isolated Timbuktu region sometimes receives support from the Food Security Commissariat and cereal banks in the form of large volumes of rice at prices below market levels.

On another front, the government takes measures to ban the export of cereals when there are shortages due to lack of rain or soaring international prices. These measures, which might be justified on the grounds of achieving domestic food security, inhibit the competitive operation of the market and have perverse unintended effects on competition as well as on incentive to produce and trade by rural producers.

Overall, the way the grain market operates today remains broadly unsatisfactory in terms of competition. The vast majority of those surveyed attribute their dissatisfaction to the withdrawal of the government from the commercial process and the liberalization of prices. The country continues to suffer from a lack of well-organized distribution networks, failure of small and medium-sized producers in remote regions to organize and the presence of numerous intermediaries between producers and consumers leading to excessive margins and causing higher retail prices. So far, the expected benefits for consumers of a liberalized, private sector-led cereal market are still to be seen.

NOTES

1. OPAM is the French acronym for Office des Produits Agricoles du Mali.
2. Direction nationale des statistiques et de l'informatique (DNSI), Mali
3. The field study is based on a convenience-sampling procedure as no formal lists of targeted populations (officials, merchants and transporters) were available to carry out random sampling. The results need to be treated with caution due to the inherent bias in convenience sampling. The findings are indicative but should not be systematically generalized.

4. The figures are based on the integrated household survey undertaken by the Malian National Institute of Statistics in 2006.
5. RM40 and RM25 refer, respectively, to the unsorted Malian rice with broken grains not exceeding 40 and 25 per cent; ELB refers to polished extra-long with a percentage of broken not exceeding 5 per cent and BB refers to white broken rice.
6. Article 3 of *Ordonnance* no. 07-025/P-RM of 18 July 2007 on the organization of competition.
7. In accordance with the provisions of *Décret* no. 08-260/P-RM of 6 May 2008 (Articles 13–15) laying down the means of implementation of *Ordonnance* no. 07-025/P-RM of 18 July 2007 relating to the organization of competition.

REFERENCES

Diarra, S.B. (2008) *Analyse du Marché des céréales au Mali*, Bamako: Projet d'Appui à la Commercialisation des Céréales au Mali.

Sanogo, K.D., N.N. Dembélé, J.M. Staatz and A. Traoré (2005) *Note sur la Problématique d'Approvisionnement des Céréales au Mali*, CSA, APCAM/MSU/USAID.

5. Production and distribution in the beef, poultry and milk sectors in Zambia

Thulasoni Kaira, Samuel Bwalya, Wesley S. Kalapula and Florence Banda Muleya

BACKGROUND TO THE RESEARCH

This chapter describes how market conditions have changed for the production and distribution of important protein foods in Zambia in recent years and considers the competition implications. The study covers a turbulent period of the country's political and economic history.

At independence in 1964, many sectors of the Zambian economy, including large-scale commercial cattle farming and retail distribution, were dominated by a few multinational companies. From 1968, the government implemented a series of nationalization programmes in various economic sectors anchored on socialist economic principles of economic management. In the food distribution system, the government created a system of state-owned national retail chains stores under the umbrella of the Zambia Consumer Buying Corporation (ZCBC) and the National Import and Export Corporation (NIEC). Scattered, small-sized privately owned retail and wholesale outlets were present in the major towns but they did not offer significant competition to the retail chains. Informal retail operators such as market traders, hawkers and street vendors supplied the lower end of the market. The state of the national retail system left much to be desired in terms of both reliable supply linkages and satisfying demand.

In 1991, a new government emerged from a multiparty election that marked a turning away from the previous one-party system. The new government introduced drastic changes in economic policy. It embarked on a series of market-oriented reforms that were anchored on three principles of liberalization, deregulation and privatization under the auspices of the International Monetary Fund (IMF) and the World Bank. The principal elements were deregulation by removal of price controls, privatization of previously state-owned enterprises including state-controlled monopolies and trade liberalization. The latter led to the elimination or near elimination of tariff barriers and the opening up of domestic markets to import competition. Economic liberalization opened up the economy to foreign direct investment. Foreign private investments took place in various sectors of the economy including beef, poultry and dairy. Both the retail distribution and food production industry have seen very large changes with the privatization and liberalization of the economy. Within a relatively short period, a whole new cast of market actors emerged. Foreign investors came into retail distribution and foreign chain stores now dominate the sector in terms of value of sales, range of products sold and the scale of investment. In the production of major protein foods (beef, chicken, eggs and dairy), the reforms ushered in large-scale 'industrialization' with the establishment and growth of some very large businesses, founded in this case, however, mostly on local rather than foreign investment.

This study examines the current pattern of retail distribution of three protein foods and the production of beef, poultry and dairy in Zambia 15 years or so after the introduction of market-oriented reforms. Beef, poultry and milk are the main protein items in the Zambian consumers' diet.[1] It looks especially at vertical links between production and distribution, the structure of the markets and the level of competition within each segment and within the many stages of each production chain.

The Zambian economy as a whole, including the beef, poultry and dairy sectors, is strongly dualistic, divided between 'industrialized' commercial and traditional, low-productivity, small-scale production, partly for subsistence. In each of the three protein food segments, the production chain contains many stages. In some of those stages, two distinct systems of production – industrial and small-scale – are carried on separately in parallel, while in other stages, transactions taking place between the two systems are well-established.

One private-sector conglomerate firm, Zambeef, is a dominant player in the beef segment as well as being involved in the production, processing, distribution and retailing of various agricultural products such as edible oils. Not only does it have dominance in the beef sector, it also has a significant presence in many other parts of the production chain in the poultry and dairy segments. The competition issues raised by this study all relate to the strongly dominant position of Zambeef in the beef production segment. Is the company abusing its position in the market? There would seem to be two possible ways in which this might be manifested.

First, there is a nationwide franchise arrangement between the dominant beef company and the largest distributor, a national supermarket chain. Does this have anticompetitive effects in the beef production segment or in retail distribution of fresh meat? What is the impact on consumer welfare?

Second, Zambeef has a lesser but still significant presence in other market segments. Does its monopolistic position in beef production give it the leverage and resources to enter and act in other segments in ways that might prejudice the competition process in those markets?

These are intricate issues for which no definitive evidence of anticompetitive conduct is forthcoming. Therefore, the chapter also discusses the operational implications for the competition agency when the situation in a particular product market gives rise to competition concerns, but where nothing is found to be actionable in terms of the competition law.

THE BEEF, POULTRY AND DAIRY MARKETS

Beef

Production

Pastureland covers four times the area of arable land in Zambia and livestock accounts for about 35 per cent of agricultural production by value (Bonaglia 2008). Livestock production is far below its potential, largely because of low productivity among small farmers. Traditional small farmers own most (about 80 per cent) of the national herd. On average, livestock-owning households have only a few head of cattle (Lubungu 2013).

Between 1972 and 1991, commercial beef production was monopolized by state-owned enterprises such as the Cold Storage Board of Zambia. It set up distribution arrangements with state-owned national retail outlets including ZCBC, NIEC and Mwaiseni Stores. After the 1991 privatization reforms, many new commercial producers entered the market, notably Zambeef, Pama Meats Limited, Best Beef, King Quality Beef, Savannah Beef Limited, Real Meat Company, Kachema Meat Company and Majoru Investments Limited.

Cattle are bred extensively in Zambia, not in intensive feedlot systems. This is the case not only in the communal grazing areas used by traditional farmers but also in the ranches run by larger-scale commercial producers.

Among the commercial actors in the beef sector, Zambeef is the largest business, with around two-thirds of the market in terms of both capital and sales volumes. The company is a large conglomerate that has subsidiaries in diverse agro-based products, including poultry, dairy and animal feedstuffs. It owns several beef ranches that supply its nine abattoirs with choice meat. It also purchases live cattle from traditional cattle-keepers for slaughter in its abattoirs. The company owns a fleet of refrigerated trucks that ferry carcasses from its abattoirs to various markets located principally

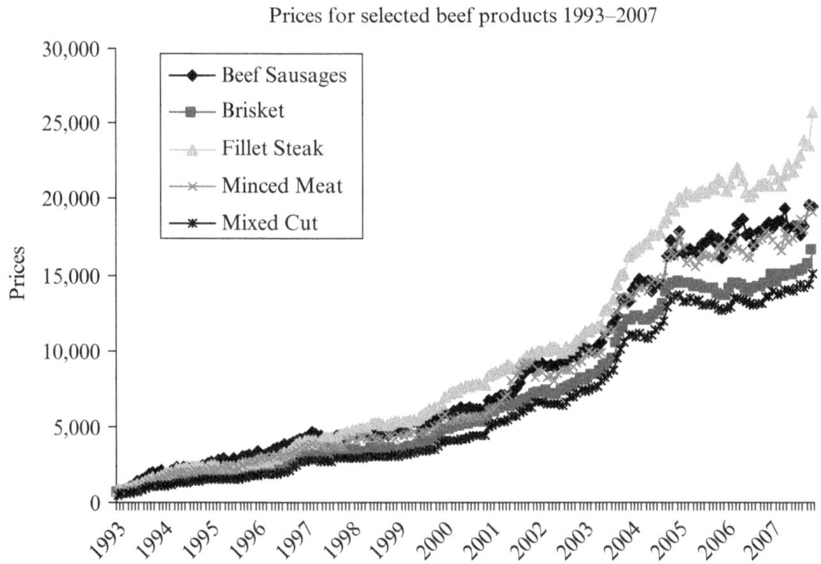

Source: Central Statistical Office.

Figure 5.1 Prices of selected beef cuts, 1993–2007

in urban areas. Transport facilities have been internalized, reducing the company's costs of supply and distribution. Management synergies have raised production efficiency among the various business units, including through reductions in the number and cost of legal contracts.

Zambeef, like other large fresh beef companies, thus has a value chain that spans production, processing and retailing of fresh meat. Smaller commercial producers also exist. Most of them have followed a different value-adding strategy, venturing downstream into processing cold meat products such as sausages, ham and polony. These include companies such as 2006 Real Meat Company, Kachema Meat Company and Majoru Investments Limited.

The price of beef has risen over the years (see Figure 5.1). The general price trend breaks down into three distinct periods. From 1993 to 2002 there was a steadily rising price trend; from 2002 to 2005 the rate of price increase gathered strength, rising steeply towards the end of that period; from 2005 to 2007 prices were much more stable.

The price hike of 2003–4 is explained by catastrophic episodes of animal disease at that time. There were massive losses of livestock and restriction of movement of live animals from one area to another by government decree. Similar restrictions were in force for two years between December 2006 to December 2008, with the same effect on prices.

Figure 5.1 also shows variations in prices of selected beef products, namely beef sausages, brisket, fillet steak, minced meat and mixed cut. The products all exhibit the same rising price trend, but the spread of prices has widened over time. Fillet steak is the most expensive type of fresh beef meat at ZMK25,000 per kilogram (US$6.58 per kilogram at the then rate of exchange). As the superior product, fillet steak is mostly consumed by high-income consumers. Mixed cut is the inferior product with the lowest price. These relative prices are consistent with the findings of a survey of retail outlets carried out for this study, covering independent outlets as well as those owned by the producers themselves.[2]

Industry informants report a strong tendency for beef to be categorized in retail outlets not just as 'beef' but in terms of the various cuts and quality grades. This 'branding', together with rising consumer incomes during a period of growth in the Zambian economy, may help account for the strongly increasing divergence of prices across products since 2005. With income growth, some consumers have been shifting demand towards higher-quality cuts. The nature of retail distribution for fresh beef meat grades, discussed below, may also have had an influence.

Market structure

The beef segment is characterized by the existence of one strongly dominant actor, Zambeef, which has a 65 per cent market share (see Table 5.1). Zambeef is a locally owned, private-sector company that began as a small butchers shop in the capital, Lusaka, in 1991. In February 2003 the company was quoted on the Lusaka stock exchange (IDE-JETRO n.d.a). Zambeef appears to be the only limited liability private-sector beef producer in Zambia whose shares can be bought and sold by the general public.

The market concentration ratio of the three largest producers (CR3) in the beef sector is 82 per cent, typifying a market that is highly concentrated, and corresponding with Zambeef's position as the dominant player. With such a large market share, Zambeef has the potential of influencing market conditions in the beef sector in Zambia through its own actions.

However, Zambeef itself has contended that its market share is significantly less, at 40 per cent, pointing to the fact that beef is graded into 'choice-choice', 'choice' and 'standard' or 'commercial' quality products. The authority found it difficult to grade beef into these categories for purposes of market share computation. By any of those metrics, however, Zambeef is the strongly dominant player in the beef sector in Zambia.

Table 5.1 also gives the value of the Herfindahl–Hirschman Index

Table 5.1 Market shares in the beef segment

Beef producer	Brand name	Ownership status	Approx. market share
Zambeef	Zambeef	Public limited liability	65%
Galaun Holdings	Luscold	Privately owned	10%
Northern Zambezi Traders	Pama	Privately owned	7%
Dar Farms	King Quality	Privately owned	3%
Best Beef Company	Best Beef	Privately owned	3%
Savannah Beef	Savannah	Privately owned	2%
Others	Micro and informal producers	Privately owned	10%
HHI			4,496

Note: 'Privately owned' here means owned by managers or family, and company stock/shares are not traded on the stock exchange.

Source: Zambia Competition Commission Survey 2006.

(HHI) of the level of concentration in the market.[3] Three discrete values are usually taken as a guide in the interpretation of the HHI values (Viscusi et al. 2005). For the levels of concentration in any given industry, a HHI value below 1,000 signifies a competitive or unconcentrated market, a HHI value of between 1,000 to 1,800 indicates a moderately concentrated market and a HHI value of above 1,800 signifies a highly concentrated market. The HHI value for the commercial beef industry stands at 4,496, which makes the beef industry in Zambia a highly concentrated market.

Zambeef's dominant position has led to a general perception that Zambeef has gained monopoly power in the beef sector. Have the arrangements that Zambeef has made for the distribution of its products contributed to its dominance as well?

The distribution of fresh beef meat

The formal distribution channels for beef meat in Zambia take supplies from both commercial and traditional livestock farmers, but the latter only indirectly. Traditional farmers sell their live animals to beef traders, who transport them for sale to butcheries or to processing companies in urban areas. Since there is a ban on movement of live animals to control disease spread, only traders with access to costly refrigerated trucks are able to supply meat to the urban markets. The movement of carcasses is cheaper than that of livestock, yet most small-scale farmers do not own refrigerated trucks, nor do they have access to abattoirs since they are located in faraway places. Thus, small-scale farmers do not participate directly in the formal distribution system. Slaughterhouses and traders offer them lower prices than they would get if they were able to sell in urban markets. Small farmers could also add value to their business by processing meat into a range of beef products, but this requires capital equipment and technology that they do not have.

Beef meat is in principle a standardized product, albeit of different quality grades. As a result of its homogenous nature, urban consumers of beef meat who live in unplanned settlements are mostly indifferent as to whether they buy from open-air markets, shops, butcheries and/or supermarkets. But higher-income urban consumers increasingly demand high-quality food products as well as hygienic standards of food preparation and handling. Increasing numbers of urban consumers are thus buying their meat from butcheries and supermarkets, where they are assured of safety. Butcheries offer beef to their customers at relatively lower prices, while supermarkets tend to aim for the higher-income consumers and charge higher prices accordingly.

At the retail level, there are some factors that may deter competition. Collaborative agreements and strategic alliances along the production chain may restrict the penetration of other firms into the retail distribution of beef. The main example of this possibility is the strategic alliance between Shoprite and Zambeef.

Shoprite is a large, multinational, South African-owned supermarket chain that was founded in 1979. It began to expand into other national markets in 1990, when it entered the market in Namibia. It first established a presence in Central Africa when it opened a store in Lusaka, Zambia in 1995. The Zambian operation is the group's largest and most mature business outside South Africa. With 39 per cent of the domestic retail market (Zambia Investment Centre) and 90 per cent of formal outlet food sales, it is the largest retailer in Zambia (IDO-JETRO n.d.b).

Shoprite operates a chain of no-frills stores, with a cost-efficient business model. It has subcontracted to Zambeef all fresh-meat butchery operations in its supermarkets. It sets high franchise standards that include packaging, weight and price considerations.[4] Zambeef has held the franchise for all 'Checkers' butchery franchises in Shoprite stores ever since the chain's launch with eight stores in 1995. Shoprite presently has 19 outlets throughout the country (Zambeef 2009).

Shoprite's volume requirements and product standards (and that of a relatively new entrant, Spar, another South African-owned chain) may be higher than many of the commercial beef producers, let alone smallholder suppliers, are able to comply with. Zambeef is said to have been awarded the franchising contract by Shoprite as it was the only company that showed willingness and capability to match Shoprite's stated specifications. Small- to medium-sized suppliers now therefore resort to securing retail sales through other, more fragmented retail outlets.

The collaboration with Shoprite has allowed Zambeef to spread out widely through the country at a low marketing cost. Given Shoprite's dominance of the retail distribution market, and the ongoing rise in household incomes in urban areas that underwrite the rise of supermarkets, the arrangement may have afforded Zambeef the possibility of monopolistically setting prices on its higher-grade beef meat to higher-income, one-stop shoppers.

Other beef products sold in Shoprite stores are frozen or processed and kept in fridges, separate from the fresh butchery counter. These are substitutes for Zambeef products only to a limited extent. In addition, Zambeef can maintain relatively high prices in their in-store butcheries by virtue of their (branded) premium quality reputation for fresh meat. Table 5.2 shows that Zambeef meat prices are consistently somewhat above the average for all individual cuts but not always the highest price. The spread is greatest at the extremes, for the least as well as for the more expensive cuts. The table also illustrates the spread of prices between different cuts that is evident in Figure 5.1. The price of the highest quality product (fillet steak) is on average 224 per cent of the lowest quality product (mixed cut).

Zambeef also practices price discrimination in different Shoprite locations. Lower prices are set on beef in lower-income areas. Lower-income areas have substitute or alternative meat suppliers in the informal market, which has lower prices (and low-quality) meat products. Zambeef's marketing strategy also includes diversification upstream and downstream. It has invested into its own retail outlets and owns 77 outlets nationwide, plus the Shoprite beef franchises. These shops tend to sell lower-quality and lower-grade cuts of beef than the Shoprite franchises. All the company's products are brought to the Zambian consumer through one or other of these outlets. None are available through any other stores. The prices charged on beef products in Zambeef's own retail outlets are much lower than charged in Shoprite. There are several reasons for this. It is more exposed to competition in those small outlets than in the supermarket sector. In that sector, Shoprite's dominance may confer a market advantage on Zambeef by association; this would also allow Zambeef to exercise price discrimination towards the wealthiest consumers who purchase its priciest products such as fillet steak (see Table 5.2). Another reason is that standards are higher in the Shoprite butcheries, which translates to higher investment in quality control, hence higher prices. In its 2009 *Annual*

Table 5.2 Beef sector brand retail prices per kilogram, January 2008, Zambian Kwacha, '000

	Zambeef	Pama	Luscold	King Quality	Best Beef	Traditional	Simple average price	Zambeef price relative to average (%)
Fillet	40,940	34,950		40,000	49,500	26,800	38,438	+ 6.5
Mince meat	23,462	20,700	30,900	21,666	24,250	18,833	23,302	+ 0.7
Beef sausage	22,933	20,500	21,450	24,000	25,500	19,083	22,244	+ 3
Brisket	19,927	16,966	17,450	21,166	22,950	16,166	19,104	+ 4
Mixed cut	17,065	13,000	13,450	13,833	21,750	16,285	15,897	+ 7

Source: Primary data collected from a survey of various retail outlets, including supermarkets and independent outlets as well as those owned by the players themselves.

Report, the company stated that its core strategy for the short term was to develop its retailing network, again aiming at higher-income consumers outside supermarket locations (Zambeef 2009).

Table 5.2 shows that in all the product lines itemized in the table, Zambeef meat prices were higher than the prices offered by smaller players on the market. Zambeef products are more expensive than any other player in the beef market, with the price premium largest in the most expensive cut (fillet). The pricing strategy pursued by Zambeef is characteristic of players that offer high-value products on the market, which in turn attract premium prices.

There is a second tier of formal retailers comprising geographically limited Zambian-owned supermarkets such as Konkola in Mazabuka (Southern Province), and Melissa and Embassy in Lusaka (Kenny and Mather 2008). Through these outlets, sales opportunities exist for local small and medium-sized farmers and other suppliers who are able to adhere to specific product and supply standards set by these supermarkets. The second-tier supermarkets are more highly priced than Shoprite, perhaps because of their narrower market base and their contracts with small to medium-scale suppliers who have higher production costs. Nonetheless, these second-tier retailers are able to command a reasonable market share within their relevant geographic market, especially of the high-income earners, because they also maintain high product standards. Shoprite stores are located on the edge of towns, while the others are situated inside residential areas.

The Poultry Industry

The poultry industry has seen a great inflow of investment since 1991 and players in the industry have benefited from rapid returns on their investments.

Poultry production is a complex activity. It breaks down into two main segments whose end products are meat and eggs. Each segment is fragmented into several stages of production, which are each commercialized and contain different market actors. Informal producers are present to a greater or lesser extent at each stage.

Poultry meat (broilers)

Poultry meat is a major source of protein in the diet of Zambian households. Of meat types, aggregate consumption by weight is second only to beef (FAO 2005). Chickens intended for consumption for their meat are referred to as 'broilers' or 'table broilers'. Broiler chickens are grown from day-old (broiler) chicks, with a production cycle of six to seven weeks from day-old chick to slaughter. Entry capital costs are not particularly high. Day-old broiler chicks are the product of hatching (broiler) eggs. Thus the poultry meat segment has at least three stages with different production characteristics at each stage, and market transactions are involved all along the chain.

Approximately 24.4 million broiler chickens are produced per annum – 15.86 million and 8.54 million in the formal and informal sectors respectively (PAZ 2007). Of broiler chickens sold at wet markets, 65 per cent are dressed while 35 per cent are live chickens. Commercial producers also collaborate with small-scale farmers to meet the demand for processed chickens on the market. The broiler segment is depicted in Figure 5.2, with some key data included.

Before 2000, the table broiler segment was largely a monopoly of Crest Chickens (Galaun Holdings, also present in beef production). However, the entry into the market after that of Verino (owned by Hybrid Poultry (Z) Limited) and Zamchick (owned by Zambeef) changed the situation.

The two largest producers in the production chain have pursued contrasting commercial strategies. Hybrid Poultry, the largest player, pursued a strategy of vertical integration upstream. Under a carefully regulated and licensed system, Hybrid Poultry imports the parents that produce the hatching eggs and goes on to produce full-grown broilers, giving it a prominent position in the broiler segment. While the upstream imports of parents and hatching eggs are permitted under licence, the day-old chicks, fully grown table chickens (live or dressed) are subjected to an import ban. Therefore, the downstream industry is not subject to foreign competition.

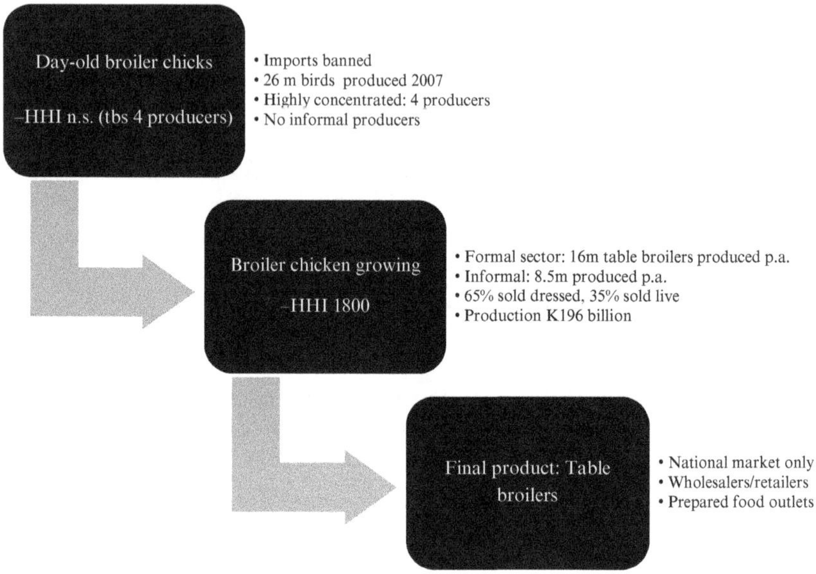

Figure 5.2 Broiler chicken production chain

Since the late 1990s, Zambia has upheld the ban on movement of all livestock within the country and barred imports of poultry in a bid to control spread of poultry diseases. The ban on importation of poultry and poultry products has been justified on grounds that lack of control would wipe out the local poultry stock and result in huge job and income losses for many small-scale farmers. This ban was still in force at the time of writing.

The second biggest producer, with 20 per cent of the market, is Zamchick, an operating division of Zambeef. As in beef, this company has practised forward (or downstream) integration by using the company's own distribution trucks and nationwide retail outlets. To add further value, it has established a fast-food fried-chicken and chips chain, Zamchick Inn, with eight outlets (Zambeef 2009). Substantial cost-reduction synergies are likely exploited along this value chain. If Zamchick were also to integrate backwards by producing day-old chicks, it might be able to realize even greater efficiencies and consolidate its competitive advantage in this segment.[5]

The price trend of processed chickens between 1993 and 2007 is evident from Figure 5.3. It shows a similar trend to beef prices, at a price per kilo somewhat less than the lower-quality beef cuts but suggesting some substitution possibilities between beef and chicken. The price rose sharply between 1993 and 2004. This may be attributed to the limited supply

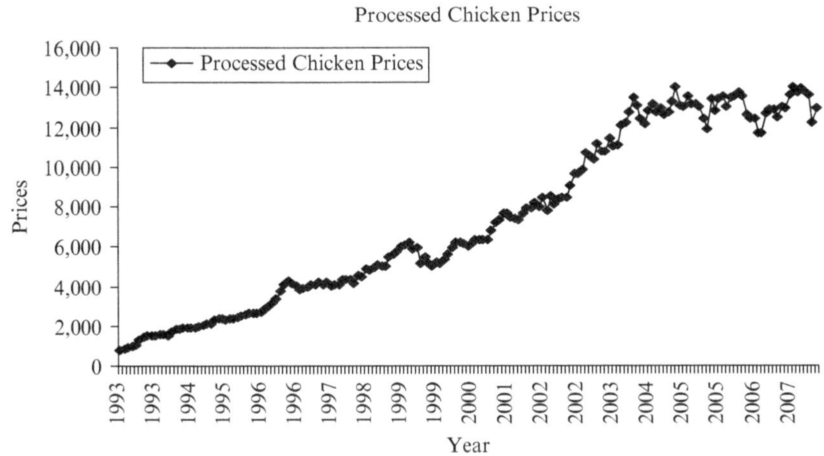

Source: Central Statistical Office and primary field data.

Figure 5.3 Prices of processed chicken per kilogram, 1993–2007, Zambian Kwacha

of day-old chicks, the ban on poultry imports, rising demand and the relatively high production costs occasioned by high stock feed prices and veterinary costs.

Since 2004, shortly after the ending of Crest's monopoly, the trend price of broiler chickens has plateaued – earlier than was the case with beef – although with considerable fluctuations. This pattern is mainly attributed to increased competition in the market from 2003. New entrants came into the day-old chicks production stage (Ross breeders took over Tamba Chicks in 2000 and Hybrid took over Bokomo), and allowed increased breeding of broilers at both large- and small-scale out-grower operations.

The broiler market structure is much more competitive than the beef segment. There are four players with 10 per cent or more of the market (see Table 5.3). The HHI figure for the broiler segment is 1,800. This figure indicates a market structure that is moderately concentrated, with Hybrid having the largest market share. This finding is backed by the concentration ratio of the three largest producers (CR3) that stands at 60 per cent.

Table 5.4 shows the different producers' table broiler/processed chicken prices. Zamchick pricing is similar in some respects to its pricing policy in the beef meat market. In two-thirds of its product categories, its prices are around 6 per cent above competitors, but in one location, Mazabuka, they are significantly lower. In respect of beef, apart from having its own retail outlets, Zambeef beef meat products are not on sale in any other outlet

Table 5.3 Market shares for processed table broiler brands

Producer	Brand name	Ownership status	Market share
Hybrid Poultry	Verino	Private	25%
Zambeef	Zamchick	Public limited liability	20%
Galaun Holdings	Crest	Public	15%
Eureka Chickens	Eureka	Private	10%
Savannah Chickens	Savannah	Private	5%
Zambezi Nkuku	Zambezi Nkuku	Private	5%
Informal Sector	Traditional	Informal	20%
HHI			1,800

Source: Figures estimated from Zambia Competition Commission Survey 2006, PAZ (2007) and findings of the survey.

Table 5.4 Processed chicken retail price in Zambian Kwacha per kilogram in supermarkets by producer and by location

Supermarket and location town	Crest	Eureka	Verino	Zamchick	Simple average price	Zamchick relative to average price (%)
Shoprite						
Kabwe	14,400		13,400	14,900	14,233	+ 5
Lusaka	13,980	13,980	11,280	14,400	13,410	+ 7
Livingstone	11,675	11,680	11,226		11,527	–
Mazabuka	11,680		11,580	10,980	11,413	– 4
Spar						
Choma		9,433			9,433	–
Livingstone		13,280			13,280	–
Lusaka		15,330			15,330	–
Konkola						
Mazabuka			13,200		13,200	–
Mellisa						
Lusaka	16,000	15,300	18,000		16,433	–
Embassy						
Lusaka		16,500			16,500	–

Source: Primary data collected from Zambia Competition Commission Survey 2006; data from suppliers with less than 10 per cent market share are omitted.

Table 5.5 Market actors, ownership and market shares for day-old broiler chicks

Producer	Brand name	Ownership status	Market share (%)
Hybrid	Cobb/Bovans	Foreign	45
Ross Breeders	Ross	Foreign	40
Bokomo	Ross/Lohnman	Foreign	10
Panda	Hubbarb	Local	5

Source: Figures estimated from Zambia Competition Commission Survey 2006, PAZ (2007), as well as findings from the survey.

except Shoprite, where it is granted exclusivity in fresh beef products. However, it does not have exclusivity in poultry products.

Day-old broiler chicks

By contrast, the day-old broiler chicks market is highly concentrated, with four commercial producers supplying broiler chicks (see Table 5.5). There is no informal sector production in this segment. Leading players in broiler chicks are Hybrid Poultry and Ross Breeders. Hybrid Poultry has a standing order to supply Eureka Chickens. Ross Breeders is vertically integrated at three stages, i.e., they import the parents that produce the hatching eggs and have their own hatcheries as well. The biggest customers for day-old chicks are Zamchick, Crest Chickens and Bokomo. In addition, export opportunities are exploited in Tanzania, Kenya and the Democratic Republic of Congo on a surplus production basis.

In this segment, the quality of the product is very important. The breed and genetics influence whether a chick will withstand the pressures of disease and the weather, as well as its compatibility with feed brands. Product branding also indicates whether the supplying firm will provide strong support services such as capacity-building, technical assistance and seminars.

More competition in this segment might succeed in bringing down the prices of day-old broiler chicks. There could then be knock-on effects down the whole value chain and, assuming no supra-normal margins or collusion by other market actors at later stages, reductions in the final retail prices of broiler chickens to the advantage of consumers.

Table eggs

As in the broiler segment, the production of table eggs is broken down into several stages, with commercial transactions at each threshold. The production chain is illustrated in Figure 5.4. The level of concentration (HHI value) is noted for each stage

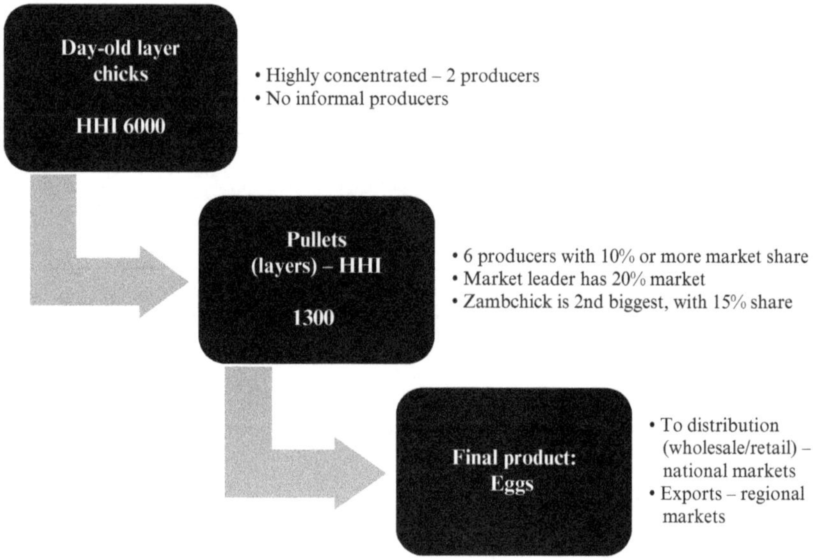

Figure 5.4 Table eggs production chain

Table 5.6 Market shares and HHI for layer pullet chicks

Producer	Market share
Bokomo	60%
Hybrid	40%
HHI	6,000

Source: Zambia Competition Commission Survey.

As for broiler chickens, production is specialized between egg-hatching to produce day-old chicks and management of layer pullets (chickens). There are only two suppliers to the market in day-old (laying) chicks: Bokomo and Hybrid (see Table 5.6). Bokomo entered the market in 1998 taking over an existing producer (Nulaid) and now has 60 per cent of this market. The second producer is Hybrid. Both are also in the day-old broiler chick market where the situation is reversed: in that case, Hybrid is the market leader.

This market is a duopoly with a HHI of 6,000. There is clearly no effective competition in this segment compared to day-old broiler chicks. On the other hand, Zambeef and perhaps other large egg-producers do not

Table 5.7 Market shares and HHI in table eggs

Producer	Brand name	Ownership status	Market share
Flamingo	Golden Lay	49% foreign	20%
Mega Farms	Mega Eggs	Private	15%
Zambeef	Zamchick Eggs	Publicly owned	15%
Cedrics Farm	Cedrics	Private/foreign	10%
Simonga Farms	Simonga	Locally owned	10%
Collet		Local/foreign	10%
Bokomo		Local/foreign	5%
Sunrise		Local/foreign	5%
Others		Locally owned	10%
HHI			1300

Source: Estimated from Zambia Competition Commission Survey 2006 and PAZ (2007).

have recourse to this market because they produce their own laying hens from in-house hatcheries.

The demand for table eggs has been growing and prices have been rising. Exports of eggs have been on the rise. Eggs have widespread market potential as long as they are transported efficiently, being vulnerable to breakages. Zambia has been a major exporter of eggs to neighbouring countries.

Table 5.7 shows market shares of the industry players in egg production. Six producers have a market share of 10 per cent or more. Flamingo has the highest market share of 20 per cent. Zamchick, with a 15 per cent market share, claims to be the only producer with national spread (Zambeef 2009). The HHI of 1,300 indicates that the table eggs industry demonstrates a moderate level of concentration. The market structure for broilers has a direct bearing on the table egg market, with possible cross-subsidization of prices.

Dairy (Milk) Industry

Market liberalization has led to a rapid and fundamental transformation of the Zambian dairy sector. Considerable foreign direct investment (FDI) has come into this industry, and a number of international partnerships have been formed. The result is a new formal dairy sector characterized by changing institutional and organizational forms as well as technological innovation. Prices have come down and marketing and production improvements in the sector have brought about increases in efficiency, capacity and quality of raw milk production. The sector has expanded based on increased consumption attributable to rise in national population and incomes. There is also increased awareness among consumers of the nutritional value and the importance of dairy products.

Milk producers and processors

The milk production system includes three types of dairy farmers (producers) and one set of market actors (processors) that are not reliant on supplies from the agricultural sector in Zambia.

Large commercial producers run capital intensive operations with herds of pure-bred, high-yielding dairy cattle, producing up to 28 litres per cow per day. Emergent or medium-sized dairy farmers can sell raw milk down the production chain in excess of domestic requirements and local informal market demand, if any; their cows typically produce only two to five litres per day. Medium-sized producers have been growing in number and the volume of milk produced.

The third type, traditional small-scale farmers, have such low productivity (partly because their cattle are not special dairy breeds) that they rarely sell their milk and then only in informal rural markets. The great majority of the national cattle herd consists of animals owned by smallholders and less than 10 per cent of the total national cattle herd are milked (FAO 2005).

Traditional and emergent farmers have a huge role to play in improving milk production in Zambia. Without them, the ever-increasing demand for dairy products cannot be met from local suppliers. The perishability of milk and associated health concerns mean that milk production presents a number of interesting challenges to smallholders for accessing the formal retail dairy market. Medium-sized producers are mainly located in peri-urban areas and resettlement schemes, and organized in associations around milk collection centres from where processors collect raw milk and some milk is sold directly to consumers. But setting up quality-controlled collection and distribution centres for them and smaller-scale traditional farmers is a huge challenge. Many technical and infrastructural improvements are needed, including cold storage collection tanks and milking parlours, and improved breeds of cattle. Some smaller farmers receive assistance in dairy production from processor buyers of their milk in the form of training in hygiene and access to dairy farm inputs. Parmalat is particularly active in this respect. While it receives about 70 per cent of its milk from large commercial farmers, it also buys in milk from about 400 medium-sized and small farmers. It has invested in infrastructure to assist them improve the volumes and quality of raw milk (Kenny and Mather 2008).

Four relevant product markets

In order to assess competition concerns in the milk market, it is important to consider market definition more carefully. There is not one, but four relevant product markets in the milk industry.

In the *unprocessed (raw) fresh milk* market, the economic actors are the traditional cattle-keepers. Herd ownership is highly fragmented and cows produce little milk per animal. As a result of the small quantity of milk each farmer produces, they have organized themselves to form associations that collect milk for processor buyers. This way they are able to participate in the formal marketing of milk; otherwise the milk is sold informally in rural markets and some is for family consumption. They do not themselves process the milk, since they lack the resources and capacity to enter that market. There are no competition concerns in this market.

The *processed fresh milk* market accounts for the majority of milk sales in formal retail outlets. It is a small market with good prospects of growth, in line with Zambia's overall economic outlook. The economic actors in this product market are milk processors. Large-scale commercial farms supply about 60 per cent of the total annual volume of milk bought by processors, which then forward their products into the formal distribution channels (Mukumbuta and Sherchand 2006).

Milk processors in Zambia have formed themselves into the Zambia Dairy Processors Association, whose industry directory indicates that there are 19 processors, many of which are small to medium-size. The biggest processors in terms of capacity are Parmalat and Zammilk, another operating division of Zambeef. Parmalat has installed processing capacity of approximately 120,000 litres per day but it has very high excess capacity; it only utilizes 45 per cent of its capacity. Zammilk has upgraded its pasteurizer capacity from 3,000 to 24,000 litres per day and it operates at more or less full capacity. Accordingly, Parmalat is the biggest producer, with Zammilk taking second place. Table 5.8 shows the market shares of the main commercial milk producers in this product market.[6]

At the time of this research, the third relevant product market, the *reconstituted milk market*, included only one monopoly actor. This was Finta, a local company located in Southern Province that imported powdered milk from the international market and manufactured reconstituted (liquid) milk locally. It was expected that more players would enter this market owing to the low costs of manufacturing reconstituted milk.

The final relevant product market was in *powdered milk*. There were no local producers at the time of this study. All powdered milk on the market was imported.[7] Two brands of powdered milk were common, Cow Bell and Needle, both targeted at higher-income groups and mainly marketed

Table 5.8 Market shares in processed fresh milk

Producer	Brand name	Status of firm	Market share of total milk market
Parmalat	Parmalat	71.5% foreign	50%
Zambeef	Zammilk	Publicly owned	20%
Galaun Holdings	Diamondale	Privately owned	12%
CR3			82

Note: 'Privately owned' here means owned by managers or family, and company stock/shares are not traded on the stock exchange.

Source: Figures estimated from Zambia Competition Commission Survey 2006, Zambia Dairy Producers Association as well as findings from the survey.
The top producers account for 82 per cent of the market on the CR3 measure. There is therefore a very concentrated market in the processed fresh milk market.

in big shops, especially supermarkets. Their prices are very high for those on average incomes.

Milk distribution

The large milk processors have also taken steps to ensure the growth or sustainability of their share of the downstream milk sales market. Parmalat instituted a distributorship system where refrigerated containers/cold rooms were given to selected distributors on a loan basis, exclusively to handle Parmalat dairy products. The arrangement is largely wholesale-based; appointed agents are paid on commission to sell on the stocks from the containers (Kenny and Mather 2008). Final retailing of dairy products, including milk, is fragmented through independent outlets ranging from Spar to formal and informal convenience stores.

As in the case of beef, Zambeef (Zammilk) sells its milk through Shoprite stores on an exclusive basis. Spar stores do not buy dairy products centrally and are therefore able in principle to source supplies from some smaller milk producers; but, as in the beef segment, these cannot in the main meet Shoprite's volume or quality standards (Kenny and Mather 2008).

Table 5.9 shows dairy sector retail prices by product in January 2008. As with chicken meat, Zambeef (Zammilk) generally prices its products in the midrange of its competitors. However, it sets the lowest price of all main suppliers for the largest, two-litre packages, suggesting that it may be aiming to capture higher income consumers who have refrigerators at home.

Table 5.9 Milk retail price by producer, January 2008, Zambian Kwacha

	Parmalat	Surprise Dairy	Eastwood Farm	Kaposhi	Zammilk	Finta	Galaun
Milk 250ml	1,750				1,500		1,125
Milk 500ml	2,588	2,280	2,650		2,217		2,300
Milk 1l		5,950	5,750				4,800
Milk 2l	10,145	10,000	8,680		8,531		9,000
Top life 250ml	2,447					2,100	
Top life 500ml	3,382					3,150	
Top life 1l	7,150						

Source: Primary data collected for the survey.

COMPETITION CONCERNS AND INTERVENTIONS

The principal objectives of this study were to analyze the current structure of production and distribution of the major protein foodstuffs in Zambia (beef, dairy and poultry) in the aftermath of economic liberalization in the early 1990s. The study examined the production and current pattern of retail distribution of three protein foods, beef, poultry and dairy, in Zambia 15 years or so after the introduction of market-oriented reforms. The main issue was to explore the competition implications of the existence of one, strongly dominant supplier in one of those segments (beef) that was also a major player in the market in the other segments. In policy terms, the intention was to examine existing competition policies and regulations in Zambia and recommend reforms to promote efficiency and consumer welfare in the retail sector as whole and the beef and poultry sectors in particular.

The structure of the beef, dairy and poultry sectors of the Zambian economy has changed drastically in the post-reform period. In general, there has been a large increase in the number of smaller players and improvements in the quality of products sold to the consumer. The increased number of producers in these sectors has afforded the consumer a broader choice of products. However, product prices have risen throughout the post-liberalization period and in some segments the market structure is heavily concentrated. This raises some competition concerns.

In the beef segment, Zambeef is a strongly dominant, quasi-monopolistic player with a 65 per cent market share. It is also present to a greater or lesser degree in all the other protein foods production segments, with shares of 20 per cent of the table broiler market, 15 per cent of the table eggs market and 20 per cent of the processed milk market.

In order for its products to reach the final consumer, Zambeef uses two distribution channels. It maintains its own network of retail stores selling its whole range of protein foods. There were 77 such outlets at the time of this study. Zambeef also has an exclusive fresh beef franchising contract with the main player in the supermarket sector, Shoprite. This franchising arrangement intensifies Zambeef's dominance in the beef industry at least in one market segment: the sale of higher-priced, higher-quality cuts and the custom of higher-income, urban consumers who are the clientele of supermarket chains in Zambia, as elsewhere.

The success of Zambeef in vertically integrating its production capability throughout the production chain provides a lesson to its rivals in how to bring down costs and improve efficiency and business growth. But the double basis of its dominance of the fresh beef market, by way of the tie-up between production and distribution, carries suspicions of abuse of its dominant position to consumers' disadvantage. There are three specific concerns.

The first concern is that Zambeef's direct and indirect dominance in the retail market for beef meat might allow monopolistic pricing of its products. This depends on market definition, which is dependent in particular on whether consumers have alternatives to beef. Availability of substitute products always disciplines and waters down the competitive power of an incumbent, dominant player. The competitive restraint presented by substitute products often has the effect of lowering the price the dominant player had planned it to be. For this reason, prices tend to be lower in the presence of alternative products, as well as the existence of the other products broadening the choice for the consumer.

There is some substitutability across beef meat cuts and into beef products, such as sausages, and into other protein foods such as chicken and pork. The similarity of long-term trend prices in beef meat and broilers suggests as much. The Zambeef CEO explained how consumers switch between the two in his discussion of market developments in 2008 (Zambeef 2009). In terms of choice between distribution outlets, there are close substitution possibilities within the Shoprite stores across protein foods groups; for example, between fresh beef and processed meat products and chicken meat, and possibly also frozen beef and fresh beef cuts supplied by other producers. There are also a range of alternative retail outlets where consumers may go to buy fresh beef. Consumers' options – small butcher shops, including Zambeef's own outlets (where prices are lower than in Shoprite), other beef producers' retail stores and small local supermarkets – will vary by locality. In this scenario, Zambeef can evidently charge premium prices for its top-of-the-range cuts in Shoprite franchise butcheries serving higher-income supermarket customers who may see no substitute for those products sold in the largest, most 'modern' outlets. It may also be able to trade on its reputation for quality and charge slightly above-average prices across the whole range of beef cuts. But there are clearly market limits to the extent to which it can raise prices on its beef meat in general. Therefore its monopolistic powers are constrained in this respect.

Second is the potentially anticompetitive nature of the vertical agreement between Zambeef and Shoprite. Does it prevent entry of new beef producers or of new suppliers of meat into the distribution sector? The long-lasting nature of the franchising agreement is suggestive of an open-ended exclusionary understanding between the two dominant players in the beef segment and in retailing. In other jurisdictions, vertical agreements are usually exempted from prosecution under the competition law. Nevertheless, in the case of the UK, for example, exemptions for franchises are not automatically granted. They can be scrutinized for possible anticompetitive effects if the market share of either the supplier or the buyer business exceeds 30 per cent (Office of Fair Trading 2004).

In Zambia, franchises are not specifically mentioned in the 1994 competition law. Vertical agreements are permitted as long as they do not permit the distributor to dictate the level of prices charged by a franchisee. It would therefore be necessary to demonstrate that the Zambeef–Shoprite franchise arrangement included price-fixing. This could be demonstrated definitively if price-fixing was mentioned in the terms of the franchising contract. On 18 September 2014, the commission requested that African Supermarkets, trading as Shoprite, notifies the agreement that they have with Zambeef Products Plc. The commission instituted investigations under Sections 8 and 14 of the Competition and Commission Protection Act, No. 24 of 2010 ('the Act') to establish the facts surrounding the effects of the transaction in the relevant market. The investigations revealed that Shoprite had an exclusive concession with Zambeef, whereby it (Zambeef) was not allowed to enter into a similar concessionary agreement with any entity deemed by Shoprite to be a direct competitor for the duration of the agreement without Shoprite's prior written consent, which consent would not be unreasonably withheld. Following its competition assessment tests, the commission decided that this exclusivity clause should be excluded from the agreement. Zambeef should be at liberty to supply Shoprite competitors without consulting Shoprite. The commission further decided that Shoprite should use a competitive bidding process to allow Zambeef competitors also to make an offer if they have the capacity to meet the requirements of Shoprite. This outcome may seem paradoxical, in the light of Zambeef's dominant position in the beef market. But it did carry the potential for promoting competitive pressure on the dominant player in the retail market.

The third competition concern is Zambeef's potential use of its business resources, generated primarily in the beef segment, to cross-subsidize sales of its products in other production segments. For instance, in Shoprite, it appears that Zambeef sets a relatively higher price premium on fresh beef meat where it has exclusivity of supply (that is, in the franchise butcheries) and a lower price on chicken products relative to other suppliers. The issue is whether those lower prices on chicken are possible because they are compensated from the profits generated by beef sales through cross-subsidization.

Cross subsidization has a strict definition in this context. It refers to the subsidization of production costs in one line of production from the profits generated in another line of production within the same business (Viscusi et al. 2005). Thus the evidence needed to demonstrate cross-subsidization is not lower prices in themselves, but the below-cost pricing of a product (Faulhaber 2005). In the case of Zambeef, the allegation would therefore be that profits generated in beef production are used to offset the production costs of chicken and facilitate below-cost pricing.

Moreover, there is some debate in the literature as to whether, even where this condition is met, cross-subsidization is anticompetitive. Some argue that banning below-cost pricing would lead to higher profits and higher prices for one-stop shoppers and reduce consumer surplus (Chen and Rey 2013).

To pursue this allegation in Zambia under the competition law, two types of information would be needed. First, the study revealed that although Zambeef's chicken pricing seems to be aggressively low in one location (Mazabuka), it sets product prices above those of its rivals in other locations. A lengthy effort to monitor prices in a larger number of retail outlets would be required to establish sustained anticompetitive strategic pricing of broilers on the company's part.

In addition, information would be needed on production costs and the profitability of broiler production. Beef is certainly among the most profitable production lines within Zambeef. According to the company's *Annual Report 2009*, in 2007 the gross profit rate of beef production was 37 per cent (its 'normal' level), but trading conditions the following year were difficult and the rate declined to 27 per cent. In broiler chicken production, the fall in profitability was even more severe during that period, from 22 per cent to 9 per cent. Nevertheless the profit rate apparently remained positive in that segment. So there is no immediate evidence of below-cost pricing of broiler meat. In connection with the real cost of production of broilers, it would not be difficult to establish whether broiler production costs were in fact subsidised, since the major part of broiler-specific feedstuffs are imported and the prices paid for those inputs would be equivalent or close to the world market price at the time of purchase. The matter could also be investigated by examining Zambeef's financial transactions as well as its shipping and trading prices.

These issues could, in principle, be explored in the context of a case investigation that might be brought under Section 7.2(b) of the 1994 competition law on discriminatory pricing. The provision relates to the nature of transactions between affiliated enterprises that 'overcharge or undercharge for goods or services purchased or supplied as compared with prices for similar or comparable transactions outside the affiliated enterprises'. However, unless precise and comprehensive data on broiler prices became available, there would be no *prima facie* case of cross-subsidization and a case investigation would be unlikely to be launched.

Zambia's 1994 competition law has been criticized for weaknesses addressing certain anticompetitive trade practices; the law is more reactive than proactive in this respect (UNCTAD 2013). With respect to mergers and acquisitions, for instance, parties signing agreements are not expressly required to seek the clearance of the commission before effecting them in the market place. At the time of this study, the enforcement agency, the Zambian Competition Commission was in fact in the process of amending the competition legislation (and the law was subsequently changed). Among other things, the commission wished to prescribe a statutory threshold that would compel all firms meeting that threshold to seek the commission's clearance of their agreements before they were effected, as in the 'negative clearance' concept of the European Commission Competition Directorate. The proposed revision is clearly germane to protein foods production in Zambia, which this study shows needs to be seen as a set of distinct, although interrelated, segments. Many of those segments display heavy market concentration and the whole sector is overshadowed by the extremely dominant position of one market player, which is based in the beef segment but significantly present across all segments. The commission should therefore be especially concerned to promote the competition process in the provision of protein foods to the Zambian consumer. The new notification procedure would enable the commission to monitor the competition implications of any proposed consolidation of businesses in any part of this industry. Two merger notifications have been made in recent years following the introduction of the new provision.

First, in 2013 the Competition and Consumer Protection Commission reviewed the takeover of Mega Eggs Limited by Bokomo Zambia Limited. Bokomo Zambia specialized in the selling of day-old chicks and rearing of laying chickens and Mega Eggs specialized in the rearing of laying chicken for the production and sale of eggs. In respect of the eggs market, the commission established that the transaction would not result in substantial lessening of competition because of high countervailing power and low barriers to entry as well as considerable number of suppliers. In addition, the commission established that the transaction would not result in the creation or strengthening of dominance in the relevant market. In connection with the supply of day-old chicks, the commission observed that only Bokomo Zambia of the merging parties was in that line of business and the merger was a vertical one in that respect. As such, the commission established that there would be no change in the relevant market structure post-merger and approved the merger. Later in 2013, the commission received a merger application involving Zamchick Limited and Rainbow Chicken Limited. The transaction involved the sale to Rainbow of 49 per cent of Zambeef's shareholding in its wholly owned subsidiary Zamchick Limited, which specialized in the growing, slaughtering and processing, distribution and retailing of broiler chickens. Rainbow Chickens Limited is a South African incorporated processor and marketer of chicken, listed on the Johannesburg Stock Exchange. The commission conducted investigations and allowed the merger to go through. It was observed that the transaction would not lead to substantial lessening of competition in the relevant market in view of the fact that there were low entry barriers into the market and that the consumers had high countervailing power in view of the presence of various suppliers of broiler chickens in the relevant market. In addition, the commission established that the transaction would not result in creation or strengthening of dominance in the relevant market.

NOTES

1. Levels of consumption of all forms of protein in Zambia are among the lowest in southern Africa (World Bank 2012). The main protein foods consumed in Zambia are (in descending order, by weight) milk, poultry (chicken meat) and beef (FAO 2005). Pork is another, less important source of protein in people's diet in Zambia, but this industry is not examined in this chapter.
2. The survey respondents were all the companies listed in Table 5.1.
3. See Chapter 2 in this volume on Costa Rica for the method of calculation of the HHI.
4. See www.shoprite.co.za.
5. The Zambeef Board had approved the establishment of its own chicken hatchery during 2008, although the project was subsequently put on hold. An oversupply of day-old chicks had developed and a new hatchery had started producing day-old chicks (Zambeef 2009).
6. Another actor in the milk market, Finta, does not process fresh milk but reconstitutes liquid, long-life (UHT) milk using imported milk powder (Kenny and Mather 2008).
7. Two brands of milk for babies and infants were also imported, A26 and Lactogen.

REFERENCES

Bonaglia, F. (2008) *Business for Development Zambia: Sustaining Agricultural Diversification*, OECD, www.oecd.org/dev/40534117.pdf.

Chen, Z. and P. Rey (2013) *Competitive Cross-Subsidization*, IDEI Working Paper IDEI-808, Toulouse.

Competition and Consumer Protection Commission (n.d.) *Staff Paper on the Application for Authorization of Vertical Agreement between Africa Supermarkets trading as Shoprite and Zambeef Products Plc.*, Zambia.

Competition and Consumer Protection Commission (2013) *Staff Paper on the Proposed Merger between Bokomo Zambia Limited and Mega Eggs Limited*, Zambia.

FAO (2005) *Livestock Sector Brief: Zambia*, March, FAO-AGAL-AGAL.

Faulhaber, G.R. (2005) Cross-subsidy analysis with more than two services, *Journal of Competition Law and Economics*, **1**(3): 441–8.

IDE-JETRO (n.d.a) www.ide.go.jp/English/Data/Africa_file/Company/zambia01.html.

IDE-JETRO (n.d.b) www.ide.go.jp/English/Data/Africa_file/Company/zambia05.html#anchor6.

Kenny, B and C. Mather (2008) Milking the region? South African capital and Zambia's dairy industry, *African Sociological Review*, **12**(2): 55–66.

Lubungu, M. (2013) *Smallholder Livestock Production and Challenges in Zambia*, Indaba Agricultural Policy Research Institute presented at High Level Government Policy Meeting, Chaminuka Lodge, Lusaka.

Mukumbuta, L. and B. Sherchand (2006) *Enabling Smallholder Prosperity: Zambia's Smallholder Milk Collection Centres*, Lusaka: ZATAC.

Office of Fair Trading (2004) *Vertical Agreements: Understanding Competition Law*, www.gov.uk/government/uploads/system/uploads/attachment_data/file/284430/oft419.pdf.

PAZ (2007) Brief on Poultry Statistics.

Tembo, S. and N. Sitko (2014) *Technical Compendium: Descriptive Agricultural Statistics and Analysis for Zambia*, Working Paper 76, Indaba Agricultural Policy Research Institute (IAPRI), Lusaka.

UNCTAD (2013) *Voluntary Peer Review of Competition Law and Policy: A Tripartite Report on the United Republic of Tanzania-Zambia-Zimbabwe*, Geneva: United Nations.

Viscusi L., J. Harrington and M. Vernon (2005) *Economics of Regulation and Antitrust*, 4th edn, Cambridge, MA: MIT Press.

World Bank (2012) *Livestock Development and Animal Health Project*, Project Appraisal Document, Report no 65184-ZM, http://documents.worldbank.org/curated/en/2012/02/15785546/zambia-livestock-development-animal-health-projectZambeef (2009), *Annual Report 2009*.

PART II

The distribution of pharmaceuticals

6. The distribution of pharmaceuticals in Jamaica

Kevin Harriott

THE AFFORDABILITY OF DRUGS

Prices of pharmaceutical products have considerable implications for the quality of the consumer's life. Poor and vulnerable population segments in developing countries have relatively high incidence of certain chronic ailments. Providing them with better access to health services is of critical importance. To a large extent, achieving this objective is associated with the availability of affordable medicines. World Health Organization (WHO) figures suggest that one-third of the developing world's people are unable to receive or purchase essential medicines on a regular basis. Three factors explain this finding: their low income, their poor coverage by health insurance and excessive prices of medicines.

Generic drugs, produced without a licence from the innovator company and marketed after the patent expiry, are usually interchangeable with brand-name products and can provide greater access to healthcare for all. Generics are frequently as effective as brand-name products and much cheaper, which often make them the only option many people can afford. The evidence shows that competition between drug companies and generic producers has led to cutting down the cost of drugs more effectively than governments' talks with drug companies.

In Jamaica, patients face excessive mark-ups on pharmaceutical products at the wholesale and retail levels of the distribution chain. A market study carried out in 2004 revealed that pharmaceutical distributors make between 25 and 30 per cent mark-up and retailers' mark-up can be as high as 80 per cent. These figures are intriguing and may suggest high concentration of market power at the distribution and retail levels of the pharmaceuticals' supply chain. Other factors could also be at play.

The market power of business enterprises is the central preoccupation of competition law enforcement authorities. While having market power is not in itself in violation of the Jamaican competition law, the Fair Competition Act (FCA) limits the actions that businesses may take to acquire, maintain and extend market power (FTC 2004). For purposes of discussion, this chapter defines 'active' market power as that which accrues to businesses through their own deliberate conduct. It refers to 'passive' market power as that which accrues to businesses due to the actions (or inactions) of independent third parties. Competition law is designed to curtail the abuse of active market power that poses a threat to the competitive environment. While the focus on active market power is justified, there is little reason to suspect that passive market power is any less threatening to competition.

The issue of drug access and affordability in Jamaica is much more perplexing when one considers that innovator (branded) medication continues to be sold at a premium after market entry of generic substitutes.

This study of the pharmaceutical sector in Jamaica seeks a proper understanding of the reasons behind this situation in order to improve the efficiency with which pharmaceuticals are distributed. The level and flow of information among various actors in the sector appears to be a greater impediment to effective competition between drug companies and generic producers. The chapter argues that drug companies exploit their informational advantage over other actors to acquire and extend their market power. A large segment of the population ignores basic information on generic and branded medication. At the same time, a great deal of confusion exists among patients, physicians and pharmacists on the substitutability of generic and patented medication.

The asymmetry of information among different market players seems to be used as a barrier to entry of competing products, which limits market competition and deters patients from purchasing cheaper products. As a consequence, patented products enjoy unjustified market power and impose excessive margins.

RATIONALE AND BACKGROUND

The effect of asymmetric consumer information on equilibrium prices was first outlined by Stigler (1961). Important work into the topic by Wolinsky (1986), who explicitly models a mechanism through which consumers gather information, offers an explanation for the source of market power in these markets. He builds on previous research into monopolistically competitive markets by Hart (1985) and attributes the market power of firms to the ignorance of consumers. He theorizes that if a consumer is unaware of which variety of the product is most suited to his taste, and it is costly for him to acquire this information, then he will not necessarily compare all the varieties of the product prior to making a purchase; that is, he will make his purchase based on knowledge of a limited number of varieties regardless of the actual number available on the market. The proportion of 'informed' consumers would determine the degree to which firms are able to set prices above competitive levels. The greater the proportion of informed consumers, or alternatively the lower the cost of information acquisition, the closer prices will be to competitive levels.

Research into this line of enquiry was extended by Harriott (2005) who demonstrates the importance of simultaneously modelling information acquisition and information dissemination in terms of furthering our understanding of the nature of markets with asymmetric information. The main point of his research is that whenever there is asymmetric information in a market, there will always be an incentive for the uninformed to acquire information and for the informed not to fully disseminate information. To understand these markets, one must explicitly take account of the information acquisition and dissemination mechanisms, as failing to do so could eliminate important interaction effects between the two mechanisms. Harriott (2005) demonstrates this point by making a contribution to the debate on the effect of advertising on competition. In an attempt to explain the source of market power for firms in a monopolistically competitive market, Joan Robinson (1969) suggested that firms use persuasive advertising to manipulate the preferences of consumers and unduly attach consumers to their products. She therefore holds the view that advertising has anticompetitive effects on the market. Harriott counters this view by showing that advertising in monopolistic markets can have pro-competitive effects since advertising subsidizes the costs of information to consumers; and it is consumers' ignorance that is firms' source of (passive) market power.

Lande and Marvel (2000) identify agreements to obstruct information channels to consumers as a form of collusive conduct. Rival firms can gain or maintain market power through agreements to limit advertising by cartel members or by boycotting third parties that supply information to consumers. Further, building information channels among competing firms has been identified as a facilitating device for implementing other forms of collusive behaviour. Kaplow and Shapiro (2007) provide an extensive review of the theoretical underpinnings of competition law. They point out that there are five key elements for sustaining collusive agreements: consensus, detection, punishment, inclusion and entry barriers. Consensus refers to the fact that firms need to agree on which outcome to collude around; detection refers to mechanisms through which firms are able to discover parties that cheat on the agreed upon action; and punishment refers to credible sanctions to be imposed on firms that cheat so as to discourage cheating. Inclusion refers to a way of including as many firms as necessary so that non-participating firms do not block the agreement; and entry barriers refers to means of limiting competition from potential entrants. The first element of collusion, i.e., consensus, requires the development of a communication channel between firms. Information exchange between firms is therefore an important element of collusive conduct that invariably leads to market failures.

There is evidence of information asymmetries in the healthcare industry in Jamaica. An important research project carried out by Gossell-Williams (2005) captures the attitude of physicians in Jamaica toward generic and innovator drugs. It revealed that there is no consensus among physicians regarding the substitutability of generics and innovators.

The extent to which this attitude among physicians reflects the opinion of other stakeholders such as pharmacists and patients is unknown. It is hoped that this study will fill this gap.

The above discussion underscores the view that an examination of the information structure in a market is an important first step in assessing the extent of competition within it. It also suggests that acquiring and disseminating information should be a privileged area of public policy intervention.

THE PHARMACEUTICAL SECTOR IN JAMAICA AND THE RESEARCH METHOD

The structure of Jamaica's public health sector as reported by Industry Canada (2004) consists of 23 hospitals, 343 health centres and 353 registered pharmacies. The Pharmaceutical Council of Jamaica reveals that there were 30 registered manufacturers and distributors of pharmaceuticals in Jamaica in February 2006. The *Jamaica Gazette* of November 2004 pointed out that the number of registered doctors amounted to 2,409.

The main pieces of legislations that regulate the sale and use of pharmaceuticals in Jamaica are the Dangerous Drug Act (1948), the Food and Drug Act (1975) and the Pharmacy Act (1975). The Pharmacy Council of Jamaica (PCJ), which was established in 1975, and the Standards and Regulation Division of the Ministry of Health (MoH), established in 1999, are the main regulatory bodies of the pharmaceutical sector.

This chapter examines data collected through surveys of the four major stakeholders in the pharmaceutical sector: consumers (patients), pharmacists, distributors and physicians. For surveys involving patients, pharmacists and physicians, a questionnaire was administered to a random sample of the respective populations.

More specifically, a random sampling technique was used for the survey

Table 6.1 Determination of population of interest for the survey among patients

	Number of people
Total population	2,621,500
Adult population	1,623,106
Adult population reporting illnesses	202,035
Adult population with chronic illnesses	100,113

Source: PIOJ and STATIN.

among patients. The survey population covers all people aged 18 years and older who have purchased prescription drugs in the preceding six months and are suffering from chronic ailments. We used the incidence of chronic ailments in Jamaica as reported from the Survey of Living Conditions conducted in 2002 jointly by the Planning Institute of Jamaica (PIOJ) and the Statistical Institute of Jamaica (STATIN). The population of Jamaica for the same year was estimated at 2,621,500 persons. Table 6.1 reports the figures leading to the determination of the population of interest for the survey. The sample targeted 1,030 patients and its distribution replicates the geographical distribution of the adult population suffering from chronic illness with 30 per cent drawn from Kingstown Metropolitan Area (KMA), 17 per cent from other urban zones and 53 per cent from rural areas.

A similar sampling technique was used for the survey of physicians. The survey's population was defined as all individuals licensed to practice medicine in Jamaica based on the 2004 *Jamaica Gazette* general register, which was stratified according to physicians' location (stratum). A sample of 242 respondents was then selected, comprising approximately 10 per cent of physicians in each stratum identified.

The survey involving distributors was based on the list of distributors registered by the Pharmacy Council of Jamaica by 2005. The list contains the names and addresses of 30 enterprises that were authorized to distribute pharmaceutical products in Jamaica, 18 of which distributed medical prescriptions. The data collected reflect the responses of 14 distributors, however, as four chose not to take part in the survey.

Finally, the survey targeted a random sample of registered pharmacists stratified by location. A proportion of 10 per cent in each location was interviewed, which led to a sample of 36 pharmacists across the county.

The response rate varied across the four surveys and across questions within a given survey. The response rate was typically higher among retailers and lower among patients. Appropriate adjustment of the sampling weights was used to account for non-responding sample units.

The purpose of this set of four surveys was to map and characterize the structure of the pharmaceutical market, paying attention to the dissemination of information on pharmaceuticals within the sector.

MAIN COMPETITION-RELATED ISSUES

The focus of this study is to assess the possible sources of (active) market power in the pharmaceutical sector. First, we highlight the degree of interconnectedness among the various players at various levels of the supply chain. Second, we assess the degree to which the pharmaceutical sector is susceptible to collusive conduct. Last, the study finds some evidence of resale price maintenance (RPM) at the manufacturing level and tied-selling at the distribution level. We find it unlikely that the tied-selling is having an undue influence on competition in the sector and the effect of RPM on competition could not be ascertained from the data collected. Overall, this evidence did not suggest that firms are engaged in anticompetitive practices on this basis.

Information and Competition

In most markets, consumers independently determine which product to purchase. Further, most goods have either search or experience characteristics, whereby consumers are able to assess a product's suitability by inspecting it prior to consumption (search goods) or at consumption (experience goods). Through their consumption patterns, consumers identify and reward firms that sell the better-suited products at the most reasonable prices. The completeness or accuracy of the information available to consumers is therefore a critical feature of competitive markets.

Consequently, we analyse the information structure of the pharmaceutical sector. Specifically we explore the sector's mechanisms for disseminating information to and acquiring information from consumers. Without access to the relevant information, the consumers' role as an effective check against inefficiency and anticompetitive activity is diminished. To fulfil the role of 'competition allies', consumers must know, among other things, how to recognize suspicious behaviour and where to report it. To perform their role of 'quality checkers', consumers must be able to identify and select the 'better' firms; that is, firms that offer the lowest price, best quality and so on.

By law, generic drugs have to be chemically equivalent (bioequivalent) to their innovator counterparts. Bioequivalence requires generics to contain the identical amounts of the main active ingredients that are present in innovator drugs but permits differences in the expedients (inactive ingredients) used in the manufacturing process. The concept of therapeutic equivalence speaks to the therapeutic relief provided by the generic drugs. Therapeutic equivalence is therefore a more useful gauge of substitutability than bioequivalence.

The survey examines the extent to which there are differences in the perceived therapeutic effects of branded and generic medication among consumers, physicians and pharmacists.

There is no consensus among physicians as to whether generic drugs are therapeutically equivalent to their respective innovators. The survey highlights mixed support from physicians and pharmacists for generics. A proportion of 30 per cent of the physicians disagreed that all generics that are rated as bioequivalent can be considered therapeutically equivalent with the innovator products, while 47 per cent agreed with it. The remaining 23 per cent held a neutral position. On the other hand, 61 per cent of pharmacists agreed with the statement while 33 per cent disagreed with it. A minor proportion of 6 per cent adopted a neutral position.

Physicians and pharmacists seemed better-informed on the properties of drugs that are heavily marketed by their manufacturers (suppliers) compared to drugs that are not. The information structure seems to be shaped by the manufacturers of innovator drugs as they host seminars and market their products through sales by (drug) representatives.

The survey revealed that roughly 40 per cent of consumers have never heard the term 'generic medication' and a similar proportion were unable to name any organization they could approach in order to complain about issues they might face regarding pharmaceutical products. The level of ignorance as reported in Table 6.2 is greater among the youngest and oldest consumers, consumers living in the rural areas rather than the capital (Kingston Metropolitan Area) and other cities, consumers living in households with a relatively low monthly income and among those who do not have access to the internet.

This level of ignorance is alarmingly high. It suggests that the normal channels of information to the 'informed' consumer are not readily accessible to those consumers even though pharmacies are required under the law to inform consumers of the availability of generic medication and the government of Jamaica has an extensive public education programme aimed at educating the general public regarding the availability and use of generic medication.

The most objective assessment of the therapeutic equivalence of innovator and generic medication is the scientific testing of drugs in four pharmacological classes of antihypertensive drugs distributed in Jamaica.

Table 6.2 Proportion of consumers who have never heard the term 'generic medication'

	%
Whole sample	40
By age	
18–24	57
25–29	35
30–34	34
35–44	32
45–59	36
>60	47
By Location	
KMA	29
Other cities	38
Rural area	45
By income level (US$000s)	
Less than 20	49
20–60	36
60–100	28
More than 100	19
By access to internet	
Have access	29
No access	44

Source: Based on findings from consumers' survey.

The test finds evidence of differences in the therapeutic effects of innovator and some generic drugs in two of these classes (University of Technology 2007). Although those findings cannot be generalized to make inferences about the therapeutic equivalence of drugs used to treat other ailments in Jamaica, they serve, along with the opinion of physicians and pharmacists, to refute claims that strong consumer preference for branded drugs has entirely been driven by irrational consumers' perceptions.

The results of the testing, however, point to the possible nature of information asymmetry in Jamaica. They demonstrate that while all generic antihypertensive drugs tested offered the relief they were designed to produce and so would pass the screening of the Ministry of Health, some generic drugs in two of the four classes tested failed to provide relief as quickly as the innovator counterpart did, and so might be rejected by final consumers, physicians or pharmacists.

There is no inherent problem with having a market with products of varying qualities, as consumers would base their product selection pattern on their marginal willingness and ability to pay for higher quality products. However, consumers and physicians who find it difficult or costly to assess the qualities of generics might develop a strong preference for innovator medication. As a consequence, prevailing information asymmetries would prevent effective generics from competing with innovator products.

The information structure of the pharmaceutical industry appears to be a greater impediment to competition than the market structure of the industry. A system must be devised in order to make it relatively cheap for consumers, physicians and pharmacists to evaluate drugs that do not have the advantage of a strong marketing force. Physicians could be very efficient in channelling information to and from consumers and should be part of any education campaign. Indeed the survey revealed that 56 per cent of consumers get most of their information about the health-care sector from physicians and 77 per cent believe that physicians provide the most credible medical advice.

An examination of the source of perceived differences in the therapeutic abilities of generic and innovators is needed as these perceptions affect consumer demand and could potentially frustrate legitimate competition in the market. If the perceptions of these groups are based on factors that can be substantiated (say, the illegal distribution of fake and or inferior generic medication in Jamaica), then steps must be taken to identify and eliminate them as far as it is efficient to do so. Similarly, if the perceptions are based on factors that cannot be proven to be false, then the information structure of the industry must be rehabilitated and exploited to facilitate a greater flow of accurate information between policymakers and stakeholders.

On the other hand, the government needs to revise its public education strategy to link it with health insurance programmes. In particular, the government must review its criteria for determining which drugs are covered by public health insurance programmes to promote an effective generic substitution.

The next sections highlight the degree of interconnectedness among the various players at various levels of the supply chain and assess the degree to which the pharmaceutical sector is susceptible to collusive conduct.

Market Players' Connections

The independence of the decision-making processes of business enterprises is a crucial feature of competitive markets. Consequently, the extent of vertical and horizontal integration and restraints among business enterprises is very important in characterizing the efficiency of the distribution sector. While vertical integration and restraints may benefit or harm competition, in general, horizontal integration and restraints (especially agreements involving prices, quantities or market segmentation) pose a threat to the competitive process and hence to the efficiency of the sector.

The survey showed that six distributors (46 per cent) had business relationships with manufacturers and seven distributors (50 per cent) had business relationships with other distributors. Distributors operated as subsidiaries, agents, exclusive distributors of the manufacturer's products or 'strategic partners' of the manufacturer. On the nature of their relationship with other distributors, one distributor mentioned that they belong to the same group, while four wholesalers indicated that they are affiliated with distributors in 'other' ways.

All 36 pharmacies sampled reported they have an affiliation/business relationship with another entity in the industry. One pharmacy indicated that it was affiliated with a manufacturer, one with a health maintenance organization, two with wholesalers and four with physicians.

The physicians' survey indicates that very few physicians were linked with at least one other player in the industry: three with manufacturers, three with wholesalers, two with importers and four with 'other' players.

It seems unlikely from survey responses that drug prescription was influenced by conflict of interest arising out of business linkages between physicians and other players.

Extent of Market Power

Significant market power is the central focus of any competition law regime. While competition law does not prohibit firms from acquiring, having or extending market power, it generally restricts the steps that firms may take to do this. In evaluating such market power, competition authorities generally examine factors such as market share, market concentration and barriers to entry and exit.

In the absence of data on relevant market shares and entry/exit barriers, the survey attempted to capture the extent of market power in the pharmaceutical sector by examining the number of firms that directly compete with each other. Other things being equal, market power would be more prevalent in markets with few competing firms than in markets with many competing firms.

Thirty registered distributors and manufacturers of pharmaceuticals operated in Jamaica in 2006. 'Localized competition', however, would suggest that the number of firms directly competing with each other is less than the number of firms operating in the market. At one extreme, there are three distributors (21 per cent) who do not think they have any rival and at the other extreme there are two distributors (14 per cent) who indicate that they have as many as 28 main rivals. Overall, competition does appear to be localized, since only eight distributors indicate that they have up to six main rivals.

As far as the retail level is concerned, 353 registered pharmacies operated in 2006. The survey data suggest that competition among pharmacies is highly localized as the majority of respondents (63 per cent) declared that they face fewer than three main competitors. It would be informative to know the reason behind 'localized' competition in the pharmaceutical sector. If, for instance, it originates from an artificial segmentation of the market then it would raise serious anticompetitive issues. However, if localized competition is the outcome of a legitimate factor such as the 'product line' specialization of distributors, then there would be no competition concerns.

Markets can be segmented into geographic regions or by types of customers. Geographic segmentation refers to an arrangement whereby firms agree to actively sell products only within specified geographic boundaries while customer market segmentation refers to an arrangement in which firms agree to sell their products only to customers with specific characteristics.

To assess the incidence of market segmentation at the manufacturer level, the survey investigated the extent to which it is manifested at the distribution level through the practice of single-sourcing. At least four distributors were supplied from a single source. Distributors, however, offer legitimate commercial reasons for single-sourcing that did not relate to market segmentation by manufacturers. The survey results did not support the geographic market segmentation hypothesis in the distribution sector. In the same vein, at least nine distributors reported supplying different categories of customers, namely pharmacies, hospitals, medical centres and clinics.

There is also little evidence that localized competition is based on the type of chronic ailment. The ailments considered were restricted to the five that are the focus of the study: arthritis, asthma, high cholesterol, diabetes and hypertension. Pharmaceuticals used to treat arthritis, asthma and hypertension were supplied by at least nine different distributors; and pharmaceuticals used to treat the other two ailments were supplied by at least six distributors.

The survey also explored the extent to which localized competition could be based on the type of pharmaceutical medication, i.e., innovator or generic drugs supplied by the distributors. The relationship between type of medication and extent of localized competition was closer for prescription medication used to treat arthritis than that used to treat other ailments. The survey shows that the three firms involved in both types of arthritis medication indicate that they have fewer main rivals than firms that do not carry both types. The same cannot be said for medication used to treat the other four ailments.

Statistical analysis was used to test whether there is a significant relationship between the types of pharmaceuticals carried by distributors and their perceived number of rivals. The analysis was conducted separately for each ailment but a statistically significant relationship was found only in the case of arthritis medication.

Probable Effects of Alleged Conduct on Competition

Tied-selling

Tied-selling is the practice by which a supplier forces its customers to buy some specific good or service from it or its affiliates, as a condition to purchase another good or service that is, by its nature and according to commercial usage, distinct from and unrelated to the first good or service. In general, tied-selling does not raise any competition concerns except if the firm is dominant in the market for the tying product; and even then there could be legitimate justification (efficiencies to be gained) from tied-selling.

The survey suggests that one out of the 12 respondents appeared to be engaged in tied-selling. In this case, retailers would be required to purchase other types of drugs in order to be supplied with drugs treating asthma and hypertension. This distributor supplies only generic asthma and hypertension medication. Data indicate that seven other distributors supply generic drugs for asthma and nine other distributors offer generic drugs for hypertension.

Even if tied-selling in the distribution sector could be proved, the existence of other suppliers who do not engage in tied-selling and the fact that none of the retailers complained from tied-buying by any distributor means that there is little reason to suspect that this conduct was substantially lessening competition.

Exclusive dealing

'Exclusive dealing' generally refers to an agreement between a supplier or manufacturer and its customer, whereby the customer is restrained from dealing with any of the supplier's competitors. Exclusive deals raise competition concerns as they may foreclose the market to competitors and new entrants. The term 'exclusive dealing' includes not only explicit agreements but also arrangements that indirectly lead to the same exclusionary effect on competitors. Under certain circumstances, exclusive arrangements may have pro-competitive effects in that they may promote non-price competition and improvement in quality of service.

Eight of the 11 distributors indicated that they are exclusive distributors of pharmaceutical medication in Jamaica. There is nothing inherently problematic with firms distributing medication exclusively. The effects of tied-selling at the distributor level depend on the extent to which the distributor has market power in the tying product market. Having exclusive rights to distribute a type of medication that commands a relatively high demand would vest the distributor with market power that is sufficient to undermine the competitive process. There is no evidence to suggest that any of the distributors is abusing its dominance to unduly lessen competition in other markets through tied-selling. The single distributor that engages in tied-selling is not an exclusive distributor of any pharmaceutical medication.

Resale price maintenance (RPM)

Theoretically RPM can be either pro-competitive or anticompetitive. While most competition legislation allows manufacturers to suggest the resale price of its products, the enforcement of minimum resale prices (through reward or punishment) is generally prohibited under competition law.

The study did not include a survey of manufacturers so the incidence of RPM by manufacturers is discerned only from the survey of distributors. There is some evidence that manufacturers are engaged in RPM. Two of the four respondents who face suggested resale prices from manufacturers (which is not prohibited under the FCA) think that they would be penalized (which is prohibited) for not following the suggested price.

Two distributors indicated that while they recommend resale prices to their customers (retailers), neither of them impose penalties on retailers for not adopting the recommended prices. This is corroborated by the fact that none of the four retailers who indicated that their suppliers recommend resale prices believed that they would be penalized for not adhering to the recommendations. There is therefore no evidence that distributors are engaged in RPM.

Horizontal agreements

Horizontal agreements can be defined as arrangements among competing entities on prices, production levels or market segmentation that restrict or threaten competition.

Collusive arrangements are inherently unstable in the sense that at least one party to the arrangement will always have an incentive to deviate from the terms ('cheat') as long as the other parties do not cheat. For a collusive arrangement to be successful, the parties must be able to coordinate around an outcome, monitor each other's behaviour and effectively punish cheaters.

The structure of the market affects the ability to successfully collude. Economic literature has established that factors such as a low number of competitors, presence of entry barriers, frequent interactions among competitors, market transparency and demand growth facilitate collusion. Conversely, factors such as business cycles and demand fluctuation, innovation, cost asymmetries, asymmetries in capacity and greater differentiation of product quality tend to impede collusion.

The survey on distribution and retailing attempted to capture the extent to which the market favours collusion by focusing on two characteristics: 'market transparency' and 'public pre-announcement of changes in business strategy'.

Market transparency Market transparency refers to the ease with which the actions taken by a firm can be observed by other firms. The free flow of information is an important aspect of competition and has either anticompetitive or pro-competitive effects depending on the type of information disseminated. Information relating to firm specific price and/or quantity produced will pose a greater threat to competition than information on other aspects of business strategies.

The existence of a trade association is one mechanism that could facilitate a greater level of market transparency by providing a channel through which information can be disseminated among rival firms.

Ten of the 14 distributors surveyed indicated that they are members of at least one of three trade associations, namely the Jamaica Chamber of Commerce (JCC), the Pharmacy Council of Jamaica (PCJ) and the Pharmaceutical Society of Jamaica (PSJ).

The JCC's membership comprises not only distributors and retailers from the pharmaceutical sector but also stakeholders from most industries in Jamaica, for example, banking, agriculture, tourism sectors and so forth. The PCJ and PSJ comprise individuals and entities from the pharmaceutical sector only. Ten of the 16 members of the PCJ are appointed by the Ministry of Health, while the other six are nominated by the PSJ. On the other hand, the PSJ comprises only pharmacists and pharmacy owners. With respect to frequency of meetings, the members of the JCC meets once per year for its general meeting and at least four other times each year; the PCJ meets ten times per year; and the PSJ meets once per month. The extent to which these associations may be (ab)used to facilitate collusion is assessed based on the type of information exchanged through the association.

The information disseminated by the associations includes data on newly developed drugs, changes in the regulatory environment and other information that could only serve to improve the efficiency of the distributive sector.

Seven distributors, among the ten that are members of at least one trade association, receive distributor specific information such as market growth trends, employment data, changes in the laws and government policies as well as information on newly developed drugs, through trade associations. Only one distributor claimed that he received, in addition, distributor-specific 'price/quantity' information.

Twenty-eight of the 36 retailers are members of trade associations. The number of meetings of these trade associations ranges from one meeting per year to eight meetings per year. Seven retailers (25 per cent) confirm that retailer-specific information is disseminated through the association. It includes, information on continuing education programmes, seminars, best practices, new drugs, rules and regulations, and developments in the industry. Two of the seven retailers declare that information on the prices and/or quantities from individual entities is revealed.

Public pre-announcements The public pre-announcement of changes in business strategy is another means through which firms can implement collusive arrangements and thereby allow conspirators to undermine competition.

The survey reveals that eight of the 13 distributors who responded on this topic indicated that they pre-announce changes in their business strategies. Six of the eight distributors indicated that they pre-announce price changes while all eight said they pre-announce changes in the availability of their drugs. Despite the fact that public pre-announcements of information on quantity have the potential to distort competition in a market, such pre-announcements may convey information to the public and could serve to improve competition. The effect of public pre-announcement of price changes is ambiguous and if a consumer welfare-enhancing justification is proven, it may not be cause for concern to a competition agency. Indeed there are legitimate reasons why a distributor might want to inform actual or potential customers (retailers) of pending price changes.

Five of the six distributors communicate price changes to retailers. What initially raises concern is the fact that one of the six distributors communicates pending price changes to rival distributors. Normally, this would be considered to be highly suspicious behaviour. An examination of the data reveals, however, that in this case the distributor sources drugs from an overseas manufacturer on behalf of other distributor(s). This being the case, the distributors share a horizontal and vertical relationship that, without more evidence, precludes us from making any definitive statement about the effect of such pre-announcements on competition in the sector.

The retailer survey illustrates that three retailers (8 per cent) pre-announce changes in their business strategy. Although two of them pre-announce changes in their prices, that information is not communicated to competing retailers and therefore raises no concerns for competition at this level of the supply chain.

DISCUSSION OF THE FINDINGS AND POLICY ISSUES

This study examines possible sources of (active) market power in the pharmaceutical sector. First, the chapter highlights the degree of interconnectedness among the various players at various levels of the supply chain. There is no evidence that the stated relationships are being exploited to facilitate anticompetitive practices.

Second, the chapter assesses the degree to which the pharmaceutical sector is susceptible to collusive conduct. The survey suggests that trade associations provide valuable services to their members but they might also be facilitating collusive conduct. The Fair Trade Commission should express this concern to associations and inform them on ways they can pre-empt members from using shared information to engage in anticompetitive practices.

Lastly, the chapter finds some evidence of resale price maintenance at the manufacturing level and tied-selling at the distribution level. It is unlikely, however, that tied-selling is creating an undue influence on competition in the sector and the effect of RPM on competition could not be ascertained from the survey and needs to be investigated further by the Fair Trading Commission (FTC).

This exploratory research into competition issues of the pharmaceutical sector in Jamaica follows two discrete lines of enquiry: potential impediments to competition based on anticompetitive practices by players in the sector (the exercise of active market power) and potential impediments based on inaction of players (the exercise of passive market power). The findings suggest that impediments to greater levels of competition in the sector seem more likely to be the outcome of passive rather than active market power. Hence, addressing the high degree of information asymmetries in the pharmaceutical sector could prove effective in resolving the sector's inefficiencies.

One key concern for policymakers should be the mistrust that a non-negligible proportion of major stakeholders have in the effectiveness of domestically distributed generic drugs. The chapter argues that the lack of confidence in generic drugs originates both from incomplete or inaccurate information and therapeutic non-equivalence of some generic drugs.

In order to address the issue of information and ensure the free flow of accurate information, policymakers need to establish mechanisms for acquisition and dissemination of information to and from the major stakeholders.

The consumers show a lack of knowledge in key areas: some are completely ignorant of the existence of 'generic medication'; others think that generic medication is more expensive than branded medication. On the other hand, a significant proportion of consumers is unaware of organizations they could rely on to remedy difficulties encountered from the use of particular pharmaceutical products. The survey suggests that physicians represent the most effective means of disseminating information on pharmaceutical products to final consumers in Jamaica both in terms of the amount of information provided and its credibility. More than half of the consumers would switch the type of their medication if asked by their physicians.

In this context, the information that flows to and from healthcare professionals (physicians and pharmacists) needs to be reviewed. Specifically, drug manufacturers appear to be a major source of information for healthcare professionals and the Ministry of Health. According to the survey, seminars held by drug manufacturers are the preferred source of information for a majority of physicians. Similarly, drug manufacturers and their representatives are the top source of information for pharmacists. Representatives of the drugs manufacturers are second only to medical journals as the source deemed by pharmacists to be most credible.

To the extent that drug manufacturers tend also to be producers of innovator medication, the existing structure of information flow to the professionals would bias their opinion in favour of innovator drugs. Policymakers should, therefore, supplement the information flow to healthcare professionals to bring about a more balanced attitude towards innovator and generic medication.

A majority of physicians expressed an interest in attending a government-sponsored seminar on generic medication. Most of them would like to hear from the research community with specialized knowledge in pharmacology. The competition authority, FTC, was informed that most of the reports to the Ministry of Health on incidents of adverse drug effects are made by the manufacturers of the drugs in question. Without casting aspersions on the ethics or character of drug manufacturers, it is undeniable that the information used by the Ministry to monitor drugs being distributed in

Jamaica would be more complete if reports of adverse drug effects were also received from sources independent from the manufacturers.

To sum up, policymakers need to reduce information asymmetries in order to mitigate inefficiencies in the pharmaceutical sector as reflected in the high margins enjoyed by retailers and distributors and the excessive prices charged to consumers. To achieve this objective, policymakers need to implement the following proposals:

- Equip consumers with the relevant information required for promoting greater levels of competition in the sector. Policymakers need to establish or rehabilitate mechanisms for disseminating information to consumers and place physicians at the heart of those mechanisms.
- Provide opportunities for physicians and pharmacists to attend seminars with authoritative pharmacology experts to ensure a well-informed cadre of healthcare professionals and therefore a better implementation of the government's generic drug policy.
- Establish a drug certification programme aimed at compiling a list of drugs that meet minimum standards. Drugs' affordability and effectiveness need to be among the key criteria.
- Take steps to reduce the lengthy drug registration process. This could be achieved by hiring additional staff and/or implementing automated registration to ensure that generic drugs are being distributed as soon as the counterpart innovator drugs are out of patent.
- Develop and promote guidelines outlining best practices for trade associations as they relate to the sharing of information among their members. The objective of the guidelines is to reduce the likelihood that trade associations are used to facilitate anticompetitive practices.

REFERENCES

FTC (2004) *The Fair Competition Act: A Guide to Anticompetitive Practices*, Kingston: Fair Trade Commission.

Gossell-Williams, M. (2005) *A 2005 Survey of the Acceptance and Perceptions of Physicians in Jamaica*, Mimeo, University of the West Indies.

Harriott, K.K. (2005) *Advertising and Consumer Search in Differentiated Markets*, PhD Dissertation, Texas A&M University.

Hart, O.D. (1985) Monopolistic competition in the spirit of Chamberlin: a general model, *Review of Economic Studies*, **52**(4): 529–46.

Industry Canada (2004) *International Market Research Reports: Drugs and Pharmaceuticals*, http://strategis.ic.gc.ca/epic/site/imr-ri.nsf/en/grl21181e.html.

Kaplow, L. and C. Shapiro (2007) *Antitrust*, NBER Working Paper Series, No. 12867.
Lande, R.H. and H.P. Marvel (2000) The three types of collusion: fixing prices, rivals and rules, *Wisconsin Law Review*, p. 941.
Robinson, J. (1969) *The Economics of Imperfect Competition*, 2nd edn, London: Macmillan.
Stigler, G. (1961) The economics of information, *Journal of Political Economy*, **69**: 213–25.
University of Technology (2007) *Comparative In Vitro Dissolution and Biopharmaceutical Properties of some Multi-Source Antihypertensive Drug Products Marketed in Jamaica.*
Wolinsky, A. (1986) True monopolistic competition as a result of imperfect information, *Quarterly Journal of Economics*, **101**: 493–512.

7. The pharmaceuticals sector in Vietnam

Que Anh Pham and Tran Phuong Lan[1]

HEALTH POLICY OBJECTIVES AND COMPETITION LAW

The objective of healthcare policy regarding medicines is to guarantee the supply of safe and effective products at a reasonable price, and ensure that patients have access to and can afford them. Access to healthcare, in its broader sense, is one of the most basic needs, an inviolable right of every human as acknowledged by the Constitution of Vietnam.[2] Despite constitutional commitment, the achievement of this objective tends to be constrained by a number of factors that range from poverty and unaffordable market prices, absence of or non-binding regulation on price mark-ups, abuse of intellectual property rights, lack of an effective generic substitution policy, excessive reliance on out-of-pocket payments for health expenses and shortage of public information.

Competition policy represents a key tool, in addition to other legal provisions and institutional mechanisms, to secure access to medicines for the population and achieve healthcare policy's objectives. Indeed, by promoting fair and free competition and preventing anticompetitive practices, competition policy can contribute significantly to protect patients' interests and improve their social welfare.

This chapter reveals, in particular, that anticompetitive practices such as price-fixing, abuse of dominance, collusive agreements and tied-selling seem to prevail in the Vietnamese pharmaceutical market. Such practices force patients to pay unreasonably high prices for their medicines. With Vietnam's growing integration into the global economy and expected developments in the pharmaceutical sector, new concerns emerge; among these are the abuse of monopoly rights by the patent-holder that can push up prices, the effect of relaxing price controls on medicines' affordability and the potential impact of a burgeoning presence of multinational companies in the Vietnamese pharmaceutical market.

Interestingly, a market study on the pharmaceutical distribution sector carried out by the Vietnam Competition Authority in 2012 corroborates most of this chapter's findings. The study revealed signs of competition law violations in the relationships among foreign drug-makers and local importers and distributors. Operators seem to collude in imposing drug prices, especially the prices of special-treatment drugs.

The remainder of this chapter has four sections. The first analyzes market structure and the level of concentration in the pharmaceutical sector in Vietnam. The second examines the scope of competition law and other related regulations in dealing with the main competition concerns. The third section explores the role of the competition authority and the pharmaceutical sector regulator in dealing with anticompetitive and unfair competition practices. It also explores the ways to attain a cohesive and effective enforcement strategy. Finally, this chapter suggests some major policy directions. Beyond the government, the competition authority and the sectoral regulator, policy proposals also target the private sector operators and consumers.

MARKET STRUCTURE IN THE PHARMACEUTICAL SECTOR

The socialist Republic of Vietnam is a Southeast Asian developing country with a population of more than 90 million and a GDP per capita of US$1,200. Since the middle of the 1980s, Vietnam has shifted from a centrally planned to a more market economy with social orientation and its poverty rate decreased from 37 to 16 per cent between 1998 and 2006. Membership of the World Trade Organization (WTO) since 2007 has boosted the presence of the country in the global market and reinforced its domestic economic reforms.

Vietnam spent around 6 per cent of its GDP on healthcare in 2013,[3] a relatively high share compared to other low- and middle-income countries. Expenditure on medicines accounts for a significant share of total healthcare costs, amounting to 53.3 per cent in 2005. In absolute terms, Vietnam spent US$3.2billion on healthcare, an almost threefold increase in absolute terms compared to 2000 (Nguyen 2011). Rising prices for medicines have been reported to account for most of this increase.

About 60 per cent of the population was covered by social health insurance in 2010. Insured members have to contribute to their health expenses through a co-payment system. The co-payment rate ranges between 5 and 20 per cent, which can represent a heavy burden for patients with high healthcare costs. All in all, the share of household out-of-pocket payments for health, although declining in recent years, still accounts for some 55 per cent of total health expenditure in Vietnam (Tran Van Tien et al. 2011).

Table 7.1 Market share of top ten pharmaceutical manufacturers, 2011

No.	Name	Market share (%)
1	Hau Giang Pharma Corporation	10.8
2	Mekophar Pharma-Chemical	7.5
3	Imexpharm Pharma	7.1
4	Domesco Medical Import Export	6.3
5	Nam Ha Pharma	5.1
6	B Braun Hanoi Pharma	4.3
7	Sanofi Synthelabo Vietnam Pharma	3.9
8	Traphaco	3.4
9	Cuu Long Pharma	3.0
10	National Phytopharma	2.9

Source: Vietnam Competition Authority.

The objective of this first section is to examine the market structure and the level of concentration in the pharmaceutical distribution sector in Vietnam. The distribution system can be approached by the number of players in the market, as well as the market share of individual players based on their revenue as stipulated in the Vietnamese competition law.

Due to the large number of players in the market, competition may seem to be intensive. The pharmaceutical distribution channel in Vietnam is made up of 39,000 pharmaceutical retailers, 170 pharmaceutical producers and 800 pharmaceutical wholesalers, among which 370 are representative offices of foreign companies supplying medicines to Vietnam. The market share of the largest company, based on its revenue, hardly exceeds 10 per cent – as reported in Table 7.1 – and the concentration index of the five largest companies remains relatively low.

This approach, however, is misleading as a way of assessing the pharmaceuticals market structure for different reasons. Pharmaceuticals are made up of many different products used to treat different diseases. Even when they contain similar active ingredients and treat the same diseases, they may still have varying medical effects and they can be administered in various dosages, or prescribed to different groups of patients. The non-homogeneity of medicines requires the partitioning of the pharmaceutical market into several small segments rather than analysis of the aggregate market. Moreover, the demand curve for medicines is not elastic; it does not depend on the level of supply or prices but on doctors' prescriptions or on professional staff's purchasing decisions in the case of hospitals and clinics. Therefore, while a pharmaceutical operator may not have a large turnover compared to the overall sector, it can still hold a high market

Table 7.2 Number of registered drugs by selected therapeutic categories

Therapeutic category	No. of registered drugs
Anti-infection	1,975
Pain-relief	1,017
Respiratory medicines	362
Stomach disorders	354
Heart-related	204
Blood-related	156
Eye-related	113
Dental-related	32
Urinary-related	25
Epileptic-related	23
Antiseptics	12
Migraine-related	8
Detoxification	7
Anaesthetics	2
Anti-retroviral	2
Globulin serum	1
Anti-malarial	1
Cancer-related	1

Note: The classification is similar but not identical to that in, for example, WHO (2004).

Source: DAV.

share for one or a few specific products. Many market studies in the pharmaceutical industry throughout the world have uncovered evidence of high concentration ratios in specific market segments for particular therapeutic categories (Regan 2008). Due to the pharmaceutical market's peculiarities, having a low overall market share does not rule out the ability of an enterprise to enjoy market power and restrict market competition. Market power in Vietnam can arise from five major factors.

First, products can be hard to substitute from a therapeutic point of view. According to the Ministry of Health's regulations on drug registration, enterprises may only trade, import, export or manufacture pharmaceutical products that have been registered with the Drug Administration of Vietnam (DAV). This means that if there is only one or a few medicines registered within a therapeutic category, or if all the registered medicines in one therapeutic category are controlled by one single distributor, the market structure in that particular segment is either a monopoly or an oligopoly. From Table 7.2, it appears that, for some therapeutic categories, the number of drugs registered tends to be very limited. Some specific drugs, however, may not be widely traded in the market, being mainly imported by the government for special use, which is why only one product is registered. The presence of one single drug in a therapeutic category does not necessarily mean that a monopoly exists in its production or distribution. Instead, the monopoly may result from the exclusive distribution of some patented products that are in the hands of large multinational pharmaceutical companies that only authorize one company to distribute them in Vietnam.

Second, intellectual property rights (IPRs) granted by the national government for a limited period of time – usually up to 20 years – to promote innovation can reinforce the exclusivity and lack of substitutability among products. Owners of IPRs can legally grant exclusive licences or sole distributorship to selected enterprises. In the absence of a therapeutic equivalent, the upper limit on the price of a patented medicine is set only by consumers' ability to pay.

Third, there can be barriers that prevent or deter the entry of new firms into the medicine market, even when incumbents are making excess profits. Governments can also be a source of entry barriers through licensing and other legal or administrative regulations. The business registration process in Vietnam, even though having been simplified substantially compared to the past, remains unfriendly, costly and time-consuming, and all those factors may deter entry.

Fourth, the fact that Vietnamese importers, wholesalers and retailers of pharmaceutical products have to depend completely on foreign companies for some patented products can deter entry.

Fifth, health insurance policy through the list of reimbursed drugs tends also to impact market power in Vietnam. Full or partial coverage of the cost of drugs by health insurance changes prices perceived by patients and pushes them to behave differently. In 2008, the reimbursement drug list consisted of 750 medicines out of around 17,000 registered drugs, according to the DAV. The 750 medicines are listed by their international non-proprietary name and providers can prescribe generic and/or brand-name products. The concern, however, is that the reimbursement list has not been sufficiently developed on the basis of evidence of cost-effectiveness. On the other hand, prescribers may also receive incentives from pharmaceutical companies and drug suppliers to prescribe drugs that are not on the reimbursement list (WHO 2011).

In addition to these five factors, there are indications that a few companies enjoy market power and restrict competition through monopoly contracts they have secured with multinational pharmaceutical companies. The latter own their chains at regional and international levels and Vietnamese companies depend on them in terms of supply and price. Such market architecture seems to lead to a high degree of vertical integration that can deter new entry and market development. The issue will be further investigated in the section on competition issues.

THE LEGAL FRAMEWORK FOR DRUG DISTRIBUTION AND COMPETITION

Vietnam has promulgated a comprehensive legal framework to regulate the issues relating to the drug industry, including competition issues in the distribution as well as pricing control and parallel importation. The legal framework is built around three key pillars.

The first pillar is the competition law promulgated in 2004 by the national assembly and its implementation provisions. The government of Vietnam acknowledges the vital role of an effective competition policy in the market economy, as well as the advantages of competitive markets in supporting economic efficiency. The gradual opening up of the Vietnamese market to foreign goods, services and investment made it necessary to protect the economic benefits of regional and global trade integration from potential anticompetitive behaviours (WTO 2013). The law on competition applies to all business enterprises and professional and trade associations in Vietnam; overseas enterprises and associations registered in Vietnam; public utilities and state monopoly enterprises. It has superseding power over all the other enacted laws regarding restrictive business practices and unfair competition practices. The law applies to every business without discrimination pertaining to ownership (domestic and foreign, state-owned or privately owned). In order to ensure that the competition law's provisions are enforced, the law and its decrees stipulate specific procedures to investigate and handle suspected violations (Pham 2006). Certain practices can be investigated following complaints from those whose interests are being damaged or initiated by the competition authority.

The second pillar is the law on medicines that took effect in 2005 and its implementation provisions. It regulates the trading of pharmaceuticals, their registration and circulation, their supply and use, provision of information and advertisements, medicines' quality standards and laboratory tests as well as management of addictive and mental health-related medicines. The law applies to all organizations and individuals within and outside Vietnam and regulates the activities of trading, distributing, circulating and advertising medicines by enterprises in all economic sectors.

Some provisions of the regulatory framework on medicines could impact market competition, such as prerequisites for distributing pharmaceuticals, requirements for quality control, pricing of medicines, advertisements and promotional sale during the process of trading and distribution. In particular, direct import licences of pharmaceuticals are granted only to Vietnamese enterprises without foreign participation. Instead, foreign pharmaceutical companies are allowed to open branch offices in Vietnam and, since 2009, to import their product directly. They are, however, barred from distribution. This discrimination, while inconsistent with the competition law's objectives of promoting a level playing field, reflects the government's decision to exempt pharmaceutical distribution from the list of industries/sectors to be liberalized under Vietnam's WTO accession commitments and to support the Vietnamese domestic pharmaceutical sector.

The third pillar is other legal frameworks including investment law, enterprise law, trade law, provisions on price control, IPR law and the consumer protection law. These laws and legal documents seem to be consistent with each other. However, three issues can be highlighted as far as laws and regulations are concerned.

First is the issue of strengthening the enforcement of existing legal and regulatory provisions. Second is the issue of extending the existing provisions to accommodate certain problematic situations. In this respect, competition provisions would need to be extended to tackle cases of vertical agreements between manufacturers and distributors. There seems also to be a lack of provision for controlling drug distributors who, while they do not operate within the country, restrict competition in the domestic pharmaceutical market of Vietnam. Third, although the pharmaceutical market operates according to market mechanisms, there is a need for a stronger regulatory role to be taken by state agencies to preserve public health concerns.

COMPETITION ISSUES IN THE DISTRIBUTION OF PHARMACEUTICALS

Based on the number of pharmaceutical wholesalers and retailers, the pharmaceutical distribution sector in Vietnam appears competitive with low concentration ratios. However, as discussed earlier, some enterprises enjoy high market power that enables them to restrict competition. The present section examines the prevalence of vertical and horizontal agreements in the pharmaceutical distribution that result in price-fixing and market division among competitors. The section also deals with the issue of abuse of dominant position and other issues that can emerge from economic concentration in the pharmaceuticals market. Finally, the section addresses unfair competition practices that seem also to prevail in the Vietnamese drug market and that are mostly related to infringement of

IPRs such as fake labels, counterfeit designs or violations in advertising and sale promotion.

Vertical Agreements in the Distribution of Pharmaceuticals

In general, the drug market is structured around two lines of suppliers: manufacturers who produce drugs and distributors that focus on setting up distribution chains for all drugs. One distinctive feature of the pharmaceutical sector in Vietnam is that most producers have their own distribution networks and only a small number of enterprises specialize in distribution.

Operators who combine production and distribution have generally large-scale distribution networks that in some cases extend beyond Vietnam's borders, and other competitors are frequently dependent on them for supply. This situation favours the emergence of vertical integration, which may deter new entry and market development.

Vertical agreements involve businesses operating at successive stages of a production chain and can, in principle, occur at any stage of manufacturing or distribution. In Vietnam, vertical agreements may exist between manufacturers and distributors and between importers and distributors. Although all the players in the drugs outlet system are domestic and foreign companies are not allowed to access this system, in reality they set up formal relationships with domestic players and acquire indirect access to outlets.

Vertical Agreements between Manufacturers and Distributors

DAV figures suggest the presence of some 170 domestic pharmaceutical manufacturers in Vietnam including those producing oriental medicines, out of which 77 comply with the standards set for 'good manufacturing practices'.[4] These account for around 53 per cent of the country's demand for medicines. To reach consumers, domestically produced medicines go either through direct distribution by manufacturers themselves who have their own branches, marketing agents and pharmacies or via private enterprises that specialize in distribution. Domestic manufacturers are mostly made up of former large state-owned enterprises, whereas distributors, on the other hand, are mostly small and medium-sized enterprises, which account for a small market share even though there is a large number of them (800 companies in total). The major players in this market are the Vietnamese enterprises, with no foreign presence except those in manufacturing joint ventures. Roughly 60 per cent of medicines used in hospitals and 70 per cent of those sold in pharmacies are domestically produced. This component of the distribution sector seems to operate in line with the current laws and regulations. Prices are relatively stable and competition within this segment does not seem to be distorted by strategic behaviours of market participants.

When vertical agreements exist, they tend to be among Vietnamese pharmaceutical distributors of mostly small and medium size, and do not seem to represent a major concern for competition and consumer welfare. Meanwhile, vertical agreements can potentially be harmful from the competition law perspective only if one of the undertakings holds a dominant position in the market. This is why the competition law grants exemption to those economic concentration cases where, after merging, the new entities would not become dominant in the market.

Vertical agreements between importers and distributors

Although domestically produced medicines account for 53 per cent of the domestic demand, they make up no more than 27 therapeutic categories mainly treating common diseases.[5] Imported medicines, on the other hand, account for a relatively lower market share, but with a larger list of therapeutic formulations. In 2008, some 72 enterprises had import licences for pharmaceutical products in Vietnam. The ten largest enterprises, however, account for more than three-quarters of the total import value and the concentration ratio of the three largest companies among them reaches 48 per cent.[6] There is also a high market concentration of imports with India, the European Union and South Korea together controlling more 90 per cent of imports (DAV 2008).

Different players distribute imported medicines; these include importing companies, companies specializing in distribution, representative offices and enterprises providing storage facilities and other supporting services as portrayed in Figure 7.1. Foreign invested enterprises (FIEs) cannot participate directly in drug distribution in Vietnam, they can only provide logistics services such as marketing, storage and delivery. However, the level of their involvement and influence in the pharmaceutical distribution sector in Vietnam appears to be high. They may hold significant market power in negotiating the terms for importing medicines into Vietnam, because of their financial capacity, their commercial contacts and their experience in dealing with global multinational pharmaceutical corporations. They participate in all stages of the distribution sector, acting as intermediaries between Vietnamese importers and foreign manufacturers, registering products, marketing, organising transportation into Vietnam, storage, delivery and payment collection. Thus, if these enterprises participate in vertical agreements, they can harm competition and violate completion law's provisions. Such agreements may take the form of either fixing prices or dividing markets.

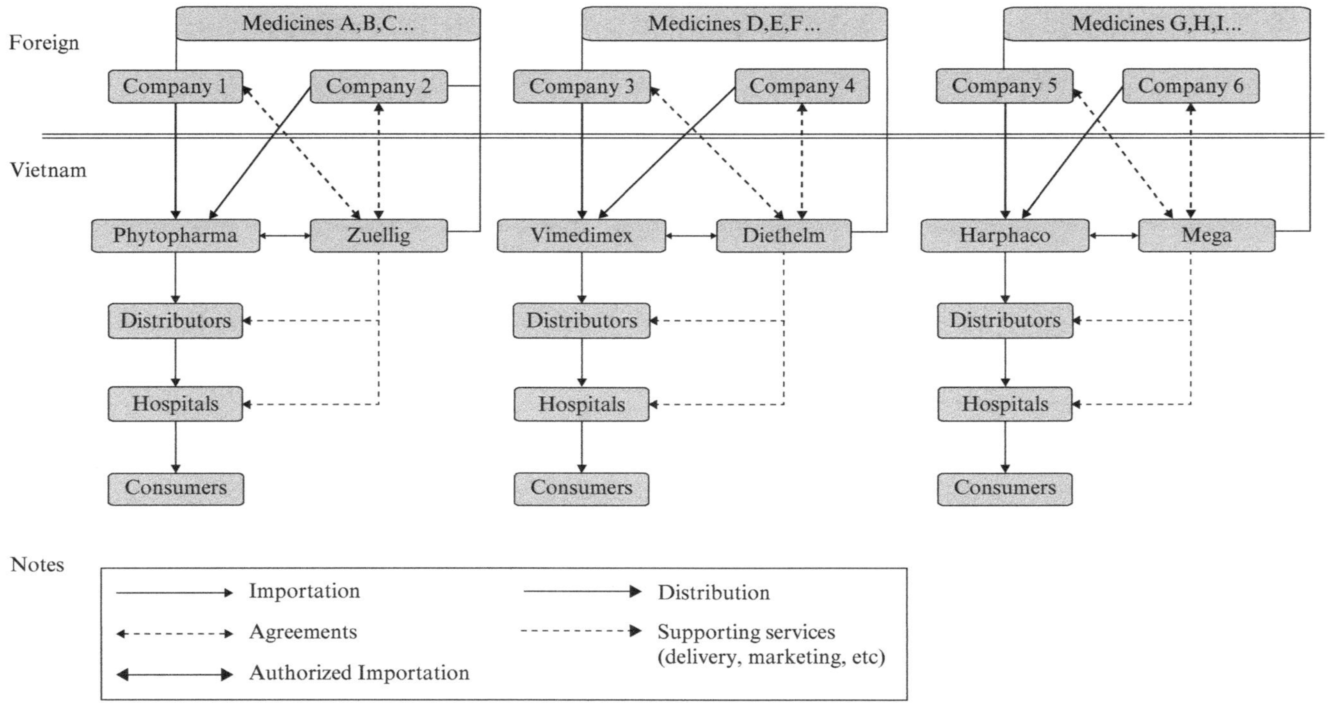

Source: DAV.

Figure 7.1 A typical pharmaceutical distribution system

Price-fixing

Some distributors, intermediaries and representative offices of foreign companies may agree to 'fix' prices. Foreign companies may set the wholesale and retail prices, amounting sometimes to two or three times international prices (DAV 2007). A 2009 study on medicine prices in Vietnam (Nguyen et al. 2009) revealed that public procurement sector prices were 8.3 times the median international reference price (IRP) for 23 innovator brand drugs (IBs) and 1.8 times the IRPs for 33 lowest-priced generic (LPG) equivalent. Prices of seven IBs and of one LPG exceeded ten times the IRPs.

Foreign enterprises argue that medicine prices were registered before importing, and wholesale and retail prices are set by Vietnamese importers and distributors themselves. Vietnamese importers and distributors, however, claim that the prices would have been 'set' by foreign companies. 'Price-fixing' practices may thus often be due to the 'pressures' exerted by companies with market power. Vietnamese importers and distributors also agree to such prices making no objection; this might reveal concerted action. According to Article 14 of the Decree No. 116/2005/ND-CP, 'agreements that fix prices of products and services directly or indirectly mean concerted actions to set the prices'.

Price-fixing can therefore be considered as an anticompetitive agreement. However, it is also a vertical agreement between enterprises at different stages of the distribution system; it needs to be investigated and addressed in combination with other factors, including a definition of the relevant market, in accordance with the competition law.

Market division

The architecture of the typical distribution system of medicines seems to indicate that the market is divided into several distribution networks almost completely independent of each other. Legally, only Vietnamese enterprises have the right to import. However, most of these companies are only authorized to make imports in response to commissions. Meanwhile, foreign pharmaceutical companies and distributors, without directly importing, hold the sole distributorships of many foreign pharmaceutical manufacturers registered in Vietnam and tend to control medicine supply.

Market division also seems to be the outcome of separate strategies employed by companies to avoid competing with each other in the same market even without explicitly 'agreeing' to divide markets. This amounts to 'tacit collusion'. The fact that companies distribute different categories or brands of products may also mean that they have 'explicit' marketing arrangements with parent foreign companies to this end.

Horizontal Agreements in the Distribution of Pharmaceuticals

Horizontal agreements can take place between operators located in the same stage of the distribution chain. This could mean agreements between manufacturers, between wholesalers, or between retailers of the same products or services. According to the competition law, only those operators in a horizontal relationship are actual competitors. In practice, however, despite the law's provisions on medicines defining wholesalers and retailers, relations among wholesalers or among retailers are not simple and most pharmaceutical distributors in Vietnam can be both wholesalers and retailers at one and the same time.

Potentially, horizontal agreements can emerge at any layer of the distribution system. Field surveys, however, suggest that there is no such agreement among similar business competitors that could potentially harm competition and operators tend to behave independently of each other. The large number of small operators as proxied by their market shares could explain such an outcome. The number of enterprises participating in pharmaceutical distribution, according to the statistics provided by the DAV, amounts to around 900 limited liability companies, joint-stock companies and private companies, approximately 30,000 retailing medical stores, some 7,500 private pharmacies and around 7,400 retailing agents in addition to 8,000 medical stores within communal-level clinics.

Abuse of a Dominant Position

The competition law stipulates that 'enterprises shall be considered to hold a dominant position on the market if they have market shares of 30 per cent or more on the relevant market or if they are able to considerably restrict competition'. In the same vein, the law instructs that 'an enterprise shall be considered to hold a monopoly position if there is no other enterprise competing with it for the provision of similar goods or services on the relevant market'. This means that enterprises enjoying a dominant position or those in a situation of monopoly possess market power.

A report on the impact of IPRs mechanisms on medicine prices in Vietnam produced under an assignment of the Ministry of Health, and supported by the World Health Organization (WHO) (Trinh et al. 2006), identified five main reasons for escalating medicine prices in Vietnam: inefficient management of businesses, consumer purchasing practices, lack of information, underdeveloped technology and, finally, pharmaceutical distributors' monopolistic behaviour. The report indicated that some foreign enterprises in pharmaceutical distribution seemed to abuse their dominant position through practices including fixing wholesale and retail prices at excessively high levels.[7]

Exclusivity over drug registration number was another factor that, until 2004, led to monopoly positions in the Vietnamese market. Before marketing any medicine, the company needed first to be registered and obtain a 'visa number' from the DAV. Once a registration number is granted to the manufacturer(s), then all importers can import and distribute the product. The registration number can also be granted to a specific distributor providing him with a legal monopoly over the product. From the competition perspective, given that the relevant market was co-terminous with the market segment of the respective drug, the distributor would enjoy a monopoly position.[8]

Monopoly positions can be acquired legally from intellectual property rights. The WTO agreement on Trade-Related Aspects of Intellectual Property Rights (TRIPS) allows states to take appropriate action to prevent the owner and holder of IPRs from abusing them unreasonably either to restrict trade or to restrict international transfer of technology.

Economic Concentration

From the perspective of the competition law, economic concentration can take different forms: mergers and acquisitions of enterprises, consolidation of enterprises, joint ventures and other forms of concentration as stipulated by law. So far, there has been no economic concentration case in the Vietnamese pharmaceutical sector that attains the market threshold for notification or prohibition by the competition law.

Some factors, however, may lead to greater concentration in the market in future. One is the possibility of foreign firms directly importing medicines. If domestic companies do not improve their infrastructure and expand their markets, they could lose market share in the domestic market to the advantage of the manufacturers and importers. Second, Vietnam's WTO commitments stipulate that, within five years following accession, average tariff level on medicines will be reduced from 5 to 2.5 per cent. Many domestic enterprises may then need to consolidate in order to be able to survive.

Unfair Competition Practices

With respect to the competition law, unfair competition practices refer to competition acts performed by enterprises in their process of doing business that run counter to common standards of business ethics and cause or can cause damage to the state's interests and legitimate rights and interests of other enterprises or consumers. Unfair competition practices in the pharmaceutical industries mostly involve misleading practices related to fake labels, fake designs or violations related to advertising and sale promotion. Field surveys undertaken by the Vietnam Competition Authority (VCA) suggest that very few unfair competition practices prevail in the pharmaceutical distribution sector in Vietnam.

State Agencies' Dealings with Competition Issues in Medicines' Market

The competition authority (VCA) and the sector regulator (DAV) are tasked with addressing different aspects of competition concerns. The competition authority is responsible for ensuring a fair and healthy competition environment via effective implementation of the competition law. It oversees the market and draws operators' attention to anticompetitive practices. It also investigates and addresses such practices. The sector regulator, on the other hand, is in charge of regulating the pharmaceutical market based on the principles of non-discrimination and transparent information in the market. It is also in charge of controlling the technical aspects of the pharmaceutical industry, cooperating with and providing information to the competition authority in specific cases.

The inter-ministerial circular between the Ministry of Health, the Ministry of Finance and the Ministry of Industry and Trade issued in 2007 sets the foundations and prescribes in detail the cooperation mechanisms between the sectoral regulator, the competition authority and the price regulator under the Ministry of Finance.

CONCLUSIONS AND POLICY RECOMMENDATIONS

The pharmaceutical distribution market in Vietnam seems competitive insofar as it contains a large number of players and low concentration ratios. The market for pharmaceuticals is unusual, however; each product, to some extent, has its own market segment and cannot readily be substituted by another product. Patients lack the technical knowledge that would allow them to shop around for alternatives to the drugs prescribed by doctors. Therefore, some distributors can potentially enjoy strong market power.

In particular, the pharmaceutical distribution sector shows signs of a high level of vertical integration, albeit cross-border. Foreign enterprises hold robust bargaining power over Vietnamese wholesalers and retailers, and a high risk exists that they may be tempted to abuse their market power to impose unreasonable conditions on domestic operators by pushing up medicine prices and causing harm to consumers. In fact, despite the large number of players that form a dense distribution network with multiple intermediary layers, drug prices in Vietnam continue to increase when they should be going down.

As highlighted earlier, although there seems to be no explicit agreements among enterprises, patented drugs imported by one local company tend to be totally different from those imported by its competitors. Each company has the propensity to supply only selected medicines of certain therapeutic groups. As a consequence, each company distributes a portfolio of seemingly exclusive products, making it possible for each of them to impose higher drug prices. Using the right to list or delist a medicine from the reimbursement system to negotiate medicine prices with suppliers can reinforce authorities' room for manoeuvre in price negotiations. Such leverage, however, can only be used when therapeutic substitutes are available.

In addition, although foreign firms are not allowed to distribute pharmaceutical products in Vietnam, they merge with and acquire domestic firms to overcome the legal barrier and become eligible to distribute their products. The heavy involvement of foreign companies in drug distribution in the local market appears to be another cause of drug price manipulation. The situation originates in foreign pharmaceutical companies' understanding that they are not subject to the Vietnamese competition law. On one hand, their commercial presence is restricted to the form of representative offices, with no business function according to the commercial law. On the other hand, competition law is only applicable to individuals and organizations doing business in Vietnam. The question is therefore whether collusion between those representative offices and domestic pharmaceutical enterprises setting market prices at two or three times the original prices could be subjected to the competition law of Vietnam. The practice of drug price stabilization prevailing in Vietnam can further reinforce monopoly positions in some market segments and prevent the enterprises involved from being subjected to the competition law.

Agreements between foreign enterprises with domestic enterprises regarding sole distributorship of some specific product can also create fertile ground for potential anticompetitive practices. Even if these enterprises do not directly take part in the distribution network, they may still influence competition via resale price maintenance.

Vietnam appears to be endowed with a fairly comprehensive regulatory framework for dealing with the pharmaceutical sector. Such a framework can be further strengthened by incorporating regulations on vertical agreements as well as other relevant provisions. Vietnam could introduce the principle of mandatory generic substitution followed, for instance, by South Africa, requiring a pharmacist to inform his customers about substitution options for their prescriptions. Amendments could also be introduced to delimit the boundaries of the distribution system and ensure that enterprises are not making use of loopholes that exist currently. In that regard, there should be a separation between registration and the granting of import licences. Decisions on which companies are allowed to participate in the distribution system should be handled by a different process from company registration.

Besides improving the legal framework, enforcement has been a major issue that can be traced back partly to the competition authority's and sector regulator's lack of experience and partly to inadequate resources and capacity in dealing with distinctive behaviours prevailing in the pharmaceutical industry.

In the short term, it is necessary to enhance the supervisory role of the state agencies (DAV and VCA) in order to oversee the market more effectively and to take swift measures to deal with practices that may restrict competition in the pharmaceutical distribution sector and thereby to protect consumers' interests. The DAV could also implement some good international practices such as conducting a general 'sector inquiry' into an industry when it suspects, based on price trends or other factors, that there may be a distortion of competition in an industry even in the absence of actual evidence of wrongdoing.

Some level of cooperation between the VCA and DAV in regulating and dealing with anticompetitive practices in the pharmaceutical sector is needed. So far, the relationship between the two agencies is quite loose due to the lack of a database on market structure and the difficulty in scrutinizing companies that may hold a dominant position and abuse such a position. On the other hand, potential risks to competition are normally not made explicit in the content of the contracts but are agreed implicitly, making them hard to detect. Detection is only made possible by the close cooperation among all relevant state agencies, and between state agencies and the private sector (through provision of information and communication of violations).

In particular, enterprises need to be advised not to include contractual clauses that may restrict competition such as fixing prices directly or indirectly, dividing customers or supplies, or preventing other enterprises from entering the market.

The pharmaceutical market in Vietnam is complex in terms of delimiting the relevant market and assessing concentration ratios. Vietnam can adopt, as most countries do, standardized systems such as the Anatomical Therapeutic Classification (ATC) recognized by the WHO, under which the drugs are grouped according to the organ of the body or physiological system on which they act and their chemical, pharmacological and therapeutic properties, and are classified in groups at five different levels. Adoption of the ATC would facilitate more product substitution between segments of the pharmaceutical market than at present.

It is also vital to build up a database on existing market players, so as to identify those holding a dominant position or a monopoly in the relevant markets or having the potential to do so. This database needs to be transparent and shared among all state agencies.

Finally, it is crucial for the VCA to engage in policy advocacy and use information and dissemination campaigns in order to promote awareness of enterprises currently doing business in the pharmaceutical sector on the competition law's provisions. More generally, public information on medicines, legal provisions and pricing policies and practices contributes in creating a transparent drug market for consumers and all stakeholders involved. Public information must provide patients with the available options in terms of efficacy, safety and cost, so they can have a more active role in the medicine decision-making process and therefore limit the discretion of the prescriber.

NOTES

1. Research and other assistance was given by Truong Thuy Linh and Tran Phuong Nhung, VCAD officials, coordinators of the project, and Ta Ngoc Dung, secretary-general of the Vietnam Association for Medical Ingredients (VIMAMES). The research team also acknowledges the valuable support of all relevant agencies, enterprises and some other experts.
2. This refers to the Constitution adopted in 1992 and amended in 2001.
3. Based on statistics on the World Health Organization website for 2013.
4. For more information, see Decision No. 47/2007/QD-BYT issued on December 24, 2007 by the Ministry of Health on the application of principles and standards regarding 'Good Manufacturing Practices'.
5. According to IMS statistics, in 2005, 61 per cent of all the medicines used in hospitals and 71 per cent of the medicines sold in pharmacies are domestically-produced. IMS health is a leading worldwide company that provides data and business solution areas for the life sciences industry including Drug Distribution Data.
6. Vietnam Pharmaceutical Industry Analysis – Vietcombank Securities 2008.
7. Zuelling Pharma (ZPV) is a case in point. From its establishment in 2001 until the DAV suspended its activities of authorized importation and distribution of final imported products in 2004, ZPV had been the sole provider of medicines providing a total of 180 active elements (out of 4,400 medicines having 900 active elements registered in Vietnam). Most of these medicines were patented products: 97 had one patented single formulation and 18 had 5 patented formulations and all were exclusively supplied by ZPV.
8. This practice disappeared from the market after the Circular No. 06/2001/TT-BYT was annulled in 2004.

REFERENCES

DAV (2007) *Official Report on Medicine Prices*, Hanoi: Drug Administration of Vietnam.

DAV (2008) *Pharmaceutical Industry Conference*, Hanoi: Drug Administration of Vietnam.

Nguyen, A.T. (2011) *Medicines Prices and Pricing Policies in Vietnam*, Doctor of Philosophy Dissertation, University of New South Wales.

Nguyen, A.T., R. Knight, A. Mant, Q.M. Cao and M. Auton (2009) Medicine prices, availability, and affordability in Vietnam, *Southern Med Review*, **2**(2): 2–9.

Pham, A. (2006) The development of competition law in Vietnam in the face of economic reforms and global integration, *Northwestern Journal of International Law and Business*, **26**: 547–64.

Regan, T.L. (2008) Generic entry, price competition and market segmentation in the prescription drug market, *International Journal of Industrial Organization*, **26**(4): 930–48.

Trinh, H.B., V.H. Tran, T.N. Nguyen, T.H. Vu and C.C. Phan (2006) *On Application of Economic Modelling of Likely Impact of Stronger Intellectual Property Rights (IPR) Protection on Medicine Prices in Vietnam*, Hanoi.

Van Tien, T., H.T. Phuong, I. Mathauer and T.K.P. Nguyen (2011) *A Health Financing Review of Vietnam*, Geneva: World Health Organization.

WHO (2004) *The World Medicines Situation*, Geneva: World Health Organization.

WHO (2011) *A Health Financing Review of Vietnam*, Geneva: World Health Organization.

WTO (2013) *Trade Policy Review: Vietnam*, WT/TPR/287.

PART III

The distribution of services: International money transfers and TV programmes

8. International money transfer services in Uzbekistan

Golib Kholjigitov[1]

SCOPE OF THE CHAPTER AND MAIN FINDINGS

One of the main competition issues in the distribution sector is that dominant companies may use restrictive practices to protect their market position, including through vertical agreements with their agents. This chapter examines this topic in the market for international money transfer services (remittance payments) in Uzbekistan. It is based on research done by the research arm (the Antimonopoly Policy Improvement Center, APIC) of the national competition authority (the State Committee of the Republic of Uzbekistan on Demonopolization, Support of Competition and Entrepreneurship). Ancillary studies and field surveys were commissioned from academic and commercial researchers in Uzbekistan.

Uzbekistan had a population of approximately 26 million people in the mid-2000s, at the time that this research was carried out. In population terms it is the third largest country, after Russia and Ukraine, of the 11 countries of the former Soviet Union that now constitute the Commonwealth of Independent States (CIS). In income terms, however, it is one of the poorest, with GDP per capita about a quarter of the level of Russia in 2005. Only Moldova, Kyrgyzstan and Tajikistan had lower income levels at that time.

International money market transfers into Uzbekistan are mainly made by temporary workers sending remittances home out of their wages earned abroad. The end of the Soviet Union led to great changes in the pattern of residence and of labour movements among the CIS member countries. Uzbekistan, like other relatively poor economies, became a high sender of migrant workers abroad in net terms. The majority (75 per cent) of migrant workers had Russia as their destination. The extent of out-migration from Uzbekistan is not known with accuracy but it may have accounted in the mid 2000s for as much as 5 per cent of the labour force. Their remittances were estimated to amount to US$1 billion in 2005, equivalent to 21 per cent of gross exports and four times as much as inflows of direct foreign investment.

The subject of this chapter is the 24-hour foreign currency transfer service. Providers organize the international transfer and arrange for collection of the funds over the counter in a secure manner in bank branches and other outlets in Uzbekistan. This is a distinct market providing a service that is not available to migrants from the banks themselves. Bank transfers are slow, much of the population of Uzbekistan is unbanked and banking services of any kind are not available to short-term migrants or those with irregular status in the host country.

The money transfers market in Uzbekistan is thus supplied by specialist, non-bank financial institutions. It developed at an extremely fast rate during the first half of the 2000s. The first provider, Western Union, arrived at the beginning of 2002. Over the next five years, another ten providers entered the market. Each new market entrant offered tariffs that were lower than those of the incumbents, resulting in a continuous decrease in the average tariff. Accordingly, the main finding of this chapter is that competition acted as a powerful force that enormously benefited consumers in this market.

The arrival of new entrants was not due to enforcement of the competition law that was enacted in 1996.[2] That law did not cover the financial services sector in the mid-2000s. However, this research indicated that it would be viable and valuable for it to do so in future and the law was duly revised to this effect. The first service provider had in fact sought to maintain its dominance – and its excessive profits – by including exclusive dealing provisions in its agreements with the commercial banks. These banks acted as its agent by enabling transfer recipients to collect the funds in their branches. Exclusive dealings with harmful effect, such as those, were not prohibited by the financial sector regulator (the Central Bank of Uzbekistan), but are proscribed under the competition law.

If the exclusive dealings provisions had stuck, they would certainly have had an anticompetitive effect. But many of the commercial banks disregarded them and the first service provider had no means of penalizing them for non-compliance. In practice, the excessively high margins of the first provider proved to be strongly pro-competitive, drawing other actors into the market and giving the banks the incentive to strike multiple deals with new providers. This dynamic was intensified in 2007 when the national Post Office network, with a very large number of branches, offered international money transfers for the first time.

The Central Bank was persuaded to bring the financial services market within the scope of the competition law for two main reasons. First, had the volume of business in the market not been growing so rapidly, a legal prohibition on exclusive dealings would have been needed to eliminate that particular barrier to entry. Second, given that the arrival of so many new private market actors had greatly diminished excessive margins in the market, a period of consolidation among the providers might occur. The market situation would need to be monitored thenceforth for potentially anticompetitive practices.

The study made some recommendations for policy. Greater transparency on the services and tariffs set by the money transfer service providers should be introduced into the market to protect consumers. To promote continued competition, the government should not let the Post Office (or any other public body) stand outside the competition law. It should also encourage the commercial banks to integrate fully into the international banking infrastructure so that they too can become service providers in the same market.

BACKGROUND

The break-up of the Soviet Union and transition to the market economy in the newly independent states led to serious disruptions to the flow and pattern of human resources. In the case of Uzbekistan, many people ended up working outside the country, while their families remained in their homeland.

International money transfers (remittances), particularly in the form of cash-to-cash transfers, are a crucial element for alleviating poverty and increasing welfare in the households of the migrants in the sending country (Taylor 1992; Van Doorn 2005; World Bank 2006). In Uzbekistan, as in many other transition countries, only a small percentage of the population had bank accounts due to historic lack of trust in the state-owned banks that constituted the banking system in the Soviet period and the recency of the financial sector reforms that saw the creation of independent commercial banks. In any event, the local banking system had weak links with the international banking system in the 1990s and early 2000s. In many parts of the former Soviet Union, specialist money transfer service providers sprang up during this period to supply a financial link between the expatriates and their families. In Uzbekistan these were totally new actors that had not been present in any sector of the national economy previously. The first service to arrive, in 2001, was the US company Western Union, founded in 1851 originally to provide telegraphic services. Western Union's share of the Uzbek international money transfers market was cut almost in half by the arrival of ten other providers in the subsequent five years, although it remained the dominant actor.

The possibility of transferring money internationally was a new phenomenon for citizens of the CIS countries. But the experience of some of those countries, including Russia and Ukraine, suggested that it was a sphere that was prone to anticompetitive and abusive behaviour, particularly in the form of exclusive contracting with cooperating banks. In addition, in Ukraine, excessively (monopolistically) high prices were charged by the service providers. The object of the current research was to examine whether the situation in Uzbekistan was similar and the extent of harm that might have been imposed on consumers of the service.

Migration Flows and Traditional Mechanisms for Remittance Payments

One of the many problems brought about by the collapse of the Soviet Union and the emergence of the independent republics was the need to manage massive population movements. Suddenly millions of people found themselves no longer citizens of the country they had been living in. Millions of other people were offered the chance to come back to the lands from where they had been forced out previously. At the time, legislation and administrative structures to regulate international migration were lacking or else operated according to the principles of the old political system.

Several countries of the former Soviet Union thus became net emigration countries. For eight countries (Armenia, Georgia, Kazakhstan, Moldova, Tajikistan, Turkmenistan, Uzbekistan and Ukraine), the level of out-migration of their citizens is very high. Migration flows out of these countries mainly comprised workers seeking employment in the Russian Federation. Among Uzbek migrants, the preferred destinations are the United States of America, Germany, the United Kingdom and the United Arab Emirates, but the majority in fact travel to work in the Russian Federation. Most go to Moscow, Saint Petersburg, Kaliningrad and cities in the Volga region. Uzbek migrants are mostly (80 per cent) male and mainly above 30 years old. They are relatively well educated and do not find opportunities to fully utilize their potential at home.

The Central Asian states have seen relatively rapid rates of population increase. The populations of Tajikistan, Turkmenistan and Uzbekistan are among the youngest in the world: approximately 40 per cent of the population in Uzbekistan is less than 15 years of age. The total population of 26 million in 2005 made Uzbekistan the third largest country in the region after Russia and Ukraine.

Uzbekistan and other former Soviet Union countries in Central Asia not only experience a high level of labour migration of their own nationals, they are also transit countries for residents of Asia and the Middle East trying to reach European Union countries.

In many cases, migrants find jobs abroad through unofficial channels or illegally, in either case bypassing the official channels of job placement abroad, with its system of guest visas and organized labour movements. The labour flow fluctuates by season. Uzbek migrants are employed overseas in a range of fields such as construction, sales, manufacturing industries, agriculture, catering and the services sector (Tyuryukanova 2005).

Reliable estimates of the number of migrant workers are lacking. According to official data, on average during the period 2003–5, labour out-migration was around 250,000 persons (Ministry of Labour and Social Security 2006). The total number of emigrants in 2005 was recorded at 266,100; this represented 2.5 per cent of the economically active population. Unofficial estimates of the real level of out-migration, however, put it at twice the official level, amounting accordingly to an outflow of 5 per cent of the labour force (Ministry of Labour and Social Security 2006).

The same official data indicate that in 2005, 20 per cent of Uzbek migrants went to neighbouring Kazakhstan and 75 per cent to Russia (Ministry of Labour and Social Security, 2006). South Korea, which also administers a work permit system, is another country destination where potential earnings are comparatively high for migrant workers. In terms of remittance mechanisms, South Korea is unusual as the only main destination country from where migrant workers use the banks to transfer money home, perhaps because the salaries of licensed foreign workers in that country are required to be paid into banks.[3]

Apart from the officially registered providers (specialist providers and the banks), what other mechanisms are used by workers abroad to transfer part of their earnings back to their households at home? One such channel is that labour migrants buy and, in person, transport to Uzbekistan expensive electronic appliances, medications, clothes, footwear and other products for their family members to use – and occasionally to sell. An informal system of remittances (*havala*) is also widely used in Uzbekistan, in two forms. Money is transferred through illegal financial structures, connected to retail businesses; the transaction is subject to commissions, which depend on the amount of the transfer and distance that money is transferred. The commission is estimated to amount to 2–3 per cent (Ministry of Labour and Social Security 2006). Another mechanism is that the transfer is embodied in goods purchased by commercial agents. Use of this mechanism seems to be limited to South Korea. Once in a few months, a Korean businessman comes to enterprises where Uzbek migrants work. He collects money from migrants, which is recorded in a register. The businessman buys goods for this money in South Korea and sends them to Uzbekistan, where they are sold on in retail markets. The revenue from these sales is distributed among receivers of remittances (the families of the migrants) according to the amount of the initial payment of the foreign worker.

Estimating the amount of remittances is problematic in general (Ghosh 2006; World Bank 2013) and also in Uzbekistan. One approach is to consider the amounts of money that migrant workers in different countries save from their earnings. According to one study, migrants from Uzbekistan working in the United States save around US$5,000 during a guest stay of six months, even at the most simple jobs that do not require a special qualification; migrant workers in South Korea may save up to US$300 monthly; and in the Russian Federation a seasonal migrant may set aside US$500–700 in a labour season of seven to eight months (Centre on Demographics and Ecology of People; Maksakova 2002; Tyuryukanova 2005).

Prior to the arrival of the international money transfer service providers, there was no data on current remittance payments. The Central Bank of Uzbekistan now provides records from these companies. The amounts they handled quadrupled between 2002 and 2006, and amounted to more than US$1 billion in 2006. More detailed data is presented below in the section analysing the market. However, the proportion of total remittance payments handled by these formal providers is unknown. The Central Bank estimates that approximately the same amount of money entered the country through routes other than the banking system. If that was the case in 2005, the income from labour migration may have amounted then to around US$1 billion, which equals 21 per cent of gross exports of the republic or four times the volume of foreign direct investment into Uzbekistan in that year.

The Regulatory Framework for Money Transfers

During the Soviet period there were no financial markets in Uzbekistan. All investment and financial decisions were made by planners and heads of state-owned enterprises. Other functions of the financial system were carried out by state-owned banks, particularly the state bank (Gosbank), which performed the functions of the Central Bank and a commercial bank at the same time. Some other specialized banks existed to service the needs of particular economic sectors, including trade financing. Non-bank institutions were extremely underdeveloped; there was only one insurance company and one pension fund, for example, which were both fully owned by the state.

Post-Soviet financial sector reforms began with the transformation of the former local branches of the Soviet banks into independent banks. Afterwards, a two-tiered banking system consisting of the Central Bank and commercial banks was introduced. The Central Bank reports to the parliament, controls the activities of the commercial banks and provides the country with its own payments system. The financial sector has continued to be developed since then, with full range of infrastructure institutions such as a banking association and a credit bureau.

Until 1994, the payments system was managed from the centre and payments from one bank to another, and also international payments, went through the postal system. Payments processing took much time – from three days to a month – because of the unpredictability of postal deliveries. From 1996, electronic payments started to be rolled out across the country along with some decentralization of the payments settlement system. The maximum time for settlements was brought down to nine days with an average settlement time of one day. Later improvements stabilized the functioning of the electronic payment system and the time taken for payment transfers between banks eventually came down to just a few minutes. Another development was the creation of an integrated national system of non-cash payments using plastic cards with SmartPay and microprocessing technology. The aims were to decrease the amount of cash in circulation, to draw in funds from households and create internationally accepted banking services for the population.

The opening up of the financial sector to specialist money transfer service providers from 2001 was another part of this move to set up the full array of financial institutions in Uzbekistan. Along with other financial sector entities, they were subject to the regulatory oversight of the Central Bank, which carries out licensing and general regulation of all banking and other financial activity.

According to Article 6 of the 1993 law on currency regulation, international money transfers are a type of currency operation. Transfer service providers coordinate closely with the commercial banks; bank retail branches serve as the outlets from which remittance recipients collect the funds that are transferred from abroad. To carry out currency operations, commercial banks have to get a license from the Central Bank. Other authorities involved in the control of currency operations along with the Central Bank are the Ministry of Finance, the State Tax Committee and the State Customs Committee.

Thus, in legal terms, money transfers are treated as currency operations carried out mainly by commercial banks having valid licences from the Central Bank to render currency operations. However, the money transfer market saw an important institutional change in July 2004 when the government of the Republic of Uzbekistan passed Decree no. 399 'On improving the activities in the sphere of postal communications'. This stipulated that one of the main tasks of the UP (the Uzbek national postal company) is to organize postal remittances, including with foreign countries. In line with this policy, in May 2005 the government passed a follow-up Decree no. 128 for the establishment of new services, including money transfers, on the basis of information-communication technologies. The technologies used included ATMs, Fram Relay, Fast Ethernet and Gigabit Ethernet in a programme funded by grants and loans from foreign financial institutions. The Central Bank also permitted international money remittance services to be done by credit unions on condition that provision of the service was mentioned in its charter.

THE INTERNATIONAL MONEY TRANSFER MARKET IN UZBEKISTAN

This section applies the standard scheme for product market analysis to the cross-border service of money transfers. It therefore examines the definition of the market and its structure and dynamics. The examination required a degree of inter-agency cooperation since the competition authority – albeit it in the arm's length guise of its research wing, APIC – had no remit over the financial services sector that was regulated by the Central Bank of Uzbekistan.

Market Definition

Defining the market was one of the challenging tasks for this research. As noted earlier, although the underlying principles for defining product and geographic market dimensions are the same for all types of markets, the Uzbek competition authority had no experience of analysing markets in financial services due to the limitations of the competition legislation. The procedure for market definition was modelled on that of the Ukrainian competition authority, which had pursued a clear and comprehensive approach to defining market boundaries of money transfers services in that country.

Hence, the relevant product market in Uzbekistan was defined as follows: 'International (cash) money transfers made without opening a bank account, with the remittance transaction taking not more than 24 hours'.

The key elements in trying to define the product market were the timeliness and ease of transfers. Although many alternatives exist to the remittance technology used by Western Union, they are not close substitutes. Postal remittances and inter-bank money transfers all fell down on one or more criterion, and were not components of the same market.

The remittances payments technology used by firms like Western Union, MoneyGram and others was unique in several aspects:

- The payment is more or less instant. Normally the operation takes about 15 minutes to carry out. Postal remittances take much longer.
- Money can be collected by the recipient at any branch of the system. Postal and bank remittances require exact destination points to send money.
- There is no need for users of the service – at either sending or receiving end – to open a bank account. Inter-bank remittances are bureaucratic and require IDs and other legal documents. For the majority of people making remittances this is an unnecessary and unfeasible burden, especially in view of the often illegal status of the sender.

In 2006 there were ten other money transfer systems rendering a service similar to that of Western Union. All of them offered almost instant transactions, although the time limit that they promised the client for collection of the money varied somewhat. A time limit of 24 hours was chosen for the definition of the market, as there is at least one company that claims on its advertisements that it guarantees clients receipt of the money within one hour on average and no later than 24 hours. Therefore, a 24-hour boundary is a reasonable time limit for money transfers services that claim to be instant.

It was found that account-to-account transfers between banks and Post Offices do not constitute close substitutes for instant cash money transfer and should not be incorporated into the relevant product market. There are a number of reasons for this. First, most of the money transfers are made by migrant workers, only a few of whom have bank accounts. Opening a bank account is often a costly procedure, quite apart from the fact that a majority of migrant workers will have legal issues opening an account in a foreign country. Account-to-account transfers cannot therefore be compared in terms of convenience to instant cash money transfers. Second, at the time of writing, although technically postal services offered instant money transfer services (as is the case in many countries), the Uzbek Post Office was not allowed to carry out foreign currency transactions using technology similar to that of the other firms in money transfers market. So the only way to transfer money abroad by post had been sending banknotes physically – in envelopes or some kind of scroll. This was by no means a close substitute to contemporary means of transferring money.

As regards the geographic market, the first consideration was that there might be some regional patterns in terms of penetration of money transfer systems. However, the data from the banks showed that the majority of the existing money transfer systems had entered contracts with the largest commercial banks in Uzbekistan, which have wide networks of branches in every region of Uzbekistan. This suggested that the spread and penetration of the money transfer systems was fairly uniform throughout the territory of Uzbekistan.

One of the peculiarities of the defining geographic boundaries for the money transfer services market is that the service is essentially carried out at two different locations, one of which is outside the territory of Uzbekistan; that is, outside the national competition protection jurisdiction. One possible definition of the market was transfer 'corridors' – such as between Uzbekistan and other former Soviet Union countries (all or selected countries, including the Baltic states), or between Uzbekistan and the rest of the world. However, that would have led to analytical difficulties because the economic actors work in two different jurisdictions and legal systems. Hence the appropriate geographic market for further analysis was defined as the whole territory of Uzbekistan.

Market Participants and Market Shares

Within the market defined as above, a considerable number of money transfer service providers operated in 2006 – a rapid structural evolution from the single market actor present five years before.

Western Union, the first-mover into the Uzbek market for money transfers, commenced operations in January 2002. It was the world leader in money transfers at that time. Western Union's main rival MoneyGram was quick to follow its lead, opening up its service three months later. The Russia-based Contact system was quick to enter the Uzbek market next, in May 2002.

From the beginning of 2004, new competitors entered the market on an almost regular basis. The newcomers were mostly from Russia, but also from the UK and UAE. The latest registered competitor is an Uzbek–Russian company JV. By the end of 2006, there were 11 money transfer providers offering the service in Uzbekistan.

Figure 8.1 shows that there was very fast growth in the volumes of money transfers both to and from Uzbekistan in the 2000s. In 2002, around US$225 million was remitted to Uzbekistan from abroad; by 2005 the amount had grown to almost US$790 million with an average year-on-year growth rate of 52 per cent. Outgoing money transfers have been growing at a slower rate (half the growth rate of incoming money transfers) and from a much smaller base. In 2002, US$86 million was sent abroad, while by 2005 the amount had increased to around US$168 million with a year-on-year growth rate of 26 per cent.

Table 8.1 Participants in the international money transfer market, Uzbekistan 2006

No.	Name of the money transfer operator and country of origin	Date of market entry
1	Western Union (USA)	January 2002
2	MoneyGram (USA)	April 2002
3	Contact (Russia)	May 2002
4	MIGOM (Russia)	February 2004
5	Anelik (Armenia)	September 2004
6	Inter Express (Russia)	November 2004
7	Travelex (UK)	February 2005
8	Xpress Money (UAE)	June 2005
9	Unistream (Russia)	August 2005
10	Bistraya Pochta (Russia)	December 2005
11	Azia Express (Uzbek-Russian JV)	June 2006

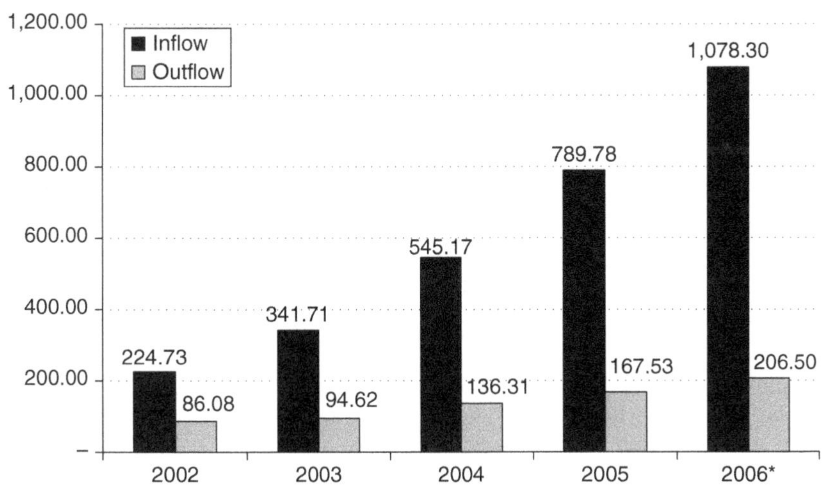

Note: *Estimate.

Source: CB Statistics.

Figure 8.1 Annual amount of money transfers (inflows and outflows in million US$), Uzbekistan, through international money transfer providers, 2002–6

As Figure 8.1 shows, Uzbekistan has been a net receiver of money transfers since the commencement of the instantaneous money transfer market. The excess of inflows over outflows is very large and has been increasing rapidly over time. Outflows represent remittances and other payments made by persons in Uzbekistan to destinations abroad. The relative values are clearly consistent with the country's status as a net sender of workers abroad. The identity of those sending money abroad is not known, but includes migrants of other Asian countries who come to Uzbekistan as a staging post to other, final destinations. Our analysis largely focuses on remittance inflows into Uzbekistan, since the beneficiaries of those flows are Uzbek personal consumers for whom we seek to estimate the level of harm (if any) of features of the market from a competition perspective. Nevertheless, the size of the market is determined by including payments in the reverse direction.

It is evident that the market for money transfers in Uzbekistan was growing remarkably fast during this period, both in terms of the number of market participants (competitors) and the size.

Once the definition of the relevant product and geographic market was decided, the next challenge was to choose the indicator(s) to use for calculating market shares of Western Union and its competitors. It was suggested earlier that to prove Western Union's dominance (which is needed, in terms of Uzbek competition legislation) its market share has to be estimated as a quantifiable measure of a firm's dominance. Several indicators were considered:

1. The number of retail points in Uzbekistan.
2. The amount of cash remitted to Uzbekistan from abroad.
3. The amount of cash remitted from Uzbekistan to abroad.
4. The cash turnover (the sum of items 2 and 3 above).
5. Total (inflow and outflow) number of transactions in Uzbekistan.

In the end, the first and second indicators were used to determine Western Union's market share. For Uzbekistan, it was considered on reflection that the most accurate indicator for calculating market shares could be the number of transactions carried out by each competitor. The idea was put forward by Western Union's local representative, who said that this was how the company had been measuring its share in various money transfers markets. The proposal was supported by the representatives of the commercial banks. A bank representative also confirmed that the data should be available, since reports on the number of transactions on money transfers were submitted by banks to the Central Bank of Uzbekistan on a quarterly basis. However, as it turned out, the Central Bank was not able to provide information on money transfer transactions except for the first half of 2006. So the final indicator from the list above could only be used to calculate market shares of remittance system only for the period January to June 2006. The results of all the calculations are presented in Tables 8.2, 8.3 and 8.4.

These calculations reveal a range of estimates – of 58, 55 and 53 per cent – for the market share of Western Union. Interestingly, the market share calculation for this company based on the single observation of the number of transactions for the first half of 2006, was similar, at 53 per cent.

Over time, Western Union's market share has been steadily decreasing from an almost monopoly position of 95 per cent share in 2002 to 53 per cent in 2006 (midyear). Clearly, for the whole period and despite its loss of market share, Western Union qualifies as being the dominant player in the market. The Uzbek competition law qualifies any firm possessing more than 35 per cent of the market as having a dominant position.

The company that has come second to the market leader's share of the market for the period covered by the analysis has been Contact. Its market share was in fact rather volatile, starting from as low as 5 per cent in 2002, getting to a record level of almost 33 per cent in 2004, only to drop down to 20 per cent by 2006 (midyear).

Anelik, Unistream, MIGOM and Bistraya Pochta are also success stories, having seen their market share grow from less than 1 per cent in the year they started (2004) up to 10, 8, 5 and 3 per cent (midyear) respectively.

Table 8.2 Market shares of money transfer service providers according to number of retail points

Name of remittance system	Starting date	Current number of partner banks	Current number of branches (retail points)	Market shares based on the number of branches (%)
WU	21.01.2002	13	755	58
MoneyGram	03.04.2002	2	29	2
Unistream	11.08.2005	3	62	5
Bistraya Pochta	30.12.2005	2	69	5
Xpress Money	15.06.2005	2	3	0
Anelik	22.09.2004	3	79	6
Contact	23.05.2002	3	88	7
MIGOM	16.02.2004	3	63	5
Travelex	03.02.2005	3	98	7
Inter-Express	17.11.2004	2	61	5
Azia Express	01.06.2006	1	n/a	0
Total			1,307	100

Table 8.3 Market shares of money transfer service providers according to money flows

Name of remittance system	Market shares based on annual inflow of money transfers (%)					Market shares based on annual outflow of money transfers (%)				
	2002	2003	2004	2005	1/2 2006	2002	2003	2004	2005	1/2 2006
WU	95	73	64	59	52	98	94	81	66	55
MoneyGram	0	1	1	1	1	2	1	2	1	1
Unistream	0	0	0	3	8	0	0	0	3	7
Bistraya Pochta	0	0	0	1	3	0	0	0	1	5
Xpress Money	0	0	0	0	0	0	0	0	0	1
Anelik	0	0	0	9	10	0	0	1	9	6
Contact	5	26	35	23	21	0	5	15	11	9
MIGOM	0	0	1	3	4	0	0	1	8	12
Travelex	0	0	0	0	0	0	0	0	2	3
Inter-Express	0	0	0	0	1	0	0	0	0	0
Azia Express	0	0	0	0	0	0	0	0	0	0
Total	100	100	100	100	100	100	100	100	100	100

Table 8.4 Market shares of money transfer service providers according to business turnover

Name of remittance system	Market shares based on annual turnover of money transfers (%)					Market shares based on the total number of transactions (%)
	2002	2003	2004	2005	1/2 2006	1/2 2006
WU	95	75	66	60	53	53
MoneyGram	0	1	1	1	1	2
Unistream	0	0	0	3	8	5
Bistraya Pochta	0	0	0	1	3	8
Xpress Money	0	0	0	0	0	0
Anelik	0	0	0	9	10	10
Contact	5	24	33	22	20	19
MIGOM	0	0	1	3	5	3
Travelex	0	0	0	0	0	0
Inter-Express	0	0	0	0	1	1
Azia Express	0	0	0	0	0	0
Total	100	100	100	100	100	100

Table 8.5 Market concentration indexes, 2002–6 (midyear)

	2002	2003	2004	2005	1/2 2006
Based on the total inflow of money transfers					
HHI	8,673	5,364	4,933	4,452	4,143
CR3 (%)	100	100	99	95	91
Based on the total outflow of money transfer					
HHI	9,379	8,420	6,305	4,852	3,871
CR3 (%)	100	100	98	87	81
Based on total money transfer turnover					
HHI	8,715	5,509	4,978	4,463	4,075
CR3 (%)	100	100	99	94	89.1

The market shares of the remaining money transfer systems (MoneyGram, Xpress Money, Travelex, Inter-Express, and Azia Express) have been around 1 per cent or less throughout the period.

Market concentration ratios (HHI and CR3) have changed over time in line with the dynamics of the market and changing numbers of players. The Herfindahl–Hirschman Index (HHI), calculated on the basis of any of the three indicators (inflow, outflow, or turnover) fell by more than half between 2002 and 2006 (from more than 8,500 to around 4,000, midyear). Competition had certainly been growing in the market, at least from a structural perspective. Yet most new entrants were not able to capture more than a minimal market share and a high CR3 index persisted throughout the period. Despite its evolution in terms of numbers of players, and the loss of half the market by the dominant company, the money transfer market remained highly concentrated by this standard measure (see Table 8.5).

To sum up, the market for money transfers in Uzbekistan has been expanding in volume at a very fast rate. This has been attracting new competitors into the market. Although Western Union's transaction volumes are still far higher than any of its competitors, its market share dropped from 100 to 53 per cent in the four years after 2002. Even so, the growth of the market was so great that its annual amount of business approximately doubled over that period. In general, the market for money transfers displayed all the typical characteristics of the introductory and growth stages of the product life cycle.

Business Practices: Western Union's Exclusive Dealing Clause

Examination of all the contracts entered into by the remittance service providers and their commercial bank partners in Uzbekistan revealed that Western Union (WU) had routinely engaged in a clearly exclusionary practice. Item 4.2.8 of Western Union's model contract stated that 'the bank is prohibited to cooperate with other companies rendering the services of online monetary transfer in a manner similar to the one used by the WU system during the period of validity of the agreement with WU'.

Unlike the Russian case, for this to qualify as an infringement of the law on competition in Uzbekistan,[4] it was necessary to prove that Western Union possessed a dominant position in the market, and that the practice (item 4.2.8 in the model contract) harmed or restricted competition. It is without a doubt that Western Union has had a significant market share in the market and that it qualifies accordingly as a dominant firm in the market. It is also evident, however, that Western Union's dominance has been falling – at least in market share terms – since 2002. Moreover, it does not seem to be the case that the item in Western Union's model contract has restricted competition considerably, for the following reasons:

- WU's market share has dropped since 2002 from more than 90 per cent to less than 60 per cent by 2006 midyear, even though its volumes of transactions had been growing almost in line with the market growth itself.
- The market has seen many new firm (competitor) entrances since 2002 and now incorporates the services of 11 money transfer systems.
- There have been no complaints to the competition authorities or the financial sector regulator from either banks or competitors against Western Union's practice. There remained other banks (retail outlets) with whom Western Union's competitors still had a chance to strike contracts for market entry. Four of the 17 commercial banks operating in Uzbekistan did not deal with Western Union (see Figure 8.2).
- Finally, the item did not stop banks that were cooperating with Western Union from entering contracts with its competitors. In fact, fewer than half (six) of the 13 banks having contracts with Western Union had abided by item 4.2.8 of the contract. The marked cells in Table 8.6 show the contracts entered into between the 11 money transfer service providers and 17 Uzbek commercial banks.

Table 8.6 Contracts between commercial banks and money transfer service providers, 2006

	Commercial banks	Money transfer systems (listed in order of market entry)											
		WU	Money Gram	Contact	MIGOM	Anelik	Inter Epxress	Travelex	Xpress Money	Unistream	Bistraya Pochta	Azia Express	Total
1	NBU	X										X	2
2	Xalq banki	X						X					2
3	Paxta bank							X					1
4	Mikrokreditbank	X											1
5	Hamkorbank	X		X		X				X	X		5
6	Kapital bank	X											1
7	PSB			X	X		X						3
8	Alp Jamol bank		X			X				X	X		4
9	Uzbek-Turkish bank	X											1
10	Universal bank	X											1
11	Gallabank		X										1
12	Savdogar bank	X			X	X	X						4
13	Ipoteka bank	X											1
14	Trastbank	X		X					X	X			4
15	Credit-Standart bank	X			X	X			X				4
16	Aloqa bank	X											1
17	Asaka bank	X						X					2
Total		13	2	3	3	4	2	3	2	3	2	1	

So the evidence is that while Western Union certainly had dominant market position, the exclusive dealing item in its model contract was not respected by the agent banks and did not in practice unreasonably restrain and did not actually harm competition.

Nevertheless – and regardless of the fact that the financial services sector was outside the remit of the Uzbek competition authority – the authority had carried out an investigation into the market for money transfers. In June 2006, State Committee of the Republic of Uzbekistan on Demonopolization, Support of Competition and Entrepreneurship (CDCE) officials had talks with the representatives of Western Union and expressed their concern over the restrictive clause in the latter's model contract. Western Union agreed to change the contract item 4.2.8 so that it would no longer violate the text of the law on competition. It implemented this commitment, annulling clause 4.2.8 of its contract with the all the commercial banks and replacing it with another that did not contain any provisions that would violate Uzbek competition legislation. In particular, the new clause did not contain any restrictions on the banks, which now can work with any number of money transfer operators other than Western Union. Thus an amicable agreement was reached between Western Union and the CDCE, which put an end to any future allegations of unlawful restriction of competition by the company.

Production Costs of International Transfer Payments

The cost of a remittance includes many elements, including the fee charged to the sender by the capturing agency, the rate of currency exchange applied, the possible tax levied and (in the case of smaller operators) the fee charged at the receiving end (Orozco 2003). In general, the costs of the remittance services consist of the following special components (as well as wage and other standard production costs to any line of business):

- Direct costs of the company related to supporting the system (software, channels of communication, system of protection (against hacking and virus attacks, etc.) and costs of occasional upgrading of the system).
- Costs related to advancement of the company's trademark (advertisements, marketing research, public relations, etc.).
- Commissions of partners (percentage ratio of income of each member of the system).
- Costs related to mutual compensations (changes in currency rates, compensating banks [SWIFT, Telex, etc.]).
- Costs related to ensuring security and guaranteeing against risks of each money transfer (conformity of AML, insuring against financial risks).

The Russian–Uzbek joint venture Azia Express charged the lowest fees for remittances sent from Russia to Uzbekistan and vice versa. Western Union also charges relatively low rates for Russia–Uzbekistan direction, because of the high volume of transactions. Sending money from Uzbekistan to Russia through Western Union costs much more than sending money in the opposite direction. Some banks offer free remittance services to attract new business (World Bank 2006), which suggests that the actual cost of remittances is fairly low. In fact, in some corridors fees for international money transfers are as low as US$1.80 per transaction.

Analysis of the profitability of market leaders using their publicly available financial statements also reveals that remittance costs are significantly lower than the fees charged to customers. Therefore, intense competition is able to force remittance service providers to lower the fees for their services; this cuts into margins but is not limited by cost constraints. The average fee for remittances was a little more than 10 per cent in 2002, when there were three companies operating in Uzbekistan (although in fact only two operated: Western Union with 95 per cent market share and Contact with 5 per cent). In 2005, the number of companies reached ten and the average fee dropped to 4–5 per cent. Taking into account the approximate 5–6 per cent decrease in average remittance fees between 2002 and 2005, it may be concluded that on average migrants from Uzbekistan saved around $40–45 million annually under reduced fees.

It was found that when setting tariffs, remittance service providers use one of the following approaches:

- Marketing approach – the tariff is defined with regard to competitors' rates – the same or lower. The level of tariffs of competitors is the main determining factor. The main goal of the company is to get maximum results in the shortest time.
- Technical approach – the service tariff is calculated as expenses of the company plus a percentage commission of the company. The goal of companies using this approach is to seize market share and hold the position thanks to its brand leadership.
- Social approach – tariff of services is defined depending on the potential of people of this or that country or territory. The income and financial opportunities of consumers are the main consideration for deciding tariffs. The main goal is that tariffs are acceptable to the consumer base.

It is for the company to decide which approach to use in setting its tariffs; the key constraint, as in any other market, is the preference of consumers.

Pricing Behaviour in the Market

Western Union's tariffs have been some of the highest in the market. This gives rise to a concern that they are 'monopolistically high' (excessive) and therefore that they may violate Article 5 of the Law on Competition ('Abuse of dominance in the form of charging monopolistically high prices'). However there are several facts that serve to refute this concern.

First of all, the analysis of the competitors' tariffs (commission for money transfer) reveals that at least one other company has applied charges within a close range to those of Western Union. That competitor is MoneyGram (see Figures 8.3 and 8.4). Moreover, at some transfer amounts, the charges by MoneyGram have been even higher than those of Western Union. Both providers offer money transfers worldwide. This may suggest that the high charges by both of them reflect, first, the fact not only that they were the first-comers to the Uzbek market, but also the costs of their maintaining worldwide networks.

Second, Western Union's tariffs on money transfers from Russia to Uzbekistan – the most popular corridor for Uzbek money transfers, constituting half of the remittance inflow to Uzbekistan in monetary terms – are almost the same as those of its competitors.

Next, Western Union's high charges have in effect been pro-competitive, insofar as they have attracted new competitors into the market. However, because most of the followers did not have such a well-known brand name as Western Union, they mostly entered the market with lower rates for their service than Western Union. In Figures 8.2 and 8.3, tariff rates for the money transfer service providers in the market in Uzbekistan are shown in the order of their market entry. Every newcomer charged lower rates on average than Western Union and other incumbents. Hence, for example, the latest market entrants – Bistraya Pochta and Azia Express – charge only 2 per cent of the sum being remitted.

Finally, the fact that many newcomers offer charges below those of Western Union indicates that consumers do have choice and may choose whichever service they afford or trust more.

Thus, despite Western Union charges being some of the highest in the market (at least on outgoing money transfers) its tariffs should be assessed in relation to the whole picture and dynamics of tariffs of other incumbents. Tariffs in the market had not stagnated but decreased on average over the course of the previous four years. This indicates that competition had been vibrant in the market and may intensify further. Western Union's charges have served more as a pro-competitive force than as an abuse of dominance because there was a growing choice of lower tariffs by alternative money transfer providers.

Nevertheless, some remaining quirks of the pricing regime suggest that tariffs still do not bear much relation to operational costs for providers.

COMPETITION INVESTIGATIONS OF THE MONEY TRANSFER MARKET IN OTHER JURISDICTIONS

Staff at APIC reviewed the literature and gathered information directly from competition authorities in other jurisdictions – mainly but not

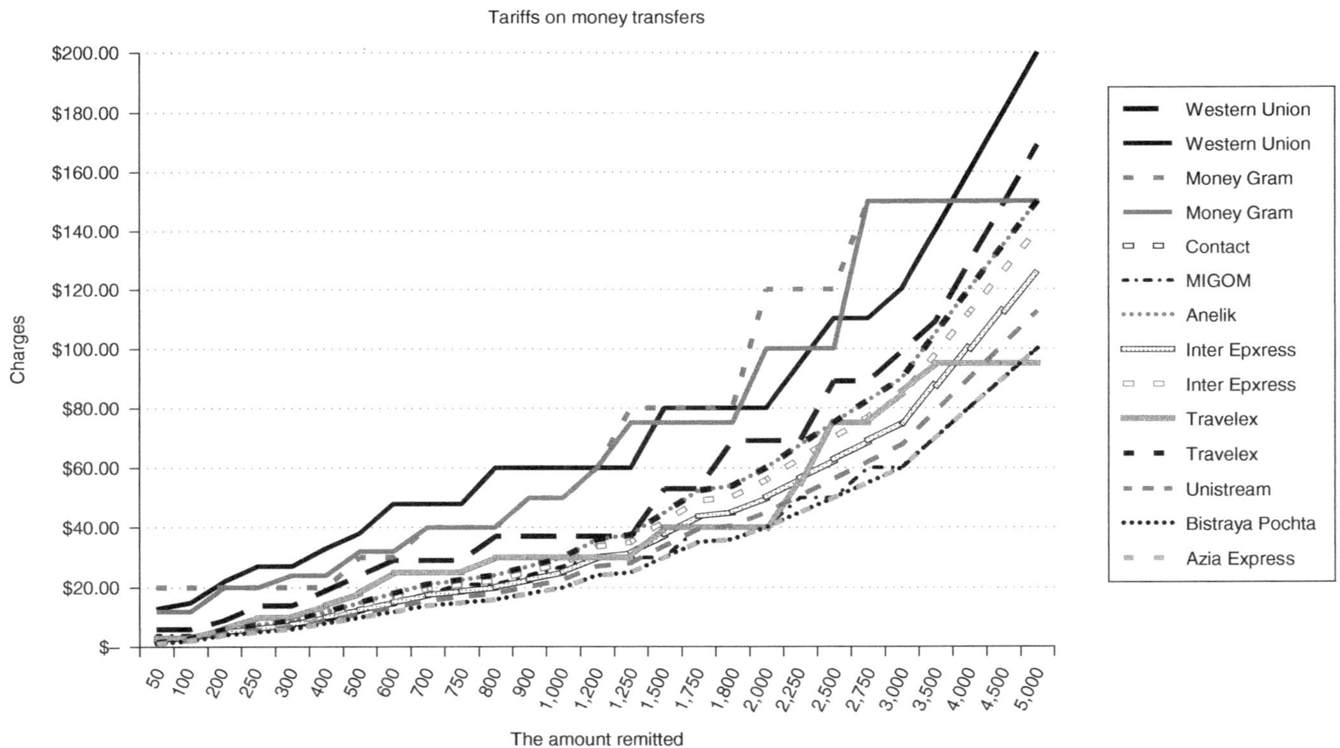

Figure 8.2 Tariffs on money transfers (amounts in US$)

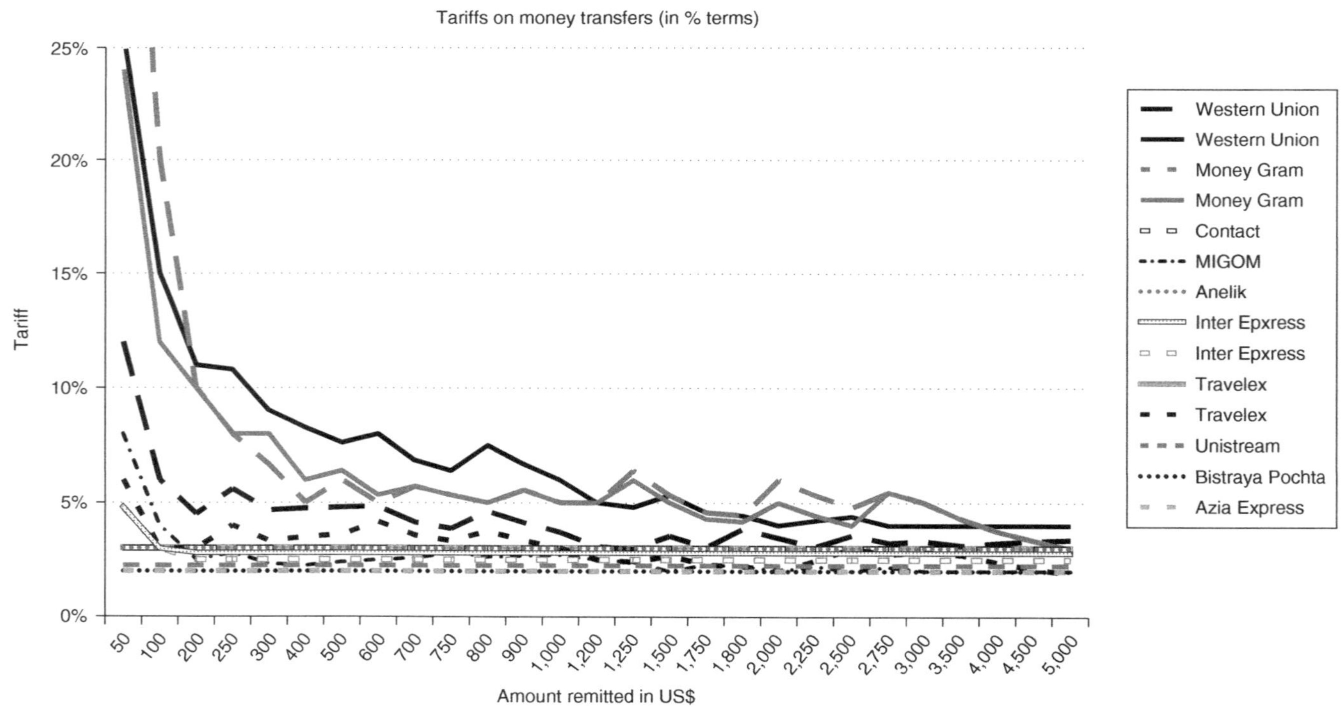

Figure 8.3 Tariff on money transfers (in per cent)

exclusively in other CIS countries – to find out about investigations that had been carried out elsewhere into the money transfer market.

Ukraine

A case had been raised by the competition authority in response to complaints from the National Bank of Ukraine alleging that Western Union had been engaging in unlawful contractual practices. The Association of Ukrainian Banks had also complained about excessive charges on remittances by Western Union. The first study of the matter revealed signs of monopoly position held by the company and thus raised suspicion of abuse of a monopoly (dominance) position forbidden under the law on protection of economic competition.

The product market was defined in this case as 'the service of paying money to physical persons in Ukraine remitted to them in foreign currency cash from abroad by instant transfer and without the need to open a bank account', noting the exclusion of commercial operations. As in Uzbekistan, the geographic market was defined as 'the territory of Ukraine', due to the fact that the remitted money could be received at any branch of the remittance system in any part of the country.

To calculate market shares as the primary indicator of dominance, the Ukrainian competition authority chose to use two indicators: the number of branches in the remittance system and the monetary amounts remitted to Ukraine. On the first indicator, it was argued that Western Union had acquired a dominant market position thanks to a wide network of direct and indirect representatives in Ukraine, including 110 banks and non-banking financial establishments. Between 2002 and 2004, Western Union increased its network of local branches from 5,500 to around 7,000, which accounted for 87 per cent of the total market. To compare, the company's closest rivals were way behind in the number of agent outlets. MoneyGram had only eight agent banks and 650 branches in 2004 (9 per cent of the total market), Anelik had 20 agent banks and more than 190 branches (2.7 per cent of the total market), and Contact had 14 agent banks and 130 branches (only 1.85 per cent of the market). Alternatively, estimating market share based on the amount of incoming remittance flows, Western Union's market share comprised more than 80 per cent during 2002–4.

It was then argued that Western Union had managed to gain a monopoly (dominant) position largely through entering exclusive contracts with its agent banks, closing the network for its competitors. During the investigation, the issue was resolved at the legislative level by amending the Ukrainian law 'On payment system and remittances in Ukraine'. Exclusive dealings were prohibited.

Comparative analysis of the tariffs charged by Western Union and its competitors gave grounds for the Ukrainian competition authority to allege that Western Union was charging monopolistically high prices. However, no official orders were issued. In March 2005, the authority sent the company a recommendation to stop violating the law, in particular by decreasing the charges on remittances to Ukraine. Realizing the seriousness of the authority's position, the company followed the recommendations and began consistently lowering its charges on the most popular routes, including those with Russia, EU member states and the USA. Despite the Ukrainian competition authority's decision to close the investigation subsequently, in recognition of the fact that Western Union was properly following the recommendations, the company continued to reduce the charges on remittances during the course of 2005 and 2006.

Russian Federation

The Russian competition authorities did not study the remittance market as such, but had investigated Western Union's exclusionary contractual practices.

The investigation was triggered by a complaint from the bank and remittance system, Contact, against item 4.2.8 of Western Union's model agreement. This item stated that a bank was prohibited from cooperating with other companies rendering the services of online monetary transfer in a manner similar to the one used by Western Union during the period of validity of the bank's agreement with Western Union. The investigation was initiated in September 2003 and lasted until the first quarter of 2004. After fact-finding, the authority arrived at a decision that item 4.2.8 of Western Union's model contract did violate the Law on Protection of Competition on the Markets of Financial Services (Article 6, 'Agreements and concerted actions of financial entities that restrict competition'), and that Western Union's contractual practices restricted competition and harmed banks and consumers.

Western Union appealed against the competition authority's decision to Moscow Arbitration Court in March 2004, but its appeal was declined. The company's objections against the decision concerned two major points:

- First, for an agreement to have some restrictive effect on competition, what needs to be proved first is that the company concluding the agreement has significant market power or market share. The Russian competition authority (at that time Ministry of Antimonopoly Policy) had done nothing to define the relevant

market and to give evidence of Western Union's significance in the market.
- Second, Western Union's exclusivity clause (item 4.2.8 of the model contract) did not restrict competition and was merely guided by safety and compliance considerations, and to avoid free-riding on its operational system.

The Moscow Arbitration Court turned down the company's appeal on the ground that proof of a violation under Article 6 of the Law on Protection of Competition on the Markets of Financial Services ('Agreements and concerted actions of financial entities that restrict competition'), did not require identification of the market power (market share) of the parties entering the agreement.

The competition authority had presented enough evidence to show that Western Union's contractual practices did block the bank network and limit entrance to the market and harmed competition significantly.

USA

In 2004 and 2005, the United States Department of Justice (DoJ) began an investigation into Western Union's contractual practices and their effect on the money transfer market. Concerns had arisen due to Western Union's persistently high market share.

The purpose of the investigation was to find out whether Western Union's contractual practices unreasonably restrained competition and hence helped the company to maintain monopoly power in the market. The evidence gathered by the DoJ was not, however, sufficient to support an allegation that Western Union's practices had any substantial anticompetitive effect. Despite its exclusionary practices, other retail locations remained available through which competitors could offer their services to consumers. Besides, in recent years, Western Union's competitors had been able to increase their transaction volumes and expand their networks. The DoJ also obtained other evidence indicating that Western Union's contractual practices did not have any substantial anticompetitive effect. The DoJ, however, specifically stressed the importance of policymakers (including those in other countries) keeping access to the network barrier-free. The growing breadth of the network (particularly through the involvement of credit unions), as well as free access to it for competitors, were found to be the major procompetitive forces in the market for money transfers (USA DoJ 2005).

CONCLUSIONS AND RECOMMENDATIONS

The main finding of this study is that intense competition in the Uzbekistan international money transfer market saw the arrival of many new service providers, each one charging lower tariffs than incumbents. That dynamic has been greatly beneficial to members of migrants' households whose remitted earnings supported their standard of living. At the outset, when the first market actor could charge a monopoly price, its tariffs were above 10 per cent; by 2006, with 14 players in the market, the average tariff had fallen below 5 per cent.

After a five-year period of reduction, the savings to consumers were very large. For example, in 2005, using the tariffs in effect at that time (4–5 per cent) rather than the average tariff of 2002 (above 10 per cent), the notional savings to consumers was around US$45 million in that year alone.

The rapid growth in the number of players in the market took place despite the fact that the first arriving company, Western Union, had imposed restrictive conditions in its contracts with a large number of national banks with extensive branch networks. It stipulated that, in line with the terms of its model contract agreement, its partners had to deal exclusively with Western Union. Provisions of this kind contradict the antimonopoly legislation of the Republic of Uzbekistan. Since the legislation did not then apply to the financial services sector, they were not in fact illegal in Uzbekistan. In any event, the banks did not all respect this provision. The broadening of the network infrastructure was also facilitated by the addition of new remittance cash collection points in credit unions and other financial organizations.

The research done for this study could have been a source of inter-agency friction between the competition authority and the Central Bank, the regulator of the financial sector. Instead the Central Bank – and the government – saw the value of the analysis of the market carried out according to the standard competition scheme. They also understood the potential of competition law enforcement to benefit consumers of financial services, as it does in other product markets. The money transfer services market can be covered by both the competition law and the financial regulatory market under the supervision of the Central Bank. The research proved its worth by way of demonstrating to the Central Bank that the competition perspective, and competition policy design and enforcement, can play a valuable part in ensuring the optimal performance of the sector. A revision of the law was duly enacted; the new law 'On competition', passed in 2011, includes the regulation of financial markets.

Some further recommendations can be made to develop the remittance money transfer market in Uzbekistan. These comprise the following:

1. Promoting the increase in the number of outlets providing money transfer services. The number was greatly increased in 2007, with the arrival of the national Post Office system in the market, described below. There is scope for further expansion in the network.
2. Making alterations to the legislation for attracting the postal services companies into the market. At the time of writing, the national Post Office had recently introduced a domestic electronic money transfer service, but it offered limited international service. At the end of 2007, the Post Office formally joined the international financial system of the Universal Postal Union, allowing it to compete in the international money transfer business. Some 3,200 Post Office counters, two-thirds of them in rural areas, were able to provide international transfer services. This added more than half as many again outlets as Western Union had contracted by 2004 (when it had 5,500 local branches in its network) and represented more than twice the total number of commercial bank branches that acted as cash collection points for remittances.
3. Taking measures for achieving more transparency in the market and promoting better understanding of options among consumers.
4. Maintaining the neutrality and impartiality of the state in regulation of the sphere of international money transfers. The Post Office and any other public body that is active in the international money transfer market must not stand outside the scope of the competition law, newly extended to cover financial services.
5. Migrant labour flows are the source of remittances. Government policy should seek to enhance collaboration with other countries in this sphere, with a view to enhancing mechanisms of social and legal protection of citizens who work abroad or desire to get a job there.
6. Uzbek banks need to be further integrated into the international bank infrastructure so that they can get involved in the market for international money transfers on more equal terms with specialist money transfer service providers.
7. Once the scope of the competition law is extended to the financial services sector, the competition authority, the CDCE, and its studies arm, APIC, need to monitor changes in the money transfer services market. After the rapid growth of the market and the increase in the number of providers in the first half of the 2000s, there may be little scope for further reduction of operational margins. A period of consolidation is thus likely among the market actors. That could bring in intensified concentration, and along with that could come different forms of anticompetitive practices among actors intended to preserve and enhance profit margins.

NOTES

1. Assistance from Zarif Jumaev, Adham Kuchkarov and Najmiddin Sharipov is gratefully acknowledged.
2. See www.globalcompetitionforum.org/regions/asia/Uzbekistan/competition.pdf.
3. http://twc2.org.sg/2015/02/09/koreas-regulatory-system-for-migrant-workers-offers-many-features-worth-emulating.
4. Abuse of dominance in the form of restricting entry into the market and/or impeding competition through exclusivity clauses in agreements/contracts (Articles 5 and/or 6 of the Law on Competition of the Republic of Uzbekistan).

REFERENCES

Centre on Demographics and Ecology of People, Institute of Prognosis of National Economy, RAN (2005) *Economy of Illegal Migration in Russia*, Moscow.

Ghosh, B. (2006) *Migrants' Remittances and Development, Myths, Rhetoric and Realities*, Geneva: International Organization for Migration and The Hague Process on Refugees and Migration.

Maksakova, L.P. (2002) *Export of Labour from Uzbekistan.*

Ministry of Labour and Social Security (2006) Information Note supplied on request to APIC for this report, Government of the Republic of Uzbekistan.

Orozco, M. (2003) *Attracting Remittances: Market, Money and Reduced Costs*, Report commissioned by the Multilateral Investment Fund of the Inter-American Development Bank, Washington, DC.

Taylor, J.E. (1992) Remittances and inequality reconsidered: direct, indirect and intertemporal effects, *Journal of Policy Modeling*, **14**: 187–208.

Tyuryukanova, E. (2005) *Forced Labour in the Russian Federation Today: Irregular Migration and Trafficking in Human Beings*, Geneva: International Labour Office.

Van Doorn, J. (2002) Migration, remittances and development, *Labour Education*, **4**(129): 48–53.

USA DoJ (2005) Statement regarding the closing of its Western Union money transfer services investigation, Department of Justice Antitrust Division, 16 March.

World Bank (2006) *Global Economic Prospects 2006: Economic Implications of Remittances and Migration*, Washington, DC: World Bank.

World Bank (2013) *Migration and Remittance Flows: Recent Trends and Outlook, 2013–2016*, Migration and Development Brief, Migration and Remittances Team, Development Prospects Group, Washington, DC: World Bank.

9. TV distribution services in Argentina

Germán Coloma, Federico Bekerman, Cecilia Castets and Marcelo D'Amore[1]

A FAST-CHANGING INDUSTRY

Between 1996 and 2006, progress in technology together with the convergence of networks, devices and services blurred boundaries inside the Argentinean TV industry and changed the way consumers accessed audio-visual content. The design of regulations and implementation of competition law underwent changes to reflect this. This chapter reviews the major cases dealt with by the Argentinean competition authority in the early 2000s and sheds light on the complexity of the television distribution sector. It provides lessons on the interactions between market structure, regulations and technology on the one hand and their impact on consumers' access and the pricing of audio-visual services on the other hand.

The distribution of television programmes in Argentina, as in other countries, takes place via free-to-air and pay-television using cable as well as satellite technologies. The sector involves a range of actors, among which are:

- TV channels (free-to-air or accessed via pay-TV systems).
- Pay-TV system operators (cable, satellite and terrestrial).
- Companies that supply TV channels to the pay-TV operators.
- Companies that produce television content and supply it to TV channels.

Those actors relate to each other through various forms and degrees of economic integration. There are cases of vertical and horizontal integration between content producers and television channels, between cable television operators and marketing firms, and between channels owned directly by cable television operators. In this complex environment, defining the relevant market is difficult for any study of the sector from a competition policy perspective.

Starting with a few cases in the mid-1990s, the sector produced a large number of cases for enforcement under antitrust legislation. This rose to several dozen cases – both conduct and merger cases – in the first decade of the twenty-first century. All cases were handled by the country's competition authority, the National Commission of Competition Defense (CNDC), although some went to appeal in the courts and were subject to judicial rulings. These cases form the basis of this chapter.

Since 2006, the Argentinean TV distribution sector has undergone more major changes following the merger of the two largest cable TV operators, Multicanal and Cablevisión, which between them control many cable TV channels. Although the merger was approved without restrictions at the time, the government subsequently raised several objections to the new integrated firm, generating much judicial activity affecting the sector. This culminated in the Argentine Congress passing a new law in 2009 regulating television in a very different way. It established major restrictions on mergers between firms operating in different communication media and in different geographic markets.

From the analysis of the competition authority's rulings in the early 2000s, five major conclusions emerge.

First, agreements such as price-fixing or market-division, restricting competition among television system actors supplying the same relevant market, harm consumers. Most horizontal mergers within the same relevant market generate similar consequences.

Second, by contrast, mergers among suppliers of television channels that do not deal directly with consumers generally do limited harm to the general economic interest.

Third, vertical agreements between television content suppliers and television system operators are, in principle, harmless from the point of view of competition law. However, anticompetitive effects may appear when there is restriction to competition in one of the industry segments (in general, retail television provision in a certain relevant market).

Such vertical agreements and mergers between TV content suppliers and television system operators can be harmful if the supplier imposes both a marketing method for its channel or content (for instance, codified pay-per-view) and also the price at which such a channel or content can be sold to the viewers. Such practices can be very harmful if used to restrict competition among operators.

Fourth, competition policy mechanisms fail to address issues that arise with natural monopolies in the provision of television content and services. This generally requires direct regulation of prices and content provision rather than the use of competition law. Certain interventions by the antitrust authority can, however, be useful, such as banning price discrimination to final customers, the obligation to give access to essential facilities, and prohibiting the sale of certain television content in bulk and resale price-fixing for some television content.

Finally, the antitrust agency can play a prominent role in competition advocacy. It can focus on the advantages of allowing programmes to be broadcast through networks other than cable television, to enable direct competition among channel suppliers in response to viewers' preferences, and to encourage the entry of new television system operators.

THE TV DISTRIBUTION SERVICES MARKET

The Argentinean regulator divides TV broadcasting services into two groups: main services and complementary services. The first group includes free-to-air (open) television, while the second group consists of community antenna television services (cable), closed television circuits, and ground and satellite television. The free-to-air television services are provided by public TV (the 'Official Broadcasting Service') plus a small number of commercial companies awarded TV channel licences via public tender. The regulator, the Federal Broadcasting Committee (COMFER), grants licenses for all other complementary services via direct awards.

Free-to-Air Television

There is only one public national channel in Argentina – Canal 7. Located in the capital, Buenos Aires, it covers the rest of the country by means of optical fibre and/or terrestrial TV transmission. Pay-television operators can receive it and include it in their channel offerings.

The most important commercial free-to-air television stations are three channels located in Buenos Aires (Canal 9, Telefé and Canal 13) and one channel in the city of La Plata (América2) 60km from Buenos Aires. These channels are directly transmitted over an area of approximately 70km radius from their originating station and in many cases with relay stations in other parts of the country. There are also a large number of regional free-to-air television channels in other parts of the country with their own programmes.

In addition to relay stations, the national free-to-air television channels are brought to consumers in the rest of the country through the sale of the distribution rights to companies that market them to pay-TV operators. There are also cases where the owners of channels sell their distribution rights directly to pay-television systems. Between them these national

Table 9.1 Ratings and viewing shares of free-to-air television channels

Channel/year	2003		2004		2005	
	Rating	Share	Rating	Share	Rating	Share
Telefé	12.5	34.4	15.0	37.4	14.3	37.8
Canal 13	10.8	29.8	10.9	27.2	9.4	24.9
Canal 9	6.2	17.1	7.2	18.0	8.3	22.0
América 2	5.5	15.1	5.5	13.7	4.7	12.4
Canal 7	1.3	3.6	1.5	3.7	1.1	2.9
Total	36.3	100	40.1	100	37.8	100

Source: IBOPE.

networks accounted for 70 per cent of all TV viewing between 2000 and 2005.

The commercial terms under which the publicly owned Canal 7 is offered to pay-television operators varies by operator. For local cable television operators in the interior of the country, the channel agrees a monthly fee based on the number of viewers. Other cable and satellite television operators, which have a wider coverage throughout the country, can usually benefit from quantity discounts.

Canal 7's main source of income, however, does not come from selling distribution rights but from advertising revenues that account for 81 per cent of its total income. The channel also receives a direct grant from the Argentinean state budget of the equivalent of 5,000,000 pesos (approximately $1.6 million) per month.

Competition among free-to-air television channels is basically over audience, i.e., viewing figures. The audience is measured either by the ratings of their programmes (which measures the audience percentage with respect to the total number of television sets in the selected universe); or by their audience share (the percentage of audience with reference to the television sets that are on at a given time). The main television audience-measuring company in Argentina (IBOPE) provides the figures for ratings and shares for the most important free-to-air television channels as shown in Table 9.1.

Pay-television

From an economic point of view, the concept of 'pay-television' encompasses cable television, satellite television and terrestrial pay-television.

Cable television is also known as closed-circuit community antenna television. Terrestrial pay-TV on the other hand, is a terrestrial television system codified in certain specific bands of the radio electric spectrum.[2] It is directly received by subscribers, and can comprise between 33 analogue channels up to 200 digitally compressed channels. Its reliance on ground stations and antennas makes transmission vulnerable to physical obstacles, natural or artificial. Terrestrial pay-TV is mainly used in rural areas, but it is becoming a more competitive service with greater use of digital technology offering more channels, and additional internet and data-transmission services.

Finally, satellite television can take two forms. The first uses telecommunications satellites (fixed satellite services) that connect the signal transmitter and the receiver and broadcasts images to targeted users by air or cable. The second form utilizes direct broadcast satellites (DBS) with a more powerful signal but with limited coverage. Users receive the television images by installing parabolic antennas of a small diameter.

Unlike free-to-air television services that can be received directly and for free by any television set, pay-TV services are only accessible to paying subscribers.

In 2001 some 5.7 million homes in Argentina had access to pay-TV, according to information from the National Institute of Statistics and the Census (INDEC) and major pay-TV system operators. That was 56.3 per cent of homes with a television set. The overwhelming majority subscribed via cable system operators, and only 3.1 per cent via satellite or terrestrial pay-TV operators. The penetration rate of cable television in Argentina was at this time higher than other Latin American and many European countries, but lower than in Canada (72 per cent), the United States (71 per cent), Denmark (68 per cent) and the United Kingdom (60 per cent).

Subscribers to pay-TV account for a significant share of free-to-air TV channels' audience. In fact many subscribers, especially those who live outside the Buenos Aires metropolitan area, can only watch free-to-air television (i.e., the country's main national networks) if they subscribe to pay-television. Ratings of pay-television's own channels were much lower than free-to-air television channels according to IBOPE.

A sector regulator (COMFER) survey found that in 2004 the only people that preferred pay-television programmes are those who either watched very few hours of television per day or who were children under 14 years of age alternating between free-to-air television channels and children's television channels.

The cable TV system operators

There were five main cable television suppliers in Argentina at the time. The two largest were Multicanal (MC) and Cablevisión (CV), which

Table 9.2 Share of the main cable television operators

Province/firm	MC	CV	TC	SC	Other
Buenos Aires (metro area)	44.6	31.8	14.5	0.0	9.1
Buenos Aires (province)	47.2	49.0	0.0	0.0	3.8
Catamarca	0.0	0.0	0.0	34.0	66.0
Chaco	45.5	39.2	0.0	0.0	15.3
Chubut	0.0	0.0	0.0	52.9	47.1
Córdoba	41.2	53.7	0.0	0.0	5.1
Corrientes	58.9	21.3	0.0	0.0	19.8
Entre Ríos	24.2	69.3	0.0	0.0	6.5
Formosa	87.7	0.0	0.0	0.0	12.3
Jujuy	0.0	0.0	0.0	0.0	100
La Pampa	48.2	51.8	0.0	0.0	0.0
La Rioja	0.0	0.0	0.0	51.9	48.1
Mendoza	0.0	0.0	0.0	76.6	23.4
Misiones	0.0	100.0	0.0	0.0	0.0
Neuquén	0.0	94.8	0.0	5.2	0.0
Río Negro	0.0	76.9	0.0	23.1	0.0
Salta	0.0	99.6	0.0	0.0	0.4
San Juan	0.0	0.0	0.0	45.7	54.3
San Luis	0.0	0.0	0.0	16.6	83.4
Santa Cruz	0.0	0.0	0.0	27.6	72.4
Santa Fe	28.0	57.9	0.0	0.5	13.6
Santiago del Estero	0.0	0.0	0.0	49.7	50.3
Tierra del Fuego	0.0	0.0	0.0	42.8	57.2
Tucumán	0.0	0.0	0.0	29.3	70.7

Source: CNDC, based on company data.

was integrated with another company called Teledigital. The others were Telecentro (TC), Supercanal (SC) and Red Intercable (RI) – not a company in itself, but a network of about 450 local independent operators. Telecentro operates in the city of Buenos Aires and its surroundings. Conversely, Supercanal does not operate in Buenos Aires but covers an important part of the interior of the country. Table 9.2 shows the market shares of the main cable operators.

The two largest cable companies in terms of users at national level, Cablevisión and Multicanal, had a large market share, both in Buenos Aires and in the rest of the country, accounting for 57 per cent of cable television users throughout the country.

The satellite TV operator

Satellite television in Argentina is provided by a single operator, DirecTV, that uses the DBS system. The main difference from cable operators lies in its capacity to offer a larger number of channels. In practice, however, the basic service offered by DirecTV is the same as the basic service offered by cable operators.

Satellite television also has a greater range of optional premium channels, and provides pay-per-view programmes, which is unusual for cable television operators. Finally, since satellite TV does not require wiring, it can reach places that cable TV cannot, mainly low population density areas.

Satellite has, however, two limitations. First, as the broadcasting of the programmes is carried out from a single location, satellite TV cannot include local television channels within the grid – unlike cable television operators. Second, it is not possible for the different television sets in a single home to watch different channels, unless there is a separate antenna connected to each television set with subsequent additional costs.

Costs of subscribing to pay-TV

Table 9.3 sets out the prices for subscribing to pay-TV. Traditionally, the price of satellite television in Argentina has been higher than the price of cable television, and where wiring is available, most people choose cable. For example, in Buenos Aires in 2005, the price of the average service provided by Multicanal and Cablevisión in the city of Buenos Aires was approximately three-quarters of the price of the basic service offered by DirecTV.

In addition, there are significant geographic price differences for cable television. The monthly fee for Cablevisión in the province of Salta was 33 per cent cheaper than in the city of Buenos Aires. Paradoxically, Cablevisión enjoys a monopoly situation in Salta, while it has several competitors in Buenos Aires. These findings need, however, to be treated with caution as data on the actual prices charged by operators in those areas where their networks overlap are not available.

Two developments are underway in pay-television that confirm the fast-changing nature of the TV sector in Argentina as well as other countries. First, as evidenced by the merger of Multicanal and Cablevisión in 2007, horizontal concentration is increasing. Second, new competitors such as telephone companies are entering the pay-TV market with the emergence of digital television.

Suppliers of TV channels to pay-TV operators

Television content goes through different stages before it reaches viewers. First, channel controllers provide resources for producers to create original programming or to purchase broadcasting rights of existing programmes,

Table 9.3 Pay-television prices in Argentine pesos (monthly fee, value added tax included)

Concept/year	2002	2003	2004	2005
Basic cable TV (Multicanal)				
Buenos Aires	47.5	55.5	56.9	60.9
Córdoba	45.6	52.9	54.0	57.9
Santa Fe	41.6	48.3	49.1	50.0
Chaco	42.3	47.7	50.4	52.7
Formosa	37.5	40.5	42.0	45.5
La Pampa	40.0	43.9	45.4	50.5
Basic cable TV (Cablevisión)				
Buenos Aires	47.5	55.0	56.0	60.0
Córdoba	42.2	47.9	48.9	52.5
Santa Fe	40.6	46.6	47.9	51.0
Chaco	44.3	52.5	53.9	54.9
Salta	34.0	35.2	36.4	40.0
Misiones	41.9	47.6	48.9	52.0
Basic satellite TV (DirecTV)	59.9	73.9	74.0	79.5
Cable/satellite price gap (%)	26.1	33.8	31.1	31.7

Source: CNDC, based on company data.

and schedule them. These channels are then supplied either to marketing companies who sell them to pay-TV operators or are supplied directly to free-to-air stations. TV programmes or channels are thus distributed to viewers through pay-TV and free-to-air television systems.

The pay-TV operators act as content distributors, choosing and purchasing the channels that will form their channel package. Viewers often also demand certain content and express their preference for channels and the time slots at which they watch them. There is a distinction between channels offered as part of the basic service and those codified requiring either a premium subscription or pay-per-view.

Pay-television systems in Argentina distribute a large number of channels. The usual grid has between 65 and 70 channels including the basic service and codified channels. The most watched are the five free-to-air television channels from the Buenos Aires metropolitan area. Thematic channels in movies, sports and children's programmes account for the remaining 30 per cent of TV viewing.

As to the suppliers of channels, the most important are Tevefé, Pramer and Artear. These companies provide pay-TV operators with both the private free-to-air television channels and other thematic channels (news,

Table 9.4 Average ratings by theme and supplier, 2001–5

Concept	Rating
Audience by theme	
Free-to-air TV	36.5
Movies	3.8
Series	1.4
Sports	2.1
Children's programmes	3.2
Music	0.6
News	2.2
Others	2.5
Audience by supplier	
Tevefé	13.2
Pramer	12.9
Artear	11.1
Imagen Satelital	3.0
Turner	2.1
Fox	1.6
ESPN	1.4
Canal 7	1.4
Discovery	1.1
HBO	1.1
LAP TV	1.0
TRISA/TSC	0.8

Source: CNDC, based on IBOPE's data.

sports and movies). Imagen Satelital and Turner are relatively smaller suppliers that focus on thematic channels.

The ratings attributed to channels can be misleading. Codified movie channels, for instance, have relatively low ratings because not all users have access to them. Nevertheless, such channels can generate large amounts of money to their suppliers and cable television operators because of their specific additional revenue. Codified soccer matches are another such case. They are broadcast by the cable channel TyC Max and are marketed by the TRISA/TSC group. These 'star channels' have triggered a large number of antitrust cases due to disagreements between suppliers and cable television operators.

TyC Max and TyC Sports are the only two channels that broadcast the Argentine first-division soccer matches live. They are also the most expensive channels and operators who offer them in their grid charge a higher subscription fees compared to those who do not.

A vertically-integrated industry

There are many vertical integration links in Argentina between pay-television operators and channel suppliers. The main cable television operator in terms of the number of users (the Cablevisión/Teledigital group) is vertically integrated with Imagen Satelital (and it was previously integrated with Pramer). The second most important cable operator, Multicanal, belongs to the same economic group as the channel supplier Artear, and is also partially integrated with the Torneos y Competencias group; and the Torneos y Competencias group controls the channels TyC Sports and TyC Max and its marketing companies TRISA/TSC.

A strategic relationship also exists between América TV (supplier of a free-to-air television channel, a news channel and a sports channel) and Supercanal (a cable television operator), between Fox and DirecTV, and between Telecentro and Canal 26, which is a news channel.

Therefore, of all the important firms taking part in the business, only Telefé, Pramer and some international channel suppliers (Turner, ESPN, HBO) are not distributed through cable or satellite television systems.

As far as ownership of channels is concerned, two of the biggest marketing firms own their channels entirely and do not market third parties' channels (Tevefé and Canal 7).

In the case of Pramer, it sells six channels of its own and nine channels belonging to third parties, among which América 2 and Canal 9 stand out. The same happens with Imagen Satelital, which markets five channels of its own and six channels that belong to third parties, and with Discovery Latin America, which sells four channels of its own and two that belong to a joint venture with BBC Worldwide.

In all these cases, the marketing of a channel belonging to a third party means the existence of exclusivity rights in a certain geographic area granted by the owner (whether it is just inside Argentina, includes neighbouring countries, all Latin American countries, or the whole world). In general, exclusivity does not apply to free-to-air television channels in the areas where they have their primary coverage or in areas endowed with relay stations of those channels.

Selling advertising and paying for channels

Channel suppliers market their advertising spaces exclusively. The satellite provision of these channels on a national basis hinders local advertising. But cable operators usually sell part of their advertising space to local advertisers.

Suppliers base the price they charge TV operators for their channels on the number of subscribers, although small cable operators charge a fixed price. Some companies offer discounts depending on the number of users, the number of channels purchased and the number assigned to each channel in the TV operator's grid (the lower the number, the greater the discount). In most contracts, the marketing firms do not themselves control the price that the operator charges its subscribers, but there has been at least one case where the contract stipulates that if the cable television operator raised the price of its basic service, then the channel supplier can increase its own price by the same proportion.

Economics of Content Production

The content used in television channels is produced by firms of different sizes and financial capacities, in various formats, for different kinds of public and for national or international markets. The producers who offer content regularly to channels with wide audiences in Argentina (e.g., series, mini-series, soap operas and magazines) are Ideas del Sur, Pol-Ka and Pensado Para Televisión (PPT). Each is connected with other media-related firms, such as film-makers.

The main client of content producers is Artear, a company majority-owned by the Clarín group, which also publishes the most widely read newspaper in Argentina. Artear is vertically integrated with the largest cable operator, Multicanal. In addition, it holds 30 per cent stakes in Ideas del Sur and Pol-Ka. Although Artear has no ownership in PPT, it buys all its output except for its production of commercials for foreign clients, which accounts for 10 per cent of PPT's revenue.

Regarding contractual terms, content producers are in charge of production while Artear holds the broadcasting rights, sometimes makes its studio available and carries the cost of advertising a programme. The producer receives payment for the content sold and additional payments from companies that wish to advertise their products or services during the programme.

A producer can market a specific number of advertising spaces linked to the programmes it produces. Against this facility, it pays a fixed amount to the channel supplier, regardless of the number of advertisers or sponsors obtained.

Content producers generate some 60 per cent of their revenue from the sale of their programmes and nearly 34 per cent from non-traditional advertising revenues. PPT, the most independent firm in the sector, receives a higher proportion (52 per cent) of its revenues from non-traditional advertising.

The overall picture of the television industry in Argentina is thus a complex web of highly vertically integrated firms, dominated by three or four large groups.

According to 2010 data from the Federal Authority for Audiovisual Communication Services (AFSCA):

> Television production is concentrated . . . in the hands of a few companies, which in turn possess most of the internal networks of the country, which broadcast their own content. Two companies (Telefónica Internacional SA–Telefé, and Clarín Group) control 65 per cent of this market. Together with Vila-Manzano-De Narvaez Group, these companies control 78 per cent of the market. In addition, TISA and Clarín Group sell their content through their own firms (Tevefé and Artear, respectively). Together with a third provider, Pramer, owned by US group Liberty, these companies share 70 per cent of the programmes sold in the country, for free-to-air television, pay-television or subscription television.[3]

MAJOR COMPETITION CASES: REVIEW AND FINDINGS

The TV programme distribution sector has produced many competition law enforcement cases in Argentina. The number of cases increased from a few cases in the mid-1990s to several dozen in the first decade of the twenty-first century. A large number centred on the supply of live sports fixtures to pay-television operators. They covered both conduct and merger cases. All cases dealt with were treated by the CNDC and decided by resolutions of the Secretary of Commerce (or the executive department in charge of the sector). Some of the decisions were appealed before different courts in the country and gave rise to judicial sentences.

Anticompetitive Conduct Cases

Four cases are reviewed in this section: the first involves concerted practices, the second and third vertical exclusionary practices and the fourth concerns exploitative abuse of a dominant position.

Case of concerted practices

The CNDC initiated a concerted practices case in February 1999. Two television channel suppliers (TRISA and TSC) set minimum resale prices for broadcasting some Argentine Football Association (AFA) matches. This was a vertical practice that affected games broadcast by the so-called 'coded system', and took place during the period 1996–8 in the Buenos Aires metropolitan area. The case also involved the three main cable television operators in that area (VCC, Multicanal and Cablevisión).

Although TRISA and TSC were separate companies, their stockholding composition was identical, and the CNDC considered them as a single economic agent. These companies purchased and sold the rights for the television broadcasting of AFA's official soccer games, and produced TV programmes in which those games were broadcast. Multicanal, Cablevisión and VCC, on the other hand, were cable television operators. Initially they were separate companies, but in 1998 VCC was bought in equal shares by the other two companies. Later, VCC was split in two units and absorbed by Multicanal and Cablevisión. At the same time, stockholders of Multicanal and Cablevisión held stock in TRISA and TSC, but the stockholding composition of these cable TV companies was sufficiently different as to consider them as independent economic agents, which were also independent from the TRISA-TSC group.

The major element that led CNDC to qualify the practice as anticompetitive behaviour followed from the definition of the relevant market and the position the companies enjoyed in that market.

The market for soccer was separated from the other sports because of the importance that the local audience assigned to it. Soccer attracted the largest amount of money, its advertising space was the most expensive and it generated the highest income for its sponsors and private advertisers.

Second, the CNDC analysed the degree of substitution between the Argentine first-division soccer and other national soccer tournaments, and concluded that they were not substitutes for soccer enthusiasts. In fact, of all the categories that competed within AFA, only the broadcasting of the first division was coded, which indicated that there was a specific demand for those matches.

Finally, the pre-recorded broadcast of soccer matches was separated from their live broadcast. Both broadcast a single event within a few hours of each other and the companies who owned the broadcasting rights (TRISA and TSC) coded the live broadcast and relayed the other on free-to-air television. This demonstrated that the two do not belong to the same market, otherwise no one would have agreed to pay the extra price to watch the live broadcast.

Therefore, TRISA and TSC had no competition for broadcasting the first-division soccer matches as they held exclusive broadcasting rights until the year 2014.

The CNDC found out that TRISA and TSC fixed a minimum resale price below which cable television operators would not market coded soccer games. The allegation of participation in minimum price-fixing was twofold. First, TRISA and TSC had set the resale prices that cable television operators would have to charge. Second, cable television operators had taken part in the anticompetitive behaviour, by meeting and jointly accepting the resale conditions for coded television programme.

The CNDC came to the conclusion that, as a consequence of the practice, competition was severely limited and the final price was artificially high and damaged cable TV users. TRISA and TSC were each sentenced with fines of 529,289 Argentine pesos (approximately US$192,000 at the prevailing exchange rate). This was the maximum amount allowed by the applicable antitrust law at that time. Cablevisión, Multicanal and VCC were sentenced with somewhat lower fines (approximately $115,000), since their involvement in the case was considered to be less.

The companies appealed the CNDC decision before the National Court of Appeals on Criminal Economic Matters, which revoked the resolution in 2003. The court did not qualify the practice as anticompetitive but as a vertical practice that had not restricted the existing competition between TRISA-TSC and other suppliers of sport television content. The court argued that the relevant market for the case was broader than the CNDC's definition. Besides, it did not assign importance to the implicit horizontal price-fixing agreement among Multicanal, Cablevisión and VCC. The case was appealed by CNDC before the Argentine Supreme Court that endorsed in 2007 the decision made by the Court of Appeals.

Cases of vertical exclusionary practices

A number of cases involving television suppliers and cable television operators are defined as exclusionary, because they were enabled by vertical relationships among the main companies in the sector. They arose because of supposed refusals to sell on the part of channel suppliers, or the imposition of prices that were seen as abusive by the plaintiffs.

Most complaints involved sports television channels. The CNDC noticed several times that the final users valued them highly and took their availability into account when choosing a television system operator. This usually implies that the sports programme suppliers enjoy a dominant position in the market reinforced sometimes by the vertical integration between them and the TV system operators.

On some occasions, the CNDC issued preliminary decisions to restore the situation that existed prior to the complaint. There still have not been any sanctions, either because the parties reached private agreements that put an end to the conflict, or because the refusal to sell was not proved.

One example of this behaviour can be found in *Multicanal vs. Fox Sports and others* (2004), where the complaint was about the supposed refusal of Fox Sports to sell Multicanal the rights to broadcast its sport channel under the same conditions it provided for its competitor, Cablevisión, which was partially owned by the Fox group. This behaviour had the potential to cause a downstream competition problem, because of Cablevisión's presence in the market as Multicanal's competitor. The CNDC pronounced a preliminary decision compelling Fox Sports to provide Multicanal with the sports channel under the same commercial terms and with the same contents as those established for Cablevisión. In its final ruling, the commission considered that the incipient discrimination was rapidly corrected by means of the cease-and-desist order, as well as by the agreement reached by both parties.

Other cases have involved TRISA and TSC, which hold the broadcasting rights of the first-division soccer games organized by the AFA. In *Teledifusora vs. TSC* (2002), for instance, a supposed refusal to sell the sports cable channel called TyC Sports was investigated, as well as the refusal to sell the soccer matches and events marketed separately by TSC. The issue was finally solved in July 1999, when the CNDC accepted the TSC's explanation that the supposed refusal to sell was a private commercial disagreement between both parties.

A similar case took place in *Decotevé vs. TRISA and TSC* (2003). A cable television operator from the city of Salta reported that the suppliers of the TyC Sports channel were refusing to sell its content, in order to exclude the operator from Salta's urban area. This exclusion was supposedly aimed at favouring its competitor, Cablevisión, whose owners also owned part of TRISA's and TSC's stock, and had vertical agreements with TRISA and TSC at a national level. This case was not sanctioned because the parties agreed to solve the conflict privately. But the CNDC considered that a potentially damaging anticompetitive practice had indeed existed, in terms of the Argentine antitrust law.

Another group of cases of vertical, supposedly exclusionary nature is related to certain exclusive dealing restrictions put into practice by the rights holders for the distribution of different television channels. In *Supercanal vs. Tevefé* (2003), for instance, the behaviour reported had to do with the alleged refusal of Tevefé to sell the television channel Telefé (for which Tevefé had the marketing rights in the city of Mendoza).

Tevefé had given the right to broadcast the channel in an exclusive way to Cuyo Televisora, which was the licensee of Channel 9 from Mendoza, a free-to-air television channel included in Supercanal's grid. In this case, the refusal to sell the channel was not related to an abusive price but to a contractual restriction, by virtue of which Tevefé refused to sell the television channel Telefé to cable television operators in areas where it had exclusive dealing agreements with a free-to-air television channel. Taking into account the absence of horizontal restraints in Mendoza and the fact that Telefé's main programmes were available through Channel 9, the CNDC understood that the suspected practice was not anticompetitive.

In *Proconsumer vs. DirecTV and HBO* (2003), on the other hand, a consumer protection organization reported the removal of movie channels

HBO and Cinemax from the cable television grid, making them exclusive to the satellite television operator DirecTV. The contract between HBO and DirecTV established the exclusive distribution of those channels through DirecTV for a specific period of time, but when that period of time elapsed, the channels could be freely licensed by HBO and marketed by the rest of the operators. HBO claimed that this was the way in which the channel was marketed in most countries where it was present, and the CNDC understood that these changes in the marketing method did not affect competition. It was concluded that market dynamics had allowed operators to replace the HBO channels for others, maintaining the number of users.

Another vertical case of exclusionary nature was *Cable Grande vs. EDEERSA* (2003). In this case, a cable television operator filed a complaint against the electricity distribution company in the province of Entre Ríos for refusing to allow them to use its electricity posts to distribute the cable TV service in the city of Paraná, despite the fact that the company allowed Cablevisión and Multicanal to make use of those posts. As had happened in other cases, the CNDC issued a preliminary decision forcing EDEERSA to make the posts available to the plaintiff whenever that was technically possible. After that decision, the two parties reached an agreement that put an end to the conflict.

Another case of vertical exclusionary conduct is *Imagen Satelital vs. Cablevisión* (2004), where the defendant was a cable television operator and the plaintiff a channel supplier that felt affected by a series of commercial practices on the part of the operator. Those practices were allegedly damaging for Imagen Satelital's erotic television channel, Venus, and were supposedly favouring a new entrant called Afrodita. The behaviour consisted of an increase of the price of Venus for the public, the free supply of Afrodita for a month to those who were already users of Venus, and a change in the position of Venus in the grid, favouring Afrodita (that took Venus's previous place in Cablevisión's grid). Although the case began with a preliminary decision in favour of the plaintiff, no sanction was finally applied, as it was understood that the behaviour of the defendant could be basically explained by Cablevisión's individual motivations. Those motivations seemed to have no relation to an intention of deliberately favouring Afrodita over Venus. It was also proved that Afrodita's supplier had no connection with Cablevisión, which meant that the exclusionary hypothesis was greatly weakened.

Cases of horizontal exclusionary practices

Cases of attempted exclusion of competitors by price reduction in strongly competitive areas tends to involve price reduction in areas in which the defendant faces competition, while prices are maintained at a higher level in other areas.

An example was the case of *Surcor TV vs. Cablevisión and Multicanal* (2002), where Multicanal was accused of offering the connection at a special price only to potential customers in the areas where Surcor TV had begun to operate. The CNDC did not qualify the behaviour as anticompetitive and saw the need to react to the competitor's offer as legitimate reason.

In another case involving L. Cabreravs VCC, Cablevisión and Multicanal (2006), the issue was the price charged by VCC (later taken over by Cablevisión and Multicanal) for the cable television service in the city of Rosario, which was higher than those charged by the same companies in other cities. Although the complaint concerned the damaging effect of this practice on consumers in Rosario, the CNDC's concern was whether higher prices charged in Rosario were used to subsidize predatory prices in other regions. This could have been true, if higher prices were coexistent with a dominant position and lower prices were concomitant with intense competition.

The CNDC conducted a series of audits and found the provision costs of the service in Rosario were higher than in other cities, and that for most cities the price charged for the cable television service was higher than the provision cost.

Exploitative abuse of dominant position

Several cases involved allegations of exploitative abuse of dominant position in the TV distribution market, but none were sanctioned. The discriminatory reduction of prices was questioned by the competitors of the alleged perpetrator. The same behaviour on the part of cable television operators had been suspected by consumers. The cases were investigated as potentially exploitative practices.

As an example, in *R. Lloveras vs. Cablevisión* (2002), Cablevisión was accused of setting different prices for cable television users in the city of Río Cuarto, reducing the price of the service in those areas where there was competition. The plaintiff, a user of the cable television service, considered that the reductions implemented by Cablevisión referred to a situation in which the users had initially paid an artificially high price for the service, generating super-normal profits for the company. The CNDC, however, closed the case because Cablevisión's reaction to new competition in reducing its prices was not seen as punishable behaviour from the competition law's point of view, as long as it was not predatory.

Another case in which abusive pricing was reported was *Dirección General de Comercio de Misiones vs. Posadas Cable and Televisión Misionera*

(2002), where the local trade authority of the province of Misiones was concerned about an increase in the price of the basic cable television service in Posadas after the merger of the two cable television operators in that city. The existence of a dominant position by the new, sole cable television operator was proven. The issue was whether the price increase represented an abuse of that position. The CNDC rejected that view and considered that the changes introduced by the operators in their service were the reason behind the price increase. The number of channels offered in the TV grid increased significantly, a large number of users had access to better reception equipment for the coded and pay-per-view channels, and the distribution network had improved.

The case of *National University of Córdoba vs. Durford* (1997) was another case of supposedly exploitative practice. It involved difficulties to access sports programmes. The licensee of a free-to-air television channel from the city of Córdoba reported abusive pricing for the purchase of the broadcasting rights of the 1998 World Cup qualifying-round soccer games, together with a situation of tying that consisted of selling a block of 46 games. The CNDC rejected the abusive pricing argument, but considered that selling the block of 46 matches was a potentially harmful practice because of the existence of a dominant position. The CNDC, however, stated that it could not remedy the damage using antitrust law instruments. The television programme supplier had found it more profitable to market its contents through cable television rather than through free-to-air television, and there was no competition argument that could make the supplier sacrifice its more profitable choice and grant its rights to an open television channel that was not willing to pay the same price for the same product.

Merger Cases

From 1999, when the procedure of antitrust merger notification was enacted in Argentina, until the middle of 2006, the CNDC investigated 26 merger cases in free-to-air, cable and satellite television markets as well as among television content producers. The majority of cases involved joint analysis of horizontal and vertical relations. The most serious concern was always an increase in the effect of increased vertical integration of the sector. There have also been cases that involved horizontal effects or market-extension with fading of real or potential competition between merged companies.

Horizontal and market-extension mergers

The CNDC authorized without restrictions the first mergers in TV distribution with horizontal effects on competition. All of them were market-extension cases in which the merging parties were not actual competitors. Teledigital carried out several mergers by purchasing firms that provided cable television services in different cities. Teledigital was also behind the only merger case prohibited by the CNDC to date in the TV distribution sector.

The case involved Teledigital/Esmeralda-Venado Tuerto Televisión (2003), where the acquiring firm, the owner of TV Interactiva, which operated in the cable television market in the city of Venado Tuerto, wanted to buy the assets of the other two cable TV companies operating in the same city. Although the merger was predominantly horizontal, it also had a vertical aspect, since Teledigital was partially integrated with several television channel suppliers such as Imagen Satelital and the TyC Sports group.

In denying authorization for the merger, the CNDC took into account the prospective establishment of a monopoly in the cable television service in Venado Tuerto. The existence of entry barriers of different kinds was also accounted for, chiefly the degree of vertical integration of the Teledigital group that could create an obstacle for entry of new entrants attempting to buy content for their broadcasting grids.

The case analysis needed also to consider the possible competition that satellite television could exert on cable television. This competition was seen as insufficient, as the two products are seen as belonging to different relevant markets.

The other predominantly horizontal case was Telefónica/AC Inversora-Atlántida Comunicaciones (2000) in which the Telefónica group proposed to acquire another company in the free-to-air television market. The CNDC imposed conditions in its approval of this merger.

Atlántida Comunicaciones controlled free-to-air television channels in eight cities. AC Inversora indirectly controlled the free-to-air television channels in two of those cities, Mar del Plata and Buenos Aires (where the merger was horizontal), and in two others. The proposed merger would also affect the markets in advertising spaces and production of certain television content.

Of these overlapping situations, the higher potential risk was associated with changes to the free-to-air television market in Mar del Plata, since AC Inversora and Atlántica Comunicaciones were the only two free-to-air television channels available in the city. In Buenos Aires, by contrast, there were three other independent free-to-air television channels, so horizontal integration taking place there would be less harmful from the competition point of view. The transaction was approved, but the Telefónica group had to sell one of the free-to-air television channels in Mar del Plata, transferring its entire stockholding to a third party.

Other mergers that affected the free-to-air television markets were

Artear/Telecor (2000) and Artear/Teledifusora Bahiense (2001). In both cases, the transactions were market-extension mergers, since the acquiring firm was a company that controlled a free-to-air television channel in the city of Buenos Aires, and the acquired firms operated in other cities. In both transactions, the CNDC took into account the fact that the purchased companies already broadcast contents marketed by Artear (and were therefore already to some extent affiliated to the main channel of that company). The acquisitions did not bring about significant changes in the existing situation and both transactions were authorized without restrictions.

Other cases of horizontal mergers that mainly affected the pay-television market were Pramer/GEMS (2000) and Pramer/Film&Arts (2000). Both transactions were approved without restrictions, as they entailed the acquisition of channels of low market share by a group that, despite controlling an important number of television channels, faced substantial competition in all the segments where it operated.

Vertical mergers

The most important merger of a predominantly vertical nature addressed by the CNDC was the case called *Liberty Media–Hicks/Cablevisión* (2001). The acquiring companies (Liberty Media and Hicks), which already controlled several cable operators and channel suppliers, jointly took over Cablevisión, one of the main cable operators in Argentina.

The CNDC approved the transaction without requesting any divestiture of assets as it did not cause a significant increase in concentration in the cable television markets. Nevertheless, to avoid potential damage to competition arising from strengthening the vertical relation following the transaction, the CNDC required the parties to ensure availability of television channels controlled by Liberty Media and Hicks, on fair commercial terms, to all those television operators requesting them. Similarly, the grid of Cablevisión and the cable TV operators that became part of the same group had to be made available, on fair commercial terms, for the television channel suppliers that competed with Liberty Media and Hicks in the television content markets.

The CNDC considered the possibility that the merger could increase incentives for a possible coordinated action in the pay-television market in order to exclude competitors or establish discriminatory clauses when marketing TV channels. In fact, the Hicks group controlled Pan American Sport Network, a sports channel, and was a stockholder in Imagen Satelital, a company that produced and marketed television channels. On the other hand, Liberty Media controlled Pramer, a company that supplied more than 20 television channels, and was a stockholder in Fox Sports,

MGM and Casa Club TV. Apart from this, Hicks and Liberty Media partially controlled TyC Sport and TyC Max, the main sports channels.

In order to protect the competitive process from practices that could have an adverse effect on competition, the Liberty Media group undertook to sell its stock in Fox Sports and made a commitment not to market those television channels where it had direct or indirect participation jointly with the Hicks group, as long as market or stockholding conditions did not change substantially.

The Liberty Media–Hicks/Cablevisión merger induced a substantial reorganization of the television programme distribution sector in Argentina, through several other transactions in the following years. The most significant one was the merger case *Liberty Media/Fox Sports* (2004). The group formed by Liberty Media and Hicks joined the Fox group to create a new company (Fox Pan American Sports) to provide mainly sports channels. The new company, in turn, entered into a contract with Torneos y Competencias, by means of which that company, owner of the main competitor of the Fox Sports channel, was in charge of selling Fox Sports contents to television system operators.

This transaction had a substantial effect on the sports channel market. The CNDC analysed several alternative relevant markets and concluded that the merger would lead to joint operation of the only channels marketing the sports channels that broadcast live soccer games played by Argentine first-division teams. The channels that did so were Fox Sports (the channel under examination) and TyC Sports and TyC Max (controlled by Torneos y Competencias).

The transaction was approved but with conditions. First, the parties planned to fully separate the stocks of Fox Pan American Sports and Torneos y Competencias. The CNDC also required Torneos y Competencias to stop marketing the Fox Sports channel to television system operators.

Another predominantly vertical merger case, *NewsCorp/DirecTV* (2005), was also related to the Fox group. The company controlling the Fox group (NewsCorp) proposed to purchase stock in Hughes, controller of the only satellite television operator in Argentina (DirecTV). The merger was approved with no restrictions. The CNDC understood that the merging parties did not have any previous horizontal relations, and that the vertical integration that would arise did not have any significant anticompetitive effect. In fact, the channels belonging to the Fox group (one specialized in series, the sports channel and the documentary channel) faced strong competition from other pay-television channels in the same segments, while DirecTV, despite being a monopolist in the satellite television segment, faced strong competition from cable television operators.

POLICY IMPLICATIONS AND POLICY CHANGES

The purpose of this section is to examine the main antitrust implications of the cases and their regulatory consequences. They can be summarized in five points.

First, price-fixing and market division can harm consumers. Agreements such as price-fixing or market-division, which lessen competition among television system operators supplying the same relevant market, harm consumers. They reinforce the operators' monopoly power such that they can increase the prices they charge their users or reduce content variety. Most horizontal mergers among television system operators present in the same relevant market generate similar consequences.

This finding originates from one of the most general principles of antitrust analysis. For example, the Argentine competition act (Act No. 25,156) prohibits all those practices that are 'intended to . . . lessen . . . competition . . . in such a way that it can be harmful to the general economic interest' (Article 1). As examples of those practices, the act mentions 'fixing . . . the price . . . of goods or services' (Article 2, subsection A) and 'distributing certain areas, markets, customers and supply sources horizontally' (Article 2, subsection B). The Argentine competition act also prohibits those mergers 'whose purpose or effect is or might be . . . to lessen . . . competition, in such a way that it can be harmful to the general economic interest' (Article 7).

In analytical terms, horizontal agreements intended to fix prices charged to users or to share customers have the effect of reducing the traded output (in our case, the number of viewers that receive the programmes). This reduces the economic surplus that those customers obtain to a greater extent than the incremental profit earned by the suppliers for undertaking the manoeuvre. This means that both consumer and total surplus are reduced.

A similar phenomenon takes place when a horizontal agreement is carried out by means of a merger among the companies that compete in the same relevant market. However, in this case, the integration may bring about cost reductions (for instance, through savings in the distribution and marketing of the programmes) that offset the surplus loss from the disappearance of competition. In these cases, the analysis must take into account this additional element, as well as the possibility that the relevant market is a natural monopoly and does therefore not allow for more than one supplier of the service.

Another issue is the difference between horizontal mergers and market-extension mergers. If the case involves television system operators that are in the same relevant market, the merger is horizontal, because it concerns companies whose integration implies the ending of the competition between them that existed previously. If, instead, the merger involves television system operators that are in different relevant markets (for instance, in two different urban areas), then the integration is not horizontal but implies an extension of the market where the companies operate. This, in principle, does not generate a competition restraint since, as the merging firms were not competitors *ex ante*, then their integration does not reduce any prior competition between them.

Argentine antitrust case law has produced several examples where collusion among television system operators was punished, as well as examples of prohibition and partial conditioning of horizontal mergers among television system operators.[4]

One was the Argentine case *CNDC vs. TRISA, TSC and others* (2002) in which one of the key elements was the implicit horizontal agreement among the three main cable television operators in the metropolitan area of Buenos Aires.

A similar problem was found in *Teledigital/Esmeralda–Venado Tuerto Televisión* (2003). That merger was forbidden by the CNDC because it implied the creation of a monopoly in the market of cable television services in the city of Venado Tuerto. The same criterion was applied in order to subject the *Telefónica/AC Inversora–Atlántida Comunicaciones* merger (2000) to divest one of the two free-to-air television channels existing in the city of Mar del Plata, which would belong to the same economic group once the merger took place.

Second, mergers among TV channel suppliers are not harmful. Mergers among suppliers of television channels that do not deal directly with consumers create limited harm to the general economic interest compared to horizontal mergers among television system operators. More suppliers of TV channels exist and it is relatively easy to replace one supplier with another. The way in which TV content and channels are marketed implies that increased market power among providers is more likely to lead to redistribution of profits among suppliers and operators than to significant changes in consumer prices.

The second implication is a particular feature of the TV distribution sector whereby suppliers' revenue from distributors takes the form of fixed amounts, as opposed to unit prices. Channel suppliers enter into agreements with operators in which they specify the global amounts to be paid, based on the operator size, but not on its exact number of subscribers. Changes in the amounts paid by operators do not have a large impact on the marginal cost of taking on new subscribers. The changes basically alter the distribution of profits between operators and suppliers but not the total amount of consumers' surplus.

The effects of a horizontal merger among content suppliers, who do not sell their products directly to the viewers, will be of an indirect nature. It can appear as if, as a consequence of the merger, the variety of available programmes decreases, or that there are important changes in the operation of TV advertising markets. One effect of reducing the content variety is a possible decline in the opinion spectrum in television programmes. This effect could be more or less important depending on whether the merger takes place among channels that specialize in news coverage or political, economic or social programmes, where it may affect the existence of a true 'information democracy'.

A less significant anticompetitive effect of a merger among TV content suppliers, in comparison to the usual effect of horizontal mergers, has to do with the fact that those suppliers do not sell their products directly to the viewers but to intermediary television system operators. When channel suppliers reach their viewers directly (as is the case with free-to-air television channels, for example), then such argument does not apply, since the effects of a merger among them are much more direct.

A review of national and international case law does not show any relevant cases that ended with the prohibition of horizontal mergers among TV content suppliers. However, as discussed, some mergers in Argentina were subject to certain divestiture requirements.

Third, vertical agreements between television content suppliers and television system operators are in principle harmless from the competition law point of view. However, potential anticompetitive effects appear when there is a restriction to competition in one of the industry segments (e.g., retail television provision in a certain relevant market). The possibility is the undermining and eventual exclusion of a rival operator from the market. This is usually due to the exclusivity in the provision of certain television content that cannot be easily substituted to one single operator. It can apply to most cases in the distribution markets of television programmes in Argentina.

The high degree of vertical integration that exists in Argentina between channel suppliers and television system operators enables operators to make use of exclusionary practices in many segments and geographic markets. The opposite phenomenon is also possible: because of a refusal to buy from an operator that is vertically integrated with a channel supplier, another non-integrated supplier may be excluded from the market, increasing the market power of the integrated supplier. Those cases are not frequent since, on a global level, each individual operator is usually a rather small client for channel suppliers (even if it holds a monopoly in its geographic area). However, as television system operators become more concentrated, this may become a more important issue, especially for local or national channel suppliers.

One case of vertical agreements and mergers with potentially exclusionary effects in Argentina was *Decotevé vs. Pramer* (2000). In accordance with CNDC's instruction, the defendant made a commitment to re-establish the provision of a group of channels to the plaintiff, a competitor of another cable television operator with which the defendant was vertically integrated.

There have also been cases of conditioned vertical mergers between a channel supplier and a TV system operator. In *Liberty Media–Hicks/Cablevisión* (2001), the CNDC imposed conduct remedies that banned price discrimination among suppliers and among television system operators, either as sellers or buyers.

One other potentially anticompetitive effect of vertical agreements and mergers between TV content suppliers and system operators appears when such arrangements help to extend the supplier's market power from the wholesale market to the retail market. This is the case when the supplier imposes a marketing method for its channel or content (for instance, codified, pay-per-view) and the price at which such channel or content can be sold to the viewers. Such practices can be very harmful if used to restrict competition among operators.

This implication of antitrust analysis arises when the restriction induced is significant for competition among operators or for the surplus of television viewers. For this to happen, the key element is the degree of market power that the TV content supplier has in its relevant market since, if it faces a strong competition itself, then the effect of its marketing strategy could be neutralized by such competition. That is why this kind of problem is generally limited to those cases where the channel supplier has an important monopoly power, and what it is looking for is to extend that power to a retail market.

The most relevant Argentine case was known as *CNDC vs. TRISA, TSC and others* (2002). The CNDC understood that the resale price maintenance imposed by a supplier of sports programmes would increase the monopoly profits of that supplier, by means of suppressing competition among the cable television operators that sold those programmes to the viewers. Therefore, the resale price maintenance exerted the same effect as organizing a cartel of cable television operators, whose supra-competitive profits were captured by the programme supplier (through the payment received from those operators).

Fourth, competition policy mechanisms fail to address issues that arise in the presence of natural monopolies in the provision of television contents and services. Such situations generally involve the need to regulate prices and provision terms directly. In this kind of situation, it is more appropriate to intervene using specific regulatory norms and mechanisms, instead of relying on the competition law and its enforcement instruments.

This implication emerges directly from the nature of competition policy as a regulatory mechanism. Antitrust is an indirect way of intervening in the markets to improve their operation in cases where such improvement can be achieved by the existence of more competition. Its ability to work is limited in markets where monopoly has certain efficiency advantages (such as natural monopolies). In such markets, market power control can only be achieved through a direct regulation of price and other provision terms, and this is an activity that is beyond the scope of competition authorities.

In *National University of Córdoba vs. Durford* (1997), for instance, the CNDC arrived at the conclusion that the market power exercised by the owner of the broadcasting rights of the games played by the Argentine national soccer team was the result of the fact that, in a way, that product was a natural monopoly (caused by the little substitutability that those games had for Argentine soccer viewers). Therefore, it was the owner's decision whether he wanted to market the games through free-to-air or cable television, and there was little that could be done from the point of view of competition law. If it was understood that the best solution for those games was that they were broadcast through free-to-air television, then the most appropriate tool that the state had was to use a specific regulation. That solution was finally adopted later, concerning the official games played by the Argentine national soccer team.

Certain interventions by the antitrust authority can, however, be useful to reduce the impact of specific problems that arise from monopoly situations. Among such interventions are the prohibition of discriminatory prices among customers, the obligation to give access to essential facilities, the prohibition of selling certain television contents in blocks, and the prohibition of fixing resale prices of certain television content.

There are some cases in which the intervention by the antitrust authority can remedy situations where the exercise of monopoly power occurs through specific practices, the disappearance of which improves the operation of the markets although it does not eliminate their monopoly nature. Most of these cases can be seen as situations of exploitative abuse of dominant position, although they can also appear in some merger cases.

Finally, the antitrust agency can play a prominent role in competition advocacy. In the TV programme distribution sector, advocacy can focus on the advantages of allowing programmes to be broadcast through networks other than cable television, to enable direct competition among channel suppliers to capture the viewers' preferences, and to encourage the entry of new television system operators.

Apart from the sanction of anticompetitive practices and of the procedures of merger control, the antitrust authorities generally have the ability to suggest regulation or deregulation of different sectors so that competition can operate in a more effective way.

Increasingly the technology exists to distribute television programmes through networks other than cable television, such as telephone lines, and perhaps, the electricity supply network. The fixed telephone network is an important potential substitute that currently competes against cable television networks in the provision of broadband internet services. One obstacle in Argentina for telephone companies to supply television services had to do with existing sectoral regulation. A change in regulation would bring about more competition both in cable television and in fixed telephone services.

Another issue in the regulatory debate is the possibility that pay-television operators begin to act as mere content transporters, which would mean that channel suppliers would offer their services directly to the viewers, in a system known as 'à la carte' programming. The advantages of that system are nevertheless ambiguous since, although it can increase competition for subscribers, it could also imply an increase in the average price of each channel and a reduction in the average number of channels received and potentially the variety of programmes.

A last issue relates to the idea that air television operators (for instance, satellite television or ground television) could represent a source of competition for cable television operators, especially in areas where there is only one cable television operator. Hence, a potential activity of competition advocacy might be to encourage new air television operators, especially because it is an activity for which the physical network is not so important and the efficiency gains of monopoly therefore smaller.

NOTES

1. Research assistance was provided in Argentina by Esteban Aguiar, Gabriel Giacobone and Germán Saller as well as staff of the CNDC; Alison Rooper assisted at the editorial stage. The study was overseen by Horacio Salerno and subsequently by Diego Povolo, commissioners at the CNDC, whose cooperation and support for the research is gratefully acknowledged.
2. Known as UHF (ultra-high frequency) and MMDS (multichannel multipoint distribution service).
3. Quoted by Laura Zommer, www.gp-digital.org/wp-content/uploads/2013/10/Argentina.pdf.
4. International case law has also produced several cases of prohibition and conditioning of horizontal mergers. In the US case *EchoStar/DirecTV* (2002) the Department of Justice objected to the merger of the only two satellite television operators that existed in the United States at that time. Conversely, in the case NewsCorp/Telepiù (2003), the European Commission only conditioned the merger of the two single Italian satellite television operators, imposing certain restrictions regarding the exclusivity contracts that the merging group signed with channel and TV content suppliers.

PART IV

Public procurement

10. Public procurement in India

Nitya Nanda, M.V. Shiju and Gaurang Meher Diljun

THE SCALE AND ECONOMIC IMPORTANCE OF PUBLIC PROCUREMENT

This chapter examines the relationship between public procurement and competition in India. It describes the regulatory framework that has been in force until recently, the procurement practices that resulted and the types of abuse that have occurred from the competition perspective. It also discusses recent efforts at reform.

Public procurement refers to the acquisition of goods and services by a public authority using public funds; this chapter deals mostly with purchase of goods. It covers both government spending and purchases by state-owned enterprises.

Public procurement covers a huge quantity of market transactions. In OECD countries, public procurement accounts for 13 per cent of total national income on average (OECD 2013). In India the level is much higher. The combined expenditure of central and state-level government departments and state-owned enterprises was estimated to be 30 per cent of GDP in 2008 (OECD 2010). The proportion of ministry and department budgets spent on procurement varies greatly. Defence and railways, among others, have very high procurement budgets, accounting for around half their total expenditure.

State-owned enterprises (known in India as PSUs, public sector undertakings), also resourced by public funds, have been estimated to have procurement budgets that amounted to approximately 3 per cent of GDP in 2010 (Sahu 2014).

Public procurement is therefore enormously important as a market activity, even more so in India than elsewhere. There is great potential both for harm from abuse of the process and for benefit to the national economy if the process is handled well and used, among other things, to promote competition.

The primary goal of procurement policy worldwide is to achieve 'value for money' in public expenditure. Poorly managed public procurement wastes public money by paying artificially high prices for supplies and diverting to private profit-making companies funds that would otherwise be available for other goods and services for public benefit. The impact is especially hard on poorer groups in the population who are disproportionately reliant on publically provided goods and services.

Second, poor procurement practices may drag down the quality and safety of public infrastructure and services. In this respect as well, the impact may be especially hard on poorer groups in the population that depend the most on publically financed services such as education, health and the railways.

Third, procurement is important to governance. The public perception of the integrity and competence of government is greatly influenced by the way in which public procurement is managed, particularly the extent to which public officials may obtain private gain from procurement activities.

Last but not least, procurement influences the capacity and structure of the economy. Government purchases of goods and services are on such a large scale that procurement affects the allocation of resources overall. Policy and practices in government procurement affect economic efficiency, competitiveness and the pace of technological innovation in the economy in general. Those outcomes are realized in large part through the competition process.

This chapter focuses on the first and last points, that is ways in which procurement, as practised, affects value for money of expenditure of these public funds and the impact on the level of competition in the markets concerned. The consumer welfare effect lies in the first instance on reduction of the realized 'purchasing power' of public expenditure. (Product safety and quality are other issues, but these are not examined in this chapter.) There is also an indirect effect by way of the impact on consumers of restraints to competition in those lines of business that also offer products for direct purchase by consumers as items of personal expenditure.

Public procurement in India is shown to be deeply flawed from the competition perspective. Failure to address competition concerns is a major cause of payment of inflated prices in procurement contracts. This chapter shows how competition failures are evident in each of the three key stages of procurement: the issuance of and responses to tenders (tender enquiries), the evaluation of bids submitted in response and the striking of contracts for the purchase transaction.

Steps are now being taken to strengthen procurement policy in India. This chapter concludes with an assessment of the likely potential of a new national procurement law and of constructive evolution in the application of the competition law to procurement markets.

THE REGULATORY FRAMEWORK FOR PUBLIC PROCUREMENT IN INDIA

Legislative and Administrative Rules

Constitutional principles

The Constitution of India does not contain any direct provision dealing with public procurement. Article 299 stipulates that procurement contracts shall be expressed as made by the president of India or by the governor of a state, as the case may be. It lays down how a contract between government and private person can be executed; and it describes what private persons are able to enter into such a contract. It does not, however, deal with how the discretion of power in entering into a contract on behalf of the authorities is exercised. Rules on that matter have been established separately by the judiciary.

In a case heard in 1979 (*R.D. Shifty vs. International Airport Authority 28*), the Supreme Court of India laid down some operational principles for procurement. It referred to Article 14 of the Constitution on the principle of equality and held that the government could not award a contract in a discriminatory or arbitrary manner.

There is no legislation at the national level on public procurement in India. Instead, procurement is subject, in a non-legally binding way, to governmental administrative regulation. An attempt was made to change the situation as the Public Procurement Bill 2012 was introduced; but it could not be enacted. The bill lapsed along with the dissolution of the 15th Lok Sabha (lower chamber of the parliament) in May 2014; a new government may reintroduce the bill.

Administrative regulations

The primary source of administrative regulation is the General Financial Rules (GFR), a set of executive orders issued by the Ministry of Finance for the central government. They are a compendium of general provisions to be followed by all offices of government while dealing with matters of a financial nature. GFR were first issued in 1947 and modified in 1963. The most recent version, GFR 2005, revises and replaces previous versions.

GFR 2005 is a voluminous document covering all aspects of financial management of central government business. Chapter 6 contains rules on the procurement of goods and services to be followed by all central ministries and departments. More detailed rules can be laid down by the individual departments so long as they are broadly in conformity with the GFR. The GFR do not apply to state-owned enterprises (PSUs).

Two main rules govern public procurement. Rule 137 lists out the fundamental principles of procurement and Rule 160 sets out practical instructions for implementing those principles.

According to Rule 137, every procuring authority is responsible and accountable for bringing in efficiency, economy and transparency into matters relating to public procurement and, most importantly for this chapter, for treating suppliers fairly and equitably and promoting competition in public procurement. General procedural measures are set out for the tendering process, in which the request for and offers of supply are framed as prelude to a contract of sale of goods or services.

Rule 160 contains specific instructions on how to bring transparency, competition, fairness, and elimination of arbitrariness into the procurement process. The items of special interest to this chapter concern the tender issuance process, the formulation of the tender invitation and bidding firms' eligibility. They include the need for clear and detailed specifications of the contract purchase, for cost to be the main criterion for evaluating bids, for prohibition of negotiations between the procurement agency and bidders on the price, and for applicants to be allowed to bid for less than the full amount of the transaction stated in the tender.

The GFR also specify the purchase mechanism to be used for tenders, which depends upon the value of the goods to be purchased. The competent authority can purchase goods as shown in Table 10.1.

There is no central procurement authority – or procurement policy setting and review body – in India. Each department or ministry has its own procurement agent and can have its own procurement rules, so long as they are broadly in conformity with the GFR. The Defence Procurement Manual 2005 and Defence Procurement Procedure 2008 are examples (OECD 2010). In addition, as noted, PSUs have their own procedures for procurement that are not required to conform to the GFR. There are hundreds of PSUs in India (Sahu 2014). One of the largest PSUs, Bharat Heavy Electricals Limited (BHEL), which is active in the power-generation sector, provides one example of how procurements are carried out in state-owned corporations. BHEL has 72 per cent of the total Indian power sector market, an international reach to its business, and annual revenues of more than US$6billion in 2014. The company has framed a general purchase policy for its units to follow. They may complement this with their own 'organizations and methods instructions' (OMI) and/or departmental procedures.

BHEL's corporate purchase policy runs contrary to the GFR and to 'good practice' norms in three main respects. First, it does not specify procurement channels to be used with reference to financial thresholds (or any other variable) as laid out for departments in Table 10.1. An external audit noted that policy guidelines lack a clear-cut framework for

Table 10.1 Mechanisms for public procurement according to the GFR

Goods purchase amount	Prescribed mechanism	Conditions
Up to INR 15,000 (US$240)	Direct purchase	
More than INR 15,000 and up to INR 100,000 (US$240–1,600)	Direct purchase	Three-person committee recommendation
More than INR 100,000 and up to INR 2,500,000 (US$1,600–40,000)	Limited tender enquiry	Enquiries sent to more than three pre-qualified suppliers; also permitted in case of emergency
More than INR 2,500,000 (US$40,000)	Advertised (open) tender enquiry	Form of advertising: in the *Indian Trade Journal*, and in one or more national daily, and on the procurement agency's website
Amt n.s.	Single tender enquiry	In case of emergency, single producer of required goods, products must match specifications of existing equipment

Note: Amounts are expressed in Indian Rupees (INR); US$ figures are quoted here at an approximate exchange rate of 62 Rupees = US$1.

inviting tenders through open tender enquiries (CAG 2010–11b). Second, it radically changes the definition of an 'open' tender: an enquiry shall be considered an open tender if it is addressed to all pre-approved vendors, so long as they are not less than six in number. Finally, advertising is optional for open tender enquiries.

These conditions greatly dampen the pro-competitive force of procurement contracts on suppliers of inputs to the main player in the heavy electricals/power industry.

State-level and Other Relevant Legislation

Procurement is subject to some additional layers of regulation, of which state-level legislation is one.

India is a union of states and state government departments also carry out large-scale procurements. Most of the states have a system similar to that of the central government whereby procurement is governed by state financial rules/codes rules issued by the finance department of each state as executive orders. However, two states, Tamil Nadu and Karnataka, have come out with specific legislations on public procurement. (Two other states are moving in this direction: Himachal Pradesh has a draft bill prepared, and in Kerala a Procurement Act was published in 2014.)

There are certain advantages in having separate legislation. Amendment of legislation is more difficult than for an executive order; this brings in an element of stability and certainty. Furthermore, an Act provides a single unitary framework, instead of the tangle of regulations that face central procurement authorities. There is a clear statement of objectives of the legislation, which is missing from the national regulations, and it lays out a stated focus on competition and transparency.

Procurement officials in Tamil Nadu report that the state Act provide a welcome safety net to them. Unlike national officials, they operate within a unified, coherent framework. Complying with the provisions of the Act shields them from audit objections and helps them avoid the inconsistencies that can occur between GFR and departmental procedures in other states. This may be beneficial in allowing for greater flexibility in the tender process, as long as officials do indeed serve the competition and other objectives of the Act. It allows them some of the greater latitude of private sector procurement processes that are not hidebound by a standard procedural framework and can therefore be responsive to competition conditions in specific markets. In other ways, the Act sets more rigorous parameters than the GFR, which are generally in line with international good practice in public procurement.

Finally, there are a number of general legislations applicable to public procurement both at the central and the state level. Among them are the Indian Contract Act 1872, the Sale of Goods Act 1930, the Central Vigilance Commission Act 2003, the Prevention of Corruption Act 1988 and the Right to Information Act 2005.

Administrative Oversight Bodies

Procurement is subject to oversight and scrutiny by two main administrative bodies of the central government, the Central Vigilance Commission (CVC) and the Comptroller and Auditor General (CAG); and by one regulatory body: the Competition Commission of India (CCI).

The CVC and the CAG focus on corruption and fraud on the part of civil servants, on the purchasing (demand) side. The CCI focuses primarily on the conduct of suppliers but the actions of procurement agencies also come under its purview in some circumstances.

The CVC regulates and monitors the conduct of public servants in all

Table 10.2 Comparison of the Tamil Nadu Act with the GFR: improvements and shared weaknesses

	Topic	Content of the Tamil Nadu Act	Stakeholder comments
a)	Improvements in the Tamil Nadu Act over the GFR		
1.	Coverage	Coverage is comprehensive. All publically funded entities in the state – including state government departments, societies and statutory boards, local bodies, cooperative institutions, universities and PSUs – are covered.	PSUs and various other publicly funded entities are not subject to the GFR. This leads to a confusing multitude of potentially inconsistent provisions. There is no guidance to officials on priority of application.
2.	Tender mechanisms	It is mandatory for all procurements to be made through a tendering process, regardless of the size of the order. Exemptions apply similar to those in the GFR (emergency, goods specifications to match existing equipment, etc.).	
3.	Reserve pricing	After evaluation of tenders, the tender accepting authority has to accept the lowest one. If the price is above the prevailing market rate or schedule of rates, the authority can negotiate for a price reduction with that tenderer. No such provision in the GFR.	Schedules of indicative rates are given in tender documents that are sometimes abysmally low and put off many genuine players from participating in the tender process.
4.	Tender cancellation and bid rejections	If the final price quoted is higher by a prescribed percentage than the schedule of rates or prevailing market price, the authority must reject the tender.	
5.	Refusal of submissions	If a tenderer has been banned by any procuring	

Table 10.2 (continued)

	Topic	Content of the Tamil Nadu Act	Stakeholder comments
		entity, the tendering authority shall not accept the tender of that tenderer even if it may be the lowest priced. No such provision under the GFR.	
6.	Grievances	There is a time-bound appellate procedure for grievances regarding acceptance of tender. Any aggrieved tenderer can approach the state government within a period of ten days of the acceptance of the tender, and the government has to decide the matter within a period of 15 days.	The appellate procedure is an empty formality, according to lawyers. Persons aggrieved finally end up in the High Court filing a writ petition, as would have happened in the absence of legislation. The Tamil Nadu Act has not brought down the number of such cases, on the contrary the number has gone up (although so also has the total value of procurements).
7.	Transparency	The Act gives some supervisory powers to the state government for the purpose of ensuring transparency in the tender process; it can ask for any information relating to transparency from the tender inviting authority and accepting authorities, as well as for records, tender documents and reports to ensure transparency in tender procedure.	
8.	Price escalation clause	Tender documents have to include a price adjustment clause to reflect any changes (upward or downward) in major cost components, e.g., labour, equipment, material and	In relevant cases the tender document often does not in fact include this mandatory clause. This has led to many disputes with suppliers and to delays in completion of projects.

Table 10.2 (continued)

	Topic	Content of the Tamil Nadu Act	Stakeholder comments
		fuel, based on a prescribed formula. The prescription applies to large contracts where the period of execution is likely to exceed 18 months.	
b)	Shared weaknesses		
9.	Contract partition	When two or more tenderers quote the same price, the tender accepting authority shall split procurement among them and the authority is prohibited from negotiating with any bidding firms except that which submits the lowest tender.	
10.	Bid prices and negotiations with suppliers	Acceptance of the lowest bid is mandatory and negotiations are prohibited with any supplier except that which has submitted the lowest bid.	Many firms do not come forward to participate; they know that unless they submit the lowest bid they will have no opportunity to negotiate. Moreover, the mandatory acceptance of the lowest bid may lead suppliers to make bids that compromise the quality of work, and may not be cost-effective for the taxpayer.

areas, including procurement. It is tasked with overseeing and correcting failures to honour the procurement regulation on the part of procurement agents.

The CAG is appointed by the Constitution of India to audit the financial accounts of the central, state and all other authorities or bodies established by the parliament. The CAG is an independent body and its audit reports and recommendations are presented before the parliament and the legislature of the states. The Parliamentary Public Accounts

Committee (PAC) reviews the audit reports and CAG observations and makes recommendations accordingly to the parliament.

The two administrative bodies do not produce a strong mechanism for monitoring the conduct of procurement in India. CAG audits are carried out well after harm is done and often do not attract the attention of the overworked PAC. The PAC normally only examines around 15–20 paragraphs out of the 1,000–1,500 paragraphs included in CAG audit reports. When actions or recommendations by the PAC are followed up by the Executive, there is a considerable time lag (between six months and one year, followed by a six-month period for the administrative units concerned to respond). This renders any attempt to sanction lapses or favouritism noted by the CAG effectively meaningless (National Institute of Public Finance and Policy 2010).

The means of redress for bidding or contracted firms under the regulations are unsatisfactory. An aggrieved party can complain to the CVC, for example, of irregularity in the tendering process or of improper exclusion of a bid submission, and may simultaneously take the issue to court. The CVC may appoint an independent external monitor and also request that someone from the aggrieved firm conduct a technical examination. These multiple processes lead to a lot of wastage of time, energy and resources (TII 2010).

Finally, the CAG and CVC are focused on the conduct of officials managing public procurements, driven by the objective of disciplining corruption. In the context of procurement, corruption does not arise solely from abuse of administrative processes. It is normally the result of interaction between suppliers seeking market advantage and procurement officials seeking private gain by facilitating the advancement of particular suppliers that will provide a pecuniary reward (bribe or side payment). The activities can be analysed separately on each side, but procurement abuses cannot successfully be tackled without identifying abuses and addressing the problem on the two sides simultaneously.

Assessment of the Regulatory Framework

The main weakness of the regulatory framework for procurement is the multiplicity of central government regulations. The regulations are not presented anywhere in a consolidated manner, most do not have the force of law and they do not cover all uses of public funds, notably by omitting procurement by state-owned enterprises. More than 150 contract formats are in use. Procurement authorities each have several variants of tender offer forms and tender auction terms. It follows that for a given piece of work – such as, for example, construction of a road – agencies differ with respect to qualification requirements, selection criteria, payment terms and dispute settlement mechanisms. There is no indication of priority of application among different rules in particular situations. Consequently, public officials can override any of the laid-down procedures in the name of obscure or subjective guidelines, citing, for example, 'expediency' or 'public interest considerations', without a credible threat of being prosecuted. Finally, mechanisms for lodging grievances and seeking redress are not transparent and are not time-bound. Recourse to the courts is expensive and slow and prejudicial to small companies. Fines are indeterminate, given that guidelines are not legally binding.

Overall, it is clear that procurement policy in India does not amount to an effective means of enabling procurement agents to bring about economy of expenditure and fairness (in the sense of consistent treatment), two of the principles to which they are accountable under the GFR. Nor can the existing set of regulations ensure equitable treatment of suppliers. Neither the CAG nor the CVC have the power to investigate or penalize malpractice on the supply side. That power rests with a third, recently constituted regulatory body, the Competition Commission of India (CCI).

Supply-side Legislation: The Competition Act 2002

Competition law is the only legislative instrument in India that addresses the behaviour of market actors in procurement as in other market situations. The Competition Act of 2002 (with later amendments) is sensitive to the potential for anticompetitive conduct in public procurement and has prepared advocacy materials to this effect (CCI n.d.). The Competition Commission of India (CCI) is the enforcement agency of the Act, which prohibits any agreement that causes, or is likely to cause, appreciable adverse effects on competition in markets in India.

Two sections of the Act address procurement markets. Section 3 states that bid-rigging or collusive bidding is one of the horizontal agreements that shall be presumed to have an appreciable adverse effect on competition. Bid-rigging is sanctioned most severely if the presence of a cartel arrangement is detected. Section 4 deals with abuse of dominant position and prohibits unfair or discriminatory conditions in purchases, sales or practices further resulting in denial of market access. Section 4 therefore addresses inter alia buyer power, that is the exclusionary, anticompetitive actions of procurement agencies insofar as they are dominant in the relevant market.

Under Section 19 of the Act, the Commission may inquire into any alleged breach of the Act that concerns bid-rigging. As in any complaint, the Commission shall direct the director general (DG) to undertake an investigation. The CCI has the powers vested in a civil court under the Code of Civil Procedure. The director general exercises those powers for the purpose of carrying out investigations, besides powers to conduct 'search and seizure'. The recommendations of the DG are then endorsed (or not) in rulings of the commission.

The Commission can impose a penalty up to 10 per cent of the average turnover for the last three preceding financial years on firms indulging in bid-rigging or collusive bidding. If bid-rigging or a collusive bidding agreement referred to in Subsection 3 of Section 3 has been entered into by a cartel, the Commission can impose a penalty of up to three times of its profit for each year or 10 per cent of its total turnover for each year of the continuance of such agreement, whichever is higher. Section 46 of the Act empowers the Commission to impose a lesser penalty to a party in a cartel if he makes true, full and vital disclosure leading to the busting of the cartel.

Up to now, six main procurement-related cases have been investigated by the CCI, covering possible barriers to entry in the terms and conditions of tenders, abuse of dominance (by procurement agencies) and bid-rigging. These are discussed in the relevant sections below.

ANTICOMPETITIVE CONDUCT IN PROCUREMENT MARKETS

This section describes the main competition concerns that arise in procurement markets and how abuses have been found in practice in India. It also discusses the findings of CCI cases. Failures of procurement can be related to competition in four ways.

First, barriers to entry are intrinsic to many aspects of procurement because procurement agents have the right to determine companies' eligibility to respond to tenders. If they impose restrictive conditions, whatever the size of the pool of potential bidders in a particular sector, only a limited number are in fact able to submit bids, weakening the force of competition. This is a *prima facie* case of erecting barriers to entry. The structural impact is greater, the higher the proportion of demand in a given market that is taken up by procurement transactions. If the conditions for participation are unreasonable then there must be suspicion of abuse of the process.

Second, a tender may be issued in a market that is weakly or non-competitive. This predisposes procurement to be wasteful of public funds because the potential suppliers are monopolistic. Conditions in their market enable them routinely to sell at prices that generate supernormal profit for them. They are not likely to change tactics in response to a procurement tender, even if they do not collude. Unless the market is extended to foreign suppliers, they are unlikely to have to confront lower-priced bids. All the bidders can refer to their previous prices as the norm. The ensuing procurement contracts thus include payment of supernormal profit to suppliers that are not under any pressure to improve the quality of their product offers.

Third, in markets where the procuring agency is a major actor in the specific product market, malpractice in its procurement practice may make it liable to scrutiny under competition law for abuse of its position as a dominant player. Such conduct lies in the area of overlap between procurement and competition policy. This is a new area of public policy that is just emerging in India. Fourth, suppliers may collude in their response to procurement tenders. The terms and conditions of procurement tenders, and more generally the way in which the procurement process is managed, may enable or facilitate anticompetitive actions (collusion) among suppliers. 'Bid-rigging' is the shorthand term for such activities. Again the consequence is the payment of supernormal profit to the suppliers.

These effects are mutually reinforcing. Repeated imposition of barriers to entry to procurement markets can prevent the emergence of any new entrants and depress competition over the long term. In weakly competitive markets, collusion is easier for suppliers. Successful collusion in the procurement market will, whatever the initial situation, enable suppliers to restrict the degree of competition in the market thereafter. Moreover, public procurement is uniquely and continually vulnerable to distortion from concerted actions across the line dividing purchasing (demand) and supply, in the form of corruption, i.e., concealed collaboration between procurement agents and suppliers. Compared to other market transactions, weak public procurement thus tends to generate a closed, static system resistant to productivity growth and innovation.

The problem of the existence of a monopolistic market structure cannot be addressed under the regulatory framework for procurement. On the other hand, barriers to entry, abuse of dominance by a procurement agency and collusion among suppliers are actionable concerns in India. Henceforth we focus on those three issues.

Barriers to Entry

The first competition concern is the possible existence in procurement markets of barriers to entry. This is likely to occur primarily (but not exclusively) on the demand side, where restrictions take effect through the terms of the tenders issued by the procurement agency.

Any curtailment of fully open tenders constitutes a barrier to entry for firms to the procurement market. The question is whether a restriction is warranted; for example, whether the eligibility conditions on firms are reasonable. In order to examine this question, we consider the distribution of tender invitations by type, the terms and conditions set in open tenders – notably suppliers' eligibility to respond to tenders – and whether unreasonable restrictions enter into the evaluation of bids. We also examine the process of registering firms in the lists of pre-qualified suppliers to which limited tender enquiries are addressed. To conclude, we consider cases of barriers to entry into procurement markets that may be erected not by the procurement agency but by other firms in the market.

Non-use of open tenders

The distribution of types of tenders issued is the main filter that affects the level of participation by suppliers in procurement events. Restrictions are clearly greatest when no tendering takes place or when limited tender enquiries are used, rather than open ones. As noted, under the GFR, open tendering is supposed to be used for purchases of goods above INR 2,500,000 (US$40,000), with few exemptions.

There is no comprehensive data on the distribution of central government procurement orders by type and value. Some information is available for the ordnance sector within the defence industry. The share of open (advertised) tenders issued is much lower in this case than the guidelines indicate.

Ordnance is produced in 41 factories round the country, constituting a giant industrial set up within the Department of Defence. It is reputedly the largest government production organization in the world, with revenues of US$2.1billion and 164,000 employees in 2010–11.

Defence sector regulation requires that 20 per cent of goods and services are obtained through open tendering. Audits reveal that, by contrast, open tenders in practice account for a miniscule share. Over a three-year period, seven factories whose accounts were examined were shown to procure only 0.07–1.91 per cent of orders through open tendering. As advertised online (http://ofb.gov.in), the vast bulk of tenders are for unconsolidated, extremely low value orders, such as individual items of stationery, soap, vehicle tyres, hand tools and so on; in these cases, limited tenders are issued to a single or two suppliers. The issuance of multiple, extremely small orders is a way of bypassing open tendering, which, according to both the GFR and the sector regulations, should be used for generic items (CAG 2010–11a).

In respect of PSUs, a study by the CAG of a sample of procurement units in BHEL revealed that limited and selected tender enquiries were the predominant channels of procurement. The percentage of orders placed through open tenders was only 6 per cent of orders by number and 8 per cent by value. In addition, many large value tenders (34 per cent by value and 19 per cent by number) were issued without any competition at all, through selected tender enquiries (CAG 2010–11b).

Failure to advertise

The purpose of open tenders is to make a bidding opportunity known to a large number of potential suppliers and the aim of the procurement authority should be to induce maximum possible relevant participation. This requires wide advertising of the intended procurement.

The GFR lay out very clearly that advertising of open tender invitations is obligatory, specifying the media channels and actual outlets to be used. Many government departments have websites to which advertised tender enquiries are to be posted, with a link to the National Informatics Centre (NIC). The provision of the link to the NIC is intended, however, to enable monitoring and archiving of tenders by the government, not to make the tenders available for viewing for the public and potential bidders in particular. The NIC did not maintain a portal for this purpose.

If there is little or no print, or no online advertising, or if advertising is confined to local markets when the relevant market is or could be more extensive, a few suppliers can become dominant over time. When potential competitors from different areas do not have information of the tender invitation, incumbents will be more likely to remain in position and maintain a collusive agreement. Appropriate advertising is thus necessary to weaken existing cartels. Corrupt officials may fail to advertise precisely in order to thwart this intention and to favour a few selected firms.

At the national level, the CVC reports that the GFR advertising requirements are not always followed in practice. In numerous instances, tender documents were not being adequately advertised. Even in cases where global tender notices were issued, the advertisements were only published in local dailies, not in a single national newspaper. In other cases, notices were published only in the evening newspapers. In some cases, although the tender notice was published in a leading national newspaper, it was not done on the page dedicated to the advertisements for tenders, thus limiting its reach (CVC 2002).

BHEL, the large PSU in the heavy electricals sector, discussed above, has a corporate procurement policy that contains no requirement for advertising to be done in *any* corporation tenders. This makes a mockery of the supposed 'open' tender enquiries that are issued.

Unreasonable terms and conditions of tender invitations

Tender documents typically set out eligibility terms concerning bidding firms' performance or capability, and the specification of the goods to be purchased. Either of these may be unreasonably presented, such that they deter firms from bidding or eliminate viable bids. The specifications set out in previous tenders may just be repeated, without amending them to different parameters according to the requirements of the new work (CVC 2007).

Several cases related to this issue have been examined by the CCI.[1] In CSR *Nanjing Puzhen Co Ltd vs. Kolkata Metro Rail Corporation Ltd*, the informant, a Chinese company, claimed that unnecessary and unreasonable conditions had been incorporated in the bid document, as a result of which the company did not qualify for the bid for supply of 200 metro train cars. The tender document imposed a prequalification criterion on the manufacturer to have supplied at least 100 cars in India before. The Commission held that the procuring authority had the right to impose the condition on the basis of specific local requirements. In M/S *Pankaj Gas Cylinders Ltd vs. Indian Oil Corporation Ltd*, the applicability of Section 4 of the Act to public procurement by a PSU came under discussion. The informant challenged a qualification criterion as unnecessary and frustrating the objective of competitive bidding. In a bid to procure 14.2kg gas cylinders, suppliers who had been blacklisted/holiday-listed by any of the liquid petroleum gas (LPG) manufacturers were disqualified. Finding a *prima facie* violation of the provisions of the Act, the Commission ordered an inquiry. The DG of CCI, after inquiry, reported that the criterion in question was restrictive and imposed unfair and discriminatory condition in procurement. The Commission then came to a majority decision in favour of rejecting the report of its DG on this question. It found it to be a reasonable condition inserted to safeguard against default by the suppliers. The basis of the Commission's decision in overruling the DG's report was not disclosed. The timeline for submissions of bids is another condition of a tender invitation. The GFR states that, for advertised tenders, the minimum time for submission of bids should not be less than three weeks (four weeks for global tender enquiries) from the date of publication of the tender notice, or availability of the bidding document for sale, whichever is later. Audit agency reports note that on occasion the response time granted for bid submission is unrealistically short (CVC 2002). Only a few firms very well-acquainted with the functioning of the department concerned and the past pattern of requirements and thus having prior knowledge of the prospective tender are able to participate in such bids.

The history of a very large turnkey hydroelectric tender invitation illustrates how an inappropriately short time for bid submission restricts participation. The response time given for submitting the tender was 45 days; the time was not extended in spite of requests from many bidders. The project was large and complex, with work running into hundreds of millions of US dollars, and it involved a lot of groundwork and research prior to submission. Only two contractors were able to submit the bids in time; they were close to the procurement agency and had done their preparatory work ahead of time. In the end, the contract was awarded at very high rates. Setting an unrealistically tight deadline defeated the purpose of seeking to gain value for expenditure of public money through competition generated by responses to a global tender (CVC 2007).

Evaluation of bids

The tender invitation itself may appear to be fully open, but the scrutiny of submissions during the evaluation stage may be biased in favour of some firms on the basis of irrelevant factors. Unrealistic prices and inappropriate criteria may not be included in the terms of reference of the tender, but brought into play improperly by the tender committee appointed to evaluate submissions. Rule 160 of the GFR (Sections ix, x and xiv) describes the methods to be used in the evaluation of bids. These are imprecise and easily abused.

A study of cases involving allegations of irregularities in the processing and award of tenders and contracts by India Railways describes how impartiality can be set aside (CVC n.d.). The Tender Committee (TC) is described as 'the villain of the piece' (when the allegations are proved to be correct). The various modus operandi adopted by the TC are reported as:

- Exaggerating the 'track record' of the 'favourite' bidder.
- Suppressing and/or downplaying its past failures.
- Exaggerating the past failures of its main rival.
- Ignoring/suppressing the otherwise satisfactory credentials of the main rival.
- Projecting, falsely, that the lower rates offered by the main rival are 'unworkable' on the basis of the estimated cost that, in the first place, was deliberately exaggerated.
- Projecting undue/artificial 'urgency' and then bypassing the lower offer on the ground that the party already has some works on hand and that, therefore, it may not to be trusted to complete the subject-work within the stipulated timeframe.
- Certifying, falsely, that the quality of the product/material offered by the 'favourite' contractor conforms to the specifications.

- Painting, deliberately, the quality of the product offered by the better-placed bidder (who has quoted lower rates) as unsatisfactory or unsuitable.
- Exaggerating the capacity/resources of a favourite contractor and downplaying that of his rival (lower bidder).

Any and all of these manoeuvres serve to promote some and exclude other suppliers from consideration for the eventual procurement order.

Limited tenders and pre-qualified suppliers

Use of limited tender invitations constitutes a per se barrier to entry. The only way to avoid barriers is for the list of pre-qualified suppliers to which invitations are sent not to be exclusionary. Key to this is the manner in which the list is drawn up.

Little guidance is given in the GFR on drawing up of lists. The CVC has commented that vague and inappropriately defined pre-qualification criteria are common lapses in procurement procedure. Pre-qualification criteria/screening can be non-transparent, vague and inappropriate. The listing process can be delayed; firms' inclusion in the list may be refused on unreasonable grounds; or updated lists may be made but not actually used for tender invitations. The exclusion of firms without any experience in the precise product market concerned is an easy way of keeping markets closed to new entrants. The process may be discriminatory. For example, small and medium-sized enterprises (SMEs) may always fail to qualify, despite an ability to fulfil small orders, either as a consequence of prior production capacity requirements or because the costs of going through the registration procedure are disproportionately high (TERI 2008, 2012). These practices may or may not be done deliberately. They may be due simply to negligence on the part of public officials. On the other hand, corrupt officials may seek to increase the probability that the rivals of a favoured firm are excluded from the tender process.

In the railways sector, the Research Design and Standards Organization (RDSO) is the research and development wing of Indian Railways (IR), responsible for vendor approval. Given the technical nature of many items required by IR, and the safety issues concerned, most of the IR procurement is allowed only through the RDSO-approved vendor list. RDSO plays a prominent role in restricting entrants into the railways procurement. There are inefficiencies, long delays and alleged corruption in both product inspections and the process of approving suppliers (TERI 2008, 2012). In 2005, the CVC had critically viewed the approving mechanism used by the RDSO and made recommendations to the Railway Board blaming the RDSO for high prices and lack of competition. A committee set up by the Ministry of Railways in 2010 noted, 'The cumbersome process being followed by RDSO delays the vendor development work and also deters the good suppliers from coming to the Railways. Railways thus continue with too few suppliers for critical items and make purchases from original equipment manufacturers at exorbitant prices'. By favouring a few suppliers, RDSO has been restricting competition, leading to cartelization and bid-rigging. IR has lost an estimated INR 500,000 million at least from overpricing in the past decade, largely due to the RDSO's non-transparent and non-competitive system of approvals (*The Statesman* 2010).

In the PSU sector, a CAG audit of BHEL stated that more than 50 per cent of procurement was through limited tender enquiries (to pre-registered firms) for which the procurement units did not have an adequate vendor base. Five units out of six surveyed had only a single registered vendor in 1,150 material groups shared between them. In other units, for a large number of products, the number of registered vendors ranged from one to three only. Furthermore, the corporate procurement policy states that press advertisements may be used for enlisting new vendors for admission into the list. In four out of the six surveyed units, however, no press advertisement had been issued for this purpose during the preceding three years; in the remaining two units, only one advertisement had been issued relating to a few product categories. The audit also revealed many cases of delay in registering vendors. Periodic updating is required but is clearly not done (CAG 2010–11b).

Another abuse of procedure occurs when tenders are not issued to all firms in the register. In defence (ordnance) procurement, even where new suppliers were registered, the department concerned did not allow them to participate in tenders. One parachute factory registered 21 new suppliers since 2006 for the supply of different stores items but none of the tenders was sent to the new entrants, despite them fulfilling all the requirements (CAG 2010–11a).

Predatory pricing

Predatory pricing can be practised by market actors to keep out new entrants or to force exits. In 2007, an ordnance factory of the Defence Department, unusually, issued an open tender. Two incumbents in the market (established suppliers) quoted INR 0.07 per unit, far less than they had in earlier limited tender channels. The last purchase price had been INR 4,401.90. This was a clear case of loss-leading predation with a view to keeping rivals out of that particular market. In the absence of any obligation under the GFR to set a reserve price, orders were subsequently placed with the two firms at the low offer price. Unsurprisingly, no supply of the item was ever received from either firm. Whether the purchase tender was relaunched, or the firms concerned were banned from taking part in later tenders – in which case their tactic misfired – is not known.

Abuse of Dominance

Sections 3 and 4 of the Competition Act can be applied in the case of suppliers of goods that resort to anticompetitive practices and abuse of dominant position in procurement markets. Dominance is defined in the Act as a position of strength enjoyed by an enterprise in the relevant market that enables it to operate independently of prevailing competitive forces. Abuse of dominance is defined as conduct that imposes an unfair or discriminatory condition in the purchase or sale of goods or service. 'Enterprises' explicitly include state-owned businesses.

Abuse of dominance by procurement agencies is exercised by the issuance of unreasonable terms and conditions in tender invitations. They have the effect of excluding possible entrants to the market; as noted above, the existence of restrictive terms and conditions has been established in some cases by the CCI. In this section, we review the investigations undertaken by the CCI into whether a procurement agency can indeed be described as a dominant player, and what constitutes abuse of its position. Three case rulings have established that government or PSU procuring agencies can indeed, in some circumstances, be brought within the ambit of the Act in that respect. But they also show that the effects of sanctions deriving from competition law enforcement may be limited.

In *Pankoj vs. IOC Ltd*, already cited, the commission held that IOC Ltd, a PSU and procurer of LPG gas cylinders, was a commercial entity and that it was a dominant player in the relevant market. From that determination, it could be assumed that a procuring agency, if it is in a dominant position, can be proceeded against for imposing restrictive conditions in the bid document.

Another, more complex case pursued the same line of argument and also illustrated some other finer points of competition enforcement in matters of procurement. It related to freight transport on the railways (Cases 64/2010 and 12/2011, *Arshiya Rail Infrastructure Limited (ARIL) vs. Ministry of Railways (MoR)/Chairman, Railway Board (RB) and Container Corporation of India Limited (CONCOR)* and Case 02/2011, *KRIBHCO Infrastructure Ltd vs. Ministry of Railways (MoR)*). The case concerned restrictions on private train freight operators newly permitted to run services on the national rail network. The ruling first established that the MoR is a government company and the CONCOR is a PSU, whose activities are economic and commercial, and thus within the purview of the Competition Law. The case then hinged on the definition of the relevant market. The CCI drew a very broad definition of the freight transport market to include road haulage. Accordingly, it found that the government parties MoR and CONCOR were not dominant players. A narrower market definition might have led to a different conclusion and opened the way for further action.

A more recent case (Cases 59/2013 and 88/2013) came to an unequivocal ruling of abuse of dominance in the procurement activities of a PSU. Coal India Ltd (CIL) was shown to operate independently of market forces and to enjoy undisputed market dominance. In the exercise of that dominance, it was found to have imposed unfair conditions upon bidders. CIL had attempted to put all liability on bid-winning companies and to impose penalties in cases where their failure to supply was in fact due to CIL's non-fulfilment of its contract terms. The commission issued a 'cease and desist' order and ordered modification of the terms and conditions of the tendering scheme, consistent with CIL accepting liability in such cases.

However, the force of the commission's rulings for improving the quality of procurement in general is undermined by the fact that, under the relevant provisions of the Act, when firms indulge in anticompetitive conduct with the assistance of public officials, the CCI lacks the power to investigate the public officials involved.

Collusion and bid-rigging

In recent years, national competition laws and law enforcement agencies round the world have found ways of offering greater incentives to cartel members, and to individuals working within them, to default. This approach has scored some notable successes and seen the break-up of many large cartels. Similarly, the pernicious influence of cartels and bid-rigging in public procurement has become much better understood. International good practice experiences have been described and many ways developed for combating cartel activities in procurement markets.

Cartels deploy a range of tactics to rig their bids and ensure that procurement contracts are secured in the way they wish (CCI n.d.; OECD 2010). Bid-rigging tactics include three main tactics designed to allocate contracts over time among cartel members, and two tactics for sharing out the business of any particular procurement purchase order. The main devices used to allocate contracts over time are bid rotation (to assure that colluding firms submit the lowest priced submissions in turn), bid covering (whereby higher priced bids are withdrawn at a late stage) and bid suppression (whereby some firms agree not to submit bids in particular procurement events). Contract-sharing is assured by submission of equal bids below the full contract value, or the making of side payments or subsequent subcontracting of part of the order by the winner to other firms.

Cartels can also attempt to limit the participation of non-member firms in the bidding process through threats of punitive action that the cartel may carry out in other (non-procurement) parts of the sector. Another form of deterrence used in some circumstances is predatory pricing. This may have relatively little appeal in procurement markets proper, however, because desired procurement contracts can be obtained by other means, without resorting to the price-cutting (and margin-cutting) entailed in this manoeuvre.

Facilitating factors in the regulatory framework

In all instances of collusion, realization of the anticompetitive effect of bid-rigging depends on either (concealed) cooperation between parties on the two sides (corruption among procurement officials) or on officials' negligence in overlooking anticompetitive conduct by suppliers. Nine characteristics of a procurement process that facilitate collusion among suppliers – and for which observers should be on the look-out – have been described as follows (OECD 2009):

- offering limited tenders
- restricted lists of registered (pre-qualified) suppliers
- unrealistic price references and inappropriate technical criteria
- failures to advertise appropriately
- overly tight submission deadlines
- absence of discussions with several bidding firms
- contract partition (market sharing) as a response to identical bids
- excessive information provision
- frequency and regularity of offers.

The only element in this list about which the regulation in India is silent, and on which no evidence is available, is the last; that is, frequent and regular procurement orders. The procurement process in India exhibits features that facilitate collusion among suppliers in respect of all the other eight elements.

The first six features have already been discussed; all are either mandatory under the regulations or have been frequently encountered in practice by monitoring bodies. There is some evidence that the two remaining features (contract partitioning and excessive information provision) are also represented in the regulations.

Contract partitioning is treated differently at different levels. At state level, in Tamil Nadu, the Act requires the procurement agency to divide up contracts where the winning bid offer does not cover the full amount of the tender order. The government regulations are not immune to the problem.

Item xiv of Rule 160 of the GFR states that where the lowest acceptable bidder is not in a position to supply the full quantity required, the remaining quantity shall, as far as possible, be ordered from the next higher responsive bidder at the rates offered by the lowest acceptable bidder. Well-informed colluding bidders, especially from a heavily cartelized industry, can easily coordinate the pricing elements of their bids in order to ensure that the contract is partitioned among them, in predetermined quantities. The amount of contracted business can be shared out appropriately over a series of contract orders; for example, made commensurate to the production capacity of the various suppliers in the cartel.

With respect to departmental procurement, the Indian Railways procurement agency directs that bids for less than 50 per cent of the procurement order must normally be dismissed by the procurement authority. This may eliminate the crudest cases of collusion in pursuit of contract-sharing; but a simple quantity restriction such as this is not effective as an anti-collusion measure. Bidding suppliers can easily agree each to bid somewhat more than 50 per cent (or whatever is the cut-off level) of the order, in the expectation that contact partition will then take place proportionately.

Finally, setting out the appropriate balance in the regulations between information transparency considerations and anticompetitive safeguards is an intriguing challenge for procurement. It is an area in which, unusually, other concerns may require limits on the 'good practices' recommended from the competition perspective.

Rules and regulations in public procurement tend to focus most strongly on rooting out corruption among officials. In order to check corruption, they impose many transparency requirements on the dealings of public departments. Yet high transparency requirements can promote collusion or strengthen existing cartels by providing them with useful information (OECD 1998 Policy Roundtables). The names and contact details of the bidders, including new entrants, are often publically available. For example, Indian Railways departmental regulations make it mandatory to publish the names and contact details of all the approved sources (bidders) on its website. New entrants are placed in a distinct (Part II) list and are eligible for restricted/limited supply; after satisfactory performance over a minimum period of 18 to 24 months they can be upgraded to regular supply category (i.e., Part I). This practice may facilitate incumbent firms bid-rigging because it ensures that there is no threat to them of surprise, undisclosed entry. Existing cartels can take appropriate steps either to negotiate with the new firms or to indulge in predatory pricing to harm them.

Evidence of collusion

There is evidence of cartel activity in procurement markets in India but its full prevalence is unknown. A CAG Defence Audit of market-sharing cites 108 cases of identical pricing (precursor to sharing out of the work) in limited tender enquiries and at least 24 cases of subdivision of contracts (CAG 2010–11a). Monitoring and audit bodies in India have identified some of the tell-tale indications that have been described most notably by the OECD (2010) and also by the CCI (n.d.). The two colluding firms in the 2007 predatory pricing case in the defence (ordnance) industry discussed above had provided the same contact fax number. That was a revealing mistake that is, taken as definitive evidence in bid-rigging trials in other jurisdictions. The CAG 2010 Defence Audit report on market sharing in the defence (ordnance) sector described a tendering process issued by a defence ordnance factory at Kanpur. Four firms responded to the tender invitation. The email addresses and fax numbers of two firms were the same. The other two firms shared identical phone numbers and requested the tender documents to be delivered to the same address. The tender documents received from three of the companies followed identical formats, had been typed on identical types of paper, showed similarities in handwriting and had similar styles of filling up the required information. These all indicated bid-rigging, which should have warranted preventive action against the firms. The audit report pointed out that 'There was enough evidence to suggest that these firms are colluding with each other to suppress competition in the procurement process. Ministry's replies (to the audit findings) do not comment on the tell-tale evidence of such collusion' (CAG 2010–11a).

A departmental audit of a bid-rigging episode in Indian Railways is another example. The case reflects the complex, multilayered strategies adopted by cartels.

In 2004–5, a tender for procurement of fully assembled bogies was issued by the Railway Board. Nine firms – eight Part I (established) and one Part II (new entrant) firm – participated in the tender. Seven firms quoted for less than 50 per cent of the quantity at a uniform price of INR 99,638 per bogie, which was a clear indication of cartel formation. The remaining Part I firm quoted for the full quantity at a rate of INR 105,000 per bogie. These eight firms were in collusion (including the firm quoting the highest price). The bid of the single Part II firm was at the lowest rate, INR 87,000, per bogie for the full quantity. Evidently, the cartel had not succeeded either in bringing this new firm on board, or had not tried to do so, perhaps being (rightly) confident that contracting conditions precluded it from obtaining much business under the contract.

The procuring authority held negotiations with the seven firms (in April

2004) but did the rate was not brought down. Nevertheless, the major part of the order was placed with those firms because the departmental regulations did not allow more than a small fraction of the order to be placed with the inexperienced Part II firm. Another twist in the case was that in order to restrict market-sharing, the Railway Board had issued a directive restricting firms from quoting below 50 per cent of the tender quantity. The seven firms with identical prices were in fact liable to be disqualified. To protect against this eventuality, the cartel had arranged that one firm in the cartel quoted for the full quantity at a higher price. Subcontracting would be done later on to compensate the other cartel members.

Several cases of alleged collusion in a procurement tendering process have been brought to the CCI under the Competition Act. Identical pricing was a feature in four cases of alleged bid-rigging (Vaid n.d.). In one such case, a complaint was lodged by a railways department against 29 parties that had responded to a goods tender (Case 50/2011, *Principal Chief Engineer, South Eastern Railway, Kolkata vs. M/s Orissa Concrete and Allied Industries Ltd and 28 other opponents*). An identical rate was quoted by almost all the firms, each quoting for a far lesser quantity than 50 per cent of the tender quantity. The sum total of their offers came to almost exactly the total quantity sought through the tender. The rate quoted by all the bid-submitting firms was about 10 per cent higher than the neighbouring railways' last purchase rate. The railway procurement authority suspected cartelization by the bidders in fixing the price and seeking to divide the procurement contract among them. Evidence was brought that the bid submissions had been coordinated and that a single person had filled in the key variables in all the submissions. The allegations were substantiated and the bidders ordered to cease and desist from indulging in anticompetitive conduct in future. The CCI did not, however, impose any penalty in the case. The grounds were that the perpetrators were largely small firms, ignorant of the fact that collusion was an offence, and that (had the rules been properly implemented) none could have won the contract in any case since offering less than 50 per cent of the tender quantity broke the terms of the tender enquiry. A warning was given that any future bid-rigging would attract penalties.

More recently, in 2013, CCI did impose a penalty in a finding of bid-rigging in the shoe industry. Eleven companies were found to have operated a cartel. They were fined US$0.9million for restricting the bidding for a Ministry of Commerce tender.[2]

In another case, three firms participated in a tender to supply of medical equipment. The tender was awarded to the lowest bidder, Safdarjung Hospital,[3] but at a high price, estimated at 160 per cent of the market rate. A complaint was brought on the basis of suspicious text (common typographical errors) in the bid submissions. The firms' bidding patterns in the past were investigated. This revealed that another of the three firms had won a previous contract, with the other two firms submitting higher (inflated) priced bids on that occasion. This bid rotation was taken as corroborating evidence of the existence of a cartel.

Finally, cartels that secure an initial contract at a low rate assure themselves of repeat business – at artificially high prices – in cases where safety sensitive, high specification or customized pieces are sought through repeat orders or as spare parts (2009 Audit Report of the RDSO). In such cases, the incumbents have a passport to indefinite contracts in the future, without any threat of challenge to their inflated margins and no risk of being outcompeted by innovative products that might have been introduced by rivals. This shows the market-stifling effect of the closed, non-competitive system that arises from mismanagement of the procurement process.

POLICY REFORM

Key Principles and Good Practice Guidelines

There is no general simple procedural framework that can address all the competition concerns that arise in procurement. Three key principles can nevertheless guide procurement policy reforms that had undoubtedly become necessary for India by 2012, when changes began to be made:

1. Maximize the participation of credible and competing firms in procurement markets.
2. Minimize the flow of competition-sensitive information so as to reduce the possibilities for collusion.
3. By extension, minimize interactions between firms, also in order to reduce the possibilities for collusion.

These principles can be applied to the different stages of the procurement process. To set the stage for the procurement contract, pre-tender market research needs to be done to establish a reference price for the goods or services to be purchased, and arrive at the most appropriate auction design. Tenders are more difficult to design for purchase of services (including construction) than for purchases of goods. In the case of services, the quality of work may be paramount and needs to be monitored as the contract proceeds. The market research stage is even more crucial in these circumstances for establishing local norms and expectations and incorporating terms and conditions into the tender documents that refer to them. The exploratory process may indicate that a two-stage tendering process would be helpful in allowing first-stage discussions on the specifications to take place with experienced suppliers (Nicholas n.d.).

At the full tender invitation stage, the driving motive should be to reduce barriers to entry and eliminate bid-rigging. The challenge is therefore to ensure proper design and implementation of tendering procedures for the purpose. In general, open tenders are the best mechanism, setting the 'gold standard' of good practice (Nicholas n.d.). While use of open tenders is generally to be preferred, they are neither necessary nor sufficient to ensure competition. The GFR recognizes some of the circumstances under which open tendering may legitimately not be needed. Abuses of the process examined earlier show that open tenders are not guaranteed to ensure competition. They can certainly be manipulated to exclude new entrants, both by procurement agents who give inadequate consideration to the need for competitive bidding, and by parties on the supply side.

For limited tender enquiries, the identification of pre-qualified suppliers needs to be managed in a continuous manner and to be as open as possible.

In open tendering, advertising needs to be widespread, the timeline for submissions needs to be appropriately generous and the specifications of the purchase order need to be to general industry standards where possible, without reference to specific brand names as a general rule (Nicholas n.d.). Procurement agencies need to have discretionary authority to specify the terms and conditions of tenders in order to optimize competition outcomes case by case, especially with respect to suspicion of collusion. The signs of collusion activity are now well understood; some individual national competition authorities have developed checklists to help their officials and the OECD has synthesized their provisions (OECD 2009). Many of the signs are obvious, such as the example of shared correspondence addresses among bidders. Provision needs to be made in the terms and conditions of tender documents for cancellation of bids on these grounds. To reduce discriminatory conditions – for example, against smaller firms and new entrants – eligibility conditions need to be thought through case by case. For example, suppliers may not need to have extensive experience in the specific field – such a stipulation favours incumbents – and there may be no justification for demanding large financial guarantees. The costs of bid submission need to be kept low – for example, by having common templates for submissions – partly so as not to give disincentives to small firms and partly to reduce the costs of the procurement process overall.

At the post-tendering stage, the most important consideration for promoting competition in the market is that evaluation criteria should be fair and transparent. The application of the criteria in the evaluation process must be recorded and open to scrutiny by outside parties. In particular, the weighting of components of the decisions needs to be chosen on a case-by-case basis but with a view to promoting competition. Without such consideration, procurement will tend to lead to concentrated markets in the long term, particularly where public purchases account for a large share of the demand in the relevant market.

E-procurement

E-procurement is a fast-spreading practice in many countries. India is well-placed to proceed in the same direction. There are many advantages, but also some drawbacks to the practice from the competition perspective.

Well-managed e-procurement can be effective against two of the main competition concerns. First, it can reduce barriers to entry and enhance participation. Online preparation and submission of bids reduces costs for suppliers and makes it easier for the authority to track responses to tender invitations.

Second, e-procurement militates against bid-rigging in a number of ways. With protocols on online correspondence in place, enquiries and responses between (anonymized) bidders and the procurement agency can be shared among all parties so that information flows are uniform. When online correspondence is archived and accessible to scrutiny, officials cannot exercise favouritism with impunity and will be protected from corporate pressure. Confidentiality in online submissions limits the flow of information to cartels about new entrants into the business; and when collusion is tacit, rather than overt, this impedes the double-guessing of rivals' intentions through their bidding tactics (Klemperer 2001). E-procurement also promotes transparency by reducing the possibility of interference and facilitating the monitoring of bids against suspicion of bid-rigging. Innovative tender designs can also be tried more easily, getting away from the single, sealed-bid procedure; for example, an agency could institute a reverse auction procedure. This would be equivalent to the procurement agency launching negotiations with several of the bidders, which is better practice than limiting negotiations to a single low-priced bidder.

The main concerns with e-procurement are the cost of implementing online systems and the difficulty of managing the procedure for smaller agencies and departments. E-procurement is also necessarily vulnerable to security concerns, i.e., information theft. In such a case, information transparency would be turned to the suppliers' advantage. A provision for cancellation of a tender would need to be in place and ready to be invoked in such circumstances.

Recent Reform Efforts

Two recent initiatives have the potential to make significant improvements to public procurement in India. Both draw on international good practice.

The first is the adoption of the 'Integrity Pact' (IP). This is an initiative of Transparency International, an international civil society organization of federated national chapters. The India chapter (Transparency International India, TII) includes many eminent persons among its advisers, notably very senior former civil servants. It has followed a unique path within Transparency International by appointing such persons as external assessors to look into complaints, rather than, as elsewhere, appointing full 'industry' outsiders such as judges or civil society activists.

The IP consists of an agreement between a government organization or department and all bidders for a contract. The IP sets out rights and obligations 'to the effect that neither side will pay, offer, demand or accept bribes and/or collude with competitors to obtain the contract'. Only those bidders that commit themselves to the IP are considered competent to participate in the bidding process, such that their signature becomes a preliminary qualification in the tendering process.

The government of India has endorsed the concept of the IP and issued instructions for its use. The CVC has issued a guideline note ('Standard Operating Procedure') for the adoption of the Integrity Pact and gives a role to independent external monitors in respect of all major procurements. The Department of Personnel and Training has suggested that all state chief secretaries are to consider adopting the IP in respect of PSUs. By May 2014, 49 central PSUs had committed to adopting the IP. The Ministry of Defence, in its 2008 Procurement Policy, has also proposed to adopt the IP in all defence deals of INR 100,000,000 and above (OECD 2010). In July 2011, the Ministry of Finance, on the advice of the Administrative Reforms Commission, issued a memorandum directing all ministries and government departments to make adherence to the IP a condition of all requests for proposals and tender documents above a certain monetary threshold.

The second initiative is the prospective enactment of a comprehensive national law on procurement. The proposed Public Procurement Law of India is based on established practice, as codified by the United Nations. UNCITRAL issued a revised Model Law on Public Procurement (the Model Law) in 2011. A formal Guide to Enactment of the text followed in 2012. UNCITRAL has also issued various informal explanatory documents to aid states in the drafting of a law appropriate to its national circumstances, with greater procedural detail than contained in the Model

Law (e.g., Nicholas n.d.). In ushering in greater standardization across jurisdictions, the Model Law is intended to facilitate international trade in procurement. Nevertheless, it does not include provisions focused on providing access to procurement opportunities for international businesses. This is the orientation of the World Trade Organization's General Procurement Agreement, to which India is not a signatory.

The proposed Indian law is an advance on previous practice in many respects:

- It streamlines and consolidates the previous regulatory framework, replacing an inchoate tangle of regulations and the multiple, fragmented guidelines to which procurement officials were supposed to conform.
- It focuses on the need to promote both competition and transparency, adopting a balanced approach. A dedicated policymaking institution will be created with centralized powers for framing regulations and reviewing certain procurements.
- Flexibility is enhanced through the introduction of two new provisions: for cancellation of tenders under suspicion of collusion (already present in the Tamil Nadu Act) and for competitive negotiations prior to contract with the top few bidders, not only with the winning bidder.
- A three-stage grievance redressal procedure is included, along the lines set out in the UNCITRAL Model Law.
- The law has provision for referral of cases to the CCI, greatly strengthening the potential for disciplining anticompetitive conduct on both supply and demand side in procurement markets.

According to the UN Office on Drugs and Crime, India's public procurement bill would enable India to achieve compliance with the stipulations contained in the UN Convention against Corruption (UNODC 2013).

The Indian law has not yet been enacted, three years after its tabling before parliament. Such a lag is normal for the passage of a national law in India. Even if the new law were passed, it might take many years before the central procurement authority becomes operational. Six years passed between the enactment of the competition law and the creation of the Competition Commission of India. At any rate, the slow passage of the law is indicative of the scale of the changes entailed in this policy reform, and perhaps also of the high degree of resistance to it – which testifies, in this context, to the need for change.

Coordination and Awareness-raising

Sound implementation of the new policies will require a high level of coordination between the various authorities concerned, notably between the new procurement authority and the CCI. There are strong complementarities between anticompetitive practices and corruption in public procurement. In India, as in many countries, enforcement of competition and mitigating of corruption is conducted separately, to the disadvantage of both. Once the new procurement agency is in place in India, a framework for joint enforcement will be needed to guide and formalize cooperation between it and the CCI as well as with the existing monitoring and vigilance bodies, notably the CAG and the CVC.

Various audiences will need to become aware of the new institutional landscape affecting procurement policy and the need to strengthen measures to promote competition in procurement markets.

The first audience comprises procurement officials at all levels. Agents will need to understand the importance of acting in accordance with the principles underlying the policy reform and of being alert to signs of bid-rigging in tender submissions. The possibility of bringing legal sanctions into play – and the importance of doing so – by way of referral of cases to the CCI constitutes a major change in administrative norms. CCI rulings are gradually refining applicable case law and creating the foundation for legal action. The process will be accelerated when referrals begin to be made by the administrative vigilance bodies. A coordination framework must include a robust process for determining sanctions against officials found to have supported anticompetitive conduct.

A pre-condition of smooth inter-agency coordination is that policy-makers understand the importance of finding ways to improve public procurement for all the reasons set out at the beginning of this chapter. In particular, economic growth and national development stand to gain from commitment to change in public procurement practices. It is also important to acknowledge that tensions exist at the heart of policymaking in this area, but that they are manageable: competition concerns should not necessarily predominate over transparency requirements, and vice versa. Last but not least, suppliers need to become aware that bid-rigging is a damaging practice that holds back efficiency and competitiveness at both firm and industry level. The judgement in the CCI bid-rigging case discussed above (*South Eastern Railway, Kolkata vs. M/s Orissa Concrete and Allied Industries Ltd and 28 other opponents*), cited the fact that the colluding suppliers did not know that such conduct was prohibited. On the introduction of the new procurement regime, all bidders will need to know that collusion and bid-rigging will be subject to legal sanction, not only from independent rulings of the CCI but through cross-agency referrals. The CCI has started work in this respect, publishing a series of advocacy booklets, including one on bid-rigging (CCI n.d.). Once the new Procurement Law is enacted, India will have a more powerful regulatory framework in place and attention will shift away from regulatory and legislated provisions towards the quality of implementation of a complex new integrated policy framework.

NOTES

1. Vaid (n.d.) notes two cases in which allegedly unreasonable terms and conditions were imposed by procurement agencies but the allegations were not upheld by the CCI (cases 15/2010 and 53/2011). See also the section on abuse of dominance.
2. www.conventuslaw.com/archive/india-behavioral-cases-cci-penalises-11-shoe-manufacturers-for-bid-rigging.
3. www.conventuslaw.com/archive/india-ccis-bid-to-curb-bid-rigging-cartels-in-india.

REFERENCES

CAG (2010–11a) *Procurement of Stores and Machinery in Ordnance Factories*, Report No 15, Comptroller and Auditor General.

CAG (2010–11b) *Bharat Heavy Electricals Ltd*, Report No 10, Comptroller and Auditor General.

CCI (n.d.) *Provisions Relating to Bid Rigging*, Advocacy Booklet No. 3, Competition Commission of India.

CVC (n.d.) *Analytical Study; Trends/Features in Cases Relating to (Indian) Railways.*

CVC (2002) *Common Irregularities/Lapses Observed in Stores/Purchase Contracts and Guidelines for Improvement in the Procurement System*, Chief Technical Examiner's Organisation.

CVC (2007) *Preventive Vigilance in Public Procurement – Study Based on the Power Sector*, CVC Office Memorandum No 12-02-1-CTE-6, Government of India, Central Vigilance Commission.

Klemperer, P. (2001) What really matters in auction design, *Journal of Economic Perspectives*, **16**(1): 169–89.

National Institute of Public Finance and Policy (2010) *Public Financial Management Performance Assessment Report*, New Delhi: National Institute of Public Finance and Policy.

Nicholas, C. (n.d.) *A Reform Tool: The 2011 UNCITRAL Model Law on Public Procurement and its Guide to Enactment*, EBRD Law in Transition, www.ebrd.com/downloads/research/law/lit113c.pdf.

OECD (2009) *Detecting Bid Rigging in Public Procurement*, Paris: Organisation for Economic Co-operation and Development.

OECD (2010) *Collusion and Corruption in Public Procurement*, DAF/COMP/GF(2101)6, Paris: Organisation for Economic Co-operation and Development.

OECD (2013) Public procurement spending, in *Government at a Glance 2013*, Paris: Organisation for Economic Co-operation and Development.

Sahu, P.K. (2014) Government procurement in India: the case of PSUs in the light of WTO procurement agreements, *Journal of Studies in Dynamics and Change*, **1**(2): 49–56.

The Statesman (2010) Panel recommends railways procurement overhaul, *The Statesman*, 31 August.

TERI (2008) Sustainable Public Procurements: Towards a Low Carbon Economy, New Delhi: The Energy and Resources Institute.

TERI (2012) *Public Procurement Policy in India and Competition Issues*, New Delhi: The Energy and Resources Institute.

TII (2010) *Implementation of Integrity Pact in India*, Transparency International India.

TII (2013) *Annual Report 2013*, www.transparencyindia.org/pdf/1420885668_Minute%20-%20FGD%20with%20IEM%20on%20IP%20-%2012%20September%202014(1).pdf.

UNODC (2013) *India: Probity in Public Procurement*, Geneva: United Nations Office on Drugs and Crime.

Vaid, S. (n.d.) *Bid Rigging in Public Procurement*, research paper, Competition Commission of India.

11. Public procurement in Morocco[1]

Lahcen Achy and Susan Joekes

SCOPE OF THE CHAPTER

Public procurement and competition law are both highly important fields of legislation and public policy. However, they have largely remained as separate compartments in respect of the design of regulation as well as intervention practices. The extent to which competition law is enforced in public procurement has received only limited attention in the literature. Instead, observers have chiefly focused on the restrictions to market competition generated by the conduct of private suppliers taking part in public procurement, through practices such as collusion and bid-rigging. The effect of public procurement regulations and administrative procedures in generating such conduct, and thus the distortions they can create in the market, were often left underexplored. This chapter is an attempt to fill part of that gap in knowledge by investigating the role of competition provisions in promoting the efficiency of public procurement and ensuring value for public money in the case of Morocco. The chapter demonstrates that, to reach its potential as engine for economic growth and to enable an efficient use of public money, the rules and procedures for public procurement need to be actively pro-competitive as far as possible, and certainly must not inhibit or distort market competition.

Public procurement accounts for about 16 per cent of GDP in Morocco and offers business opportunities to a large number of companies in different economic sectors through the country. The chapter uses a two-pronged approach to assess the state of competition in public procurement in Morocco. First, it examines existing regulatory provisions from the competition perspective. Second, the chapter draws on data from a sample of procurements awarded by selected contracting authorities to analyze their key characteristics with special reference to the structure of the particular markets involved.

The overall procurement market does not seem to suffer from lack of competition insofar as a very large number of suppliers and contracting entities are involved. The sheer size of the market may also be expected to offer opportunities for new as well as experienced bidders. Examination of contracts awarded reveals, however, that public procurement buyers operate in segmented markets comprising many niches in specific sectors that serve particular contracting authorities or particular geographical areas and exhibit different market conditions. The intensity of competition can vary greatly across such niches even within the same economic sector, depending on contracting authorities' behaviour. Similarly, the same contracting authority can face different levels of competition in its markets depending on the product or service line being purchased and on suppliers' behaviour.

The main reason cited by procurement buyers for rejecting bids in public tenders (open, restricted or two-stage tenders) is suppliers' lack of experience and poor references. Contracting authorities are risk-averse and this leads them to favour suppliers with which they have dealt in the past. Internalizing such bias, most suppliers target their bidding efforts on a limited number of procuring entities and ignore the rest.

Regarding requests for quotation and negotiated contracts, suppliers' 'connections' with contracting authorities seemed to play a major role in successful bidding. These two procedures can offer easier access than open tenders to new entrants. In practice, however, requests for quotation and negotiated contracts provided limited opportunities for suppliers that had a track record in their line of business, backed up by solid references, but with no history with the particular tendering authority involved. The lowest bidder rule that is properly embedded in public procurement may have to play a more important role in the awarding of contracts for new entrants that either lack experience or have no connections inside the contracting authority.

Both suppliers and tendering officers consider that even though public procurement provides room for competition, it is regularly marred by favouritism. In this respect, the procurement authorities are often complicit with and facilitate suppliers' market segmentation tactics. Even with a comprehensive set of regulations, policymakers may not be able to foster competition if the behaviours of procurement agents that distort competition – whether done deliberately or through serious negligence – are not effectively detected and punished.

In light of the critical role of public procurement in the Morocco's economy, the authorities should take four main steps: create at a professionally trained staff that can monitor supplier behaviour and detect non-compliance cases; grant the status of law to the rules governing public procurement; strengthen the appeals system; and better define sanctions for non-compliance by way of administrative or criminal sanctions, as appropriate.

THE PUBLIC PROCUREMENT REGULATORY FRAMEWORK

To achieve greater efficiency in public procurement, the legislator seeks to promote competition among suppliers. The various regulatory changes made over the past decade have provided, among other things, more information on markets and promoted optimization of the auction process to facilitate more competitive market conditions.

Nevertheless, Morocco's public procurement regulatory framework is still not comprehensive. It only partially covers the needs-assessment phase of procurement as well as the performance evaluation of implemented contracts. Some of the provisions tend to create entry barriers due to unreasonably restrictive selection criteria and weakness of the complaints and appeal mechanisms offered to suppliers. The regulatory framework contains no penalties for infringement of its provisions. A new decree, in which the current framework's weaknesses are addressed, is being drafted. Its approval and entry into force, however, have been subject to delay.

Morocco's public procurement is governed by decree no. 2-06-388. This entered into force in February 2007 and is based on international standards including the model of the United Nations Commission on International Trade Law (UNCITRAL), the World Trade Organization (WTO) agreement on procurement and the directives of major donors including the European Union and the World Bank Group.

The regulations cover governmental departments and local authorities and their subsidiary entities such as state-owned enterprises, public subsidiaries, joint ventures, dealerships and other organizations subject to state financial control. The Department of National Defence usually benefits from specific exemptions. Some entities are not explicitly subject to public procurement regulations but are not excluded from them either; this can create ambiguous cases where the regulations are not systematically complied with.

Procurement procedures are laid out in considerable detail in the regulations. The objective is to ensure competition among bidders and transparency in the award of contracts. Six procurement methods are defined: open tenders; restricted tenders; two-stage tenders (where only those suppliers who meet minimum technical and financial requirements in the first stage are invited to tender in the second stage); competitive procedures (in which the contracting authority selects a plan or project, such as an urban planning, architectural or engineering project, on a competitive basis); negotiated tenders (with advertising used in exceptional circumstances); and, finally, requests for quotation[2] used for small-value procurements (less than US$20,000).

An update of the 2007 decree is in preparation. The new regulatory framework is expected to give greater emphasis to transparency of procedures and value for money in government expenditure. It is also concerned with strengthening market competition – ensuring equal treatment of bidders and improving their guarantees of fair treatment – by providing better ways for registration of complaints and access to appeal mechanisms.

Public Procurement Provisions from the Competition Perspective

The importance of public procurement led the legislature to frame the regulations to comply with three principles: transparency and morality in the public sphere; competition and equal treatment of bidders; and efficiency of public expenditure including procedural simplicity.

These principles promote, directly or indirectly, competition in public procurement. Competition is explicit in the second principle and in the spirit of the first and third principles. Transparency and morality are necessary for competition as they involve fighting cartels among bidders as well as favouritism. Efficiency of public spending and simplicity of procedures stimulate competition by reducing regulatory barriers to entry.

Four main forms of anticompetitive practice arise in public procurement due directly to the behaviour of actors or indirectly by regulatory provisions designed either to ensure the morality of procurement procedures or to control expenditure.

First, there could be an agreement between a contracting authority and a supplier that involves favouritism and corruption. Second, there could be an agreement among suppliers to collude and behave as cartel. Third, there could be entry barriers that increase the cost of participation and regulatory barriers. Finally, there could be a lack of market attractiveness due to unrealistic requirements of the bidders.

Admissibility and Pre-qualification

Public procurement regulations give minimal guidance to the authorities on how to identify acceptable bids; that is, bids that can be considered for selection for the contract award. Article 18 of the decree of February 2007 stipulates a basic set of standard criteria, which are supplemented by others in particular economic sectors.

To understand how rejections are handled in practice, procurement authorities were questioned and 30 calls to tender, in which the criteria were specified and had weights are assigned to them, were analyzed.

Procurement officials reported two main reasons for rejection (non-consideration) of submissions: the bidder's lack of experience or a skill mismatch between the staff suggested by the bidder and the procuring entity's requirements. Contracting authorities appear to have a highly risk-averse approach, favouring suppliers that 'have already shown their proofs', especially in providing similar services to other entities. The criterion of 'experience and references' was granted nearly 50 per cent of the total weight, and assessment of staff skills accounted for 25 per cent. There seemed to be no operational threshold for experience on its own. Procurement staff remarked that the 'more a supplier had won bids, the better it will be placed to implement other public contracts' even if an experience-rich supplier's methods or technologies had become obsolete. This filtering process constitutes a strong barrier to entry for potential new suppliers.

A qualification system (based on a classification of building and public works companies) was established by the Ministry of Equipment and Transport by decree and adopted later by other government departments such as Agriculture, Housing, Water and Forestry. Classification and qualification is mandatory for participation in tenders exceeding 5 million dirham (approximately US$500,000). Qualification can reinforce the supplier's position for other, lower-value procurements.

Qualified companies are classified according to their production capability, the volume of work they can handle and their technical performance. A large number of these categories include only a small numbers of companies, creating market concentration in the relevant procurement market. In terms of competition, the challenge lies in the development of company capabilities in the relevant part of the economy and the entry of new players into the relevant procurement markets. This suggests that more collaboration among suppliers would be useful, partly as a way of enhancing outsourcing.

Bidding Conditions

Table 11.1 shows how bidding conditions laid down in the regulations are translated into actual tender documents and whether they serve as impediments to submission of proposals in any respect. The information comes from examination of a sample of 36 tender documents from four selected ministries.

In general, the lowest-price rule is applied in assessment of admitted and qualified bids, with one major exception. Procurement of studies and project management services is treated as a special case. These contracts can be of very different sizes and types depending on the department's specific agenda. For example, procurements of this type can be high-value if a

Table 11.1 Bidding conditions based on the regulations as found in tender documents

Cumulated documentation	Approvals and certificates	Evaluation criteria	Amount of bid security deposit
The regulations indicate that all relevant documentation has to be reproduced in the tender call (19 out of 36 regulations have this requirement). In the majority of cases, additional elements are duplicates of documents already in the dossier. The usefulness of this can be questioned.	A licence or certificate is required in more than half the cases. In the case of procurements for works, the regulations state that authorization replaces the technical file. But in almost one case out of four, the contracting authority also requests a technical proposal. In those cases, rating criteria are not given.	Systematic evaluation criteria are only specified for procurement of services. These criteria emphasize experience and knowledge of the candidate. But in some cases the tender seems to describe a person, not a profile. Some 'experience' requirements seem excessive.	The amount of security deposits required ranges from \$120 to \$60,000. The relevance of very small – or very large – bid security deposits is questionable. The bid security deposit may be used as a means of selection, but this is not regularly explained.

Source: Conseil de la Concurrence and Mazars (n.d.), based on compilation of 36 tender documents released by contracting authorities.

ministry is setting up a new strategy, making changes to its internal organization or undertaking computerization projects. Because of their complex nature, these procurements are not granted under the rule of lowest bidder. The risk that competition considerations are set aside is therefore higher in this sector. There is greater scope for favouritism by the procuring entity.

Complaints and Litigation Procedures

Tenderers can use three methods to complain and express their dissatisfaction with the procurement process. They can address a complaint to the administrative hierarchy, to the public procurement committee or to an administrative tribunal.

First, any competitor can address a complaint to the respective contracting authority for violation of the procurement procedure or it can dispute the reasons for rejecting its application. The contracting authority needs to provide an answer within a time limit of seven days. In the case of an unsatisfactory response, the competitor can submit its complaint to the relevant minister, who has the capacity to order remedial action, suspend the complaint or cancel it. In practice, since no time limit for the minister's response is mentioned in procurement regulations, such complaints lead generally only to extension of the deadline for settling disputes.

In case the minister's response is unsatisfactory for the competitor, the latter may submit a detailed request to the secretary-general of the government, which may in turn address the request to the public procurement review board (OECD 2009a). The opinion of the public procurement board is communicated to the prime minister and the minister concerned, but it is purely advisory.

There is no time limit and the article does not state how the appellant can carry forward his case in the face of non-response by the administration. Moreover, competitors cannot contest the procurement method or selection criteria. They cannot contest a decision of the procurement committee to reject all bids or a decision of the contracting authority to withdraw the tender. Such restrictions significantly reduce the force of the guarantee supposedly enabling competitors to safeguard their rights.

Finally, any discontented competitor can resort to the administrative courts to preserve its interests. In practice, applicants rarely resort to the courts in order to preserve a good relationship with the public administration.

Interviews with civil servants in charge of public procurements provided information on the character of complaints. The findings are set out in Table 11.2.

In practice, competitors rarely formally complain due to the weaknesses in and complexity of the regulatory procedure. They prefer to lodge complaints informally. Most pleas and litigation focus on the implementation of public procurement contracts, usually caused by issues related to deadlines and failure to respect contract specifications.

MARKET SIZE AND CONCENTRATION

Data on procurement procedures for this section come from Morocco's General Treasury and cover selected contracting authorities (both central

Table 11.2 Timing and frequency of supplier complaints according to procurement officials

	Before procurement award	Complaints on the award of contract	Complaints related to implementation of the contract	Complaints related to payment of the contract
Frequency	Very low (< 2 per cent of procurements)	Very low (< 2 per cent of procurements)	Moderate (5–10 per cent of procurements)	Variable depending on the department
Comments	Questions on the consultation documents are common but complaints are rare	Official complaints are rare but informal (verbal) complaints are common (10 per cent of consultations)	Complaints relate to problems in execution (delays, respect of specifications)	Informants indicated that these complaints are most likely in local procurements (municipalities)

Source: Conseil de la Concurrence and Mazars (n.d.) based on interviews with civil servants in charge of public procurements in selected contracting authorities.

and local). The available data cover uses of various tendering procedures for different procurement purposes (works, products and services) in total and disaggregated by selected lines of business.

The focus is on four ministries: the Ministries of Equipment and Transport; Agriculture and Fisheries; Energy, Mining, Water and Environment; and Health. These all have large procurement budgets, surpassed only by the Ministries of Defence and Education. Added together, they make up approximately 38 per cent of government contracts awarded during the period 2006–9. Table 11.3 shows, for each ministry, the number of contracts struck and the proportion of contracts awarded through an open tendering process (by value and by number).

In terms of procurement method, open tendering procedures were overwhelmingly predominant in all ministries. The share of procurements implemented through open tendering ranged between 87 and 98 per cent. This finding is in accordance with the Moroccan procurement regulations that require open tendering as the general procedure. However, non-open tendering procurements tended to be used for the largest contracts. For the Ministry of Agriculture, the average value of a non-open tender procurement represented two to seven times the value of an open tender contract. The Ministry of Equipment and Transport and the Ministry of Health

Table 11.3 Number of procurements issued and proportion of open tenders in, selected ministries, annual averages in the period 2006–9

	Number of procurements issued	Percentage of open tenders in all procurements (based on the value of procurements)	Percentage of open tenders in all procurements (based on the number of procurements)
Ministry of Equipment and Transport	1,670	89.4	98
Ministry of Agriculture and Fisheries	950	86.8	96
Ministry of Energy, Mining, Water and Environment	92	98.0	99
Ministry of Health	1,440	96.0	95

Source: Conseil de la Concurrence and Mazars (n.d.), based on Moroccan General Treasury data.

recorded similar patterns. The value of one of the two contracts awarded by the Ministry of Energy through negotiated tendering was 17 times greater than the average value of a procurement award; this was an extreme case.

Within the period, the trend in all four ministries was for the average value of procurement contracts to increase over time. This could have been due to a general increase in the price of services or driven by an increase in the technical elimination threshold following the entry into force of the 2007 decree. If the latter, it could mean that the cost increase was associated with better quality. However, the increases might instead (or as well) have been driven by oligopolistic situations or by supplier collusion.

Table 11.4 lists the number of procurement awarded during the period 2006–9 categorized by reference to their 'object', i.e., the sector of economic activity, defined as works, products or services. The ministries vary in the respective shares of the procurement object and the pattern is quite unstable over time. The Ministry of Energy, Mining, Water and Environment presents a particularly puzzling picture; the reasons for this are not clear. The main point is that in the other three ministries, a large number of procurements of all types, and of many different values,[3] are regularly carried out by the purchasing officers of these departments.

Table 11.4 Number of procurements by object for the selected ministries, 2006–9

	2006	2007	2008	2009
Ministry of Equipment and Transport				
Works	629	669	602	676
Supplies	454	430	321	322
Services	786	718	557	528
Ministry of Agriculture				
Works	399	339	296	303
Supplies	637	540	377	382
Services	113	182	107	135
Ministry of Energy, Mining, Water and Environment				
Works	1	1	138	160
Supplies	11	5	10	16
Services	2	7	7	17
Ministry of Health				
Works	311	246	191	207
Supplies	540	922	793	893
Services	301	278	317	391

Source: Conseil de la Concurrence and Mazars (n.d.) based on Morocco's General Treasury data.

The Size and Structure of 'Procurement Markets'

This section examines the nature of procurement markets, defined as markets in which the procurement authority is the single actor on the demand side and potential suppliers – submitting bids in response to tender invitations – are the actors on the supply side. Those suppliers that do not submit bids in a specific tender are not treated as participants in the market. On the basis of this definition, the existence of competition in the specific procurement market by object (product line) does not guarantee that the competitive process is manifest within any specific tender on the same market. Collusion and bid-rigging on the part of private entities taking part in public procurement can deter other entities from bidding and distort competition (Sánchez Graells 2015). On the other hand, the effect of public procurement regulations and administrative practices can create barriers to entry and restrain market competition.

The bid rate, which indicates the number of participants in a tender, is a first indicator of market structure. For the period 2006–9, on average three bids were submitted for every tender issued by the central procurement department of the Ministry of Agriculture and 2.6 bids were submitted for provincial department tenders.

Central departments of the Ministry of Agriculture submissions were made by 198 suppliers, of which 68 were awarded one or more contracts. One in ten of the 68 companies participated in at least two central government department bids. All of them were located in the capital city, Rabat, where the central departments are located. The capital, Rabat, and the largest commercial city in Morocco, Casablanca, are situated less than 100km apart. No supplier outside the Casablanca–Rabat axis bid for more than two central department tenders.

The Provincial Departments of Agriculture (PDA) received 1,263 bids during the period 2006–9. A total of 733 different suppliers took part in the bids, of which 322 were awarded contracts. Approximately 8 per cent of the winning companies participated in more than one PDA call for tender. Most participated in tenders located in their geographical area, but suppliers headquartered in the Casablanca–Rabat axis also participated in tenders outside their region.

The size of the tender can be a factor in determining the number of bidders. Some suppliers focus only on large-size contracts and ignore small-size contracts, leaving them to other competitors. The size of particular procurement markets may be also limited by the specific nature of the product line. For instance, only a tiny number of firms supply geological maps commissioned by the Ministry of Energy. Requirements for references can close up the market further for domestic providers, even where they have experience of supplying the relevant products on a smaller scale. For the Ministry of Energy, procurements of numerous product lines (including office supplies, computer supplies and equipment, printing works, geological studies and consultancy) essentially operate in oligopolistic market structures with a small number of companies winning 80 per cent of total value of procurements. The high level of concentration arises in part from requirements for references and certificates; this persuades suppliers to specialize. But in many cases the products are widely produced and other factors must be in play.

Suppliers tend to position themselves in well-defined business segments and make tender offers only in those segments. In respect of Ministry of Agriculture procurement, only a very small share (3 per cent) of bidding companies put in proposals in response to tenders from more than one central or provincial department.

Table 11.5 Business sectors covered in procurement events, 2006–9

Type	Code	Business sector
Works	W1	Roads
	W2	Maintenance
	W3	Road signs
	W4	Construction and development
	W5	Printing
Products	P1	Office furniture
	P2	Medical equipment
	P3	Office equipment
	P4	Hygiene and disinfection products
	P5	Computing supplies
	P6	Technical equipment and tools
	P7	Meteorological equipment
	P8	Other equipment
Services	S1	Computing services
	S2	Studies and business analysis
	S3	Security
	S4	Transportation
	S5	Accommodation and reception

Source: Conseil de la Concurrence and Mazars (n.d.) based on the classification of public procurement event by their object.

Market Concentration in 'Procurement Markets'

Using our chosen definition of the market for procurements, it is possible to calculate levels of market concentration for selected business sectors and contracting authorities (see Table 11.5).

Essentially these calculations pick up variation in the pattern of bidding about the low bid rates described earlier. Different indicators (number of bidders per public procurement, Herfindahl–Hirschman Index, etc.) are calculated for each market episode, comprising one business sector and one contracting authority, in which four contracting authorities were involved during the fiscal year 2009–10. The authorities were the Ministry of Agriculture and Fishing, the Ministry of Energy and Mining, the urban district of Casablanca and the rural commune of Sidi Yahia Zaërs (SYZ). The sample is made up of 236 suppliers awarded at least one procurement, among which 128 were with the Ministry of Agriculture; 19 with the Ministry of Energy, Mining, Water and Environment; 55 with the urban district of Casablanca; and 34 companies with the rural commune of SYZ.

Table 11.6 Sectoral concentration indexes (aggregate values)

Sector	Value of HHI	Level of concentration
P5: Computing supplies	2,178	High
P3: Office equipment	1,043	Moderate
P6: Technical equipment and tools	1,020	Moderate
S2: Studies and business analysis	758	Low
W4: Construction & Development	203	Low

Source: Conseil de la Concurrence and Mazars (n.d.). The values refer to the HHI based on the number of suppliers competing for public procurements in each business sector.

The share of suppliers that were awarded contracts in several sectors by the same contracting authority was around 12 per cent for the Ministry of Agriculture, 11.5 per cent for the urban district of Casablanca and 5 per cent for the Ministry of Energy. For the rural commune of SYZ, however, 44 per cent of the suppliers had contracts in several sectors. This finding may be explained by the fact the rural commune purchases mostly simple products, services and works that can be supplied by the same companies or due to other factors, such as that small contracts in the periphery attract a limited number of suppliers.

For the Department of Agriculture (both the central departments and provincial branches [PDA]), 10 per cent of suppliers have contracts with different central departments and 9 per cent were present in different PDAs. Only one supplier was awarded a contract with both a central and a provincial department of agriculture.

Concentration by sector was estimated by aggregating the value of procurement and market shares of different suppliers. The Herfindahl–Hirschman Index (HHI) was calculated for five sectors, as shown in Table 11.6. The value of the HHI ranges from 0 to more than 10,000. It indicates high concentration for values exceeding 1800, moderate concentration for values between 1000 and 1800 and low concentration for values less than 1000.

The sectoral concentration indexes show a situation of intense competition (low concentration) in construction and development and in 'studies and business analysis'. The sectors of 'technical equipment and tools' and 'office supplies and equipment' are characterized by moderate concentration, whereas 'computing supplies' is a highly concentrated market.

Concentration indexes by contracting authorities suggest a different pattern. In general, competition is more restricted as suppliers tend to focus on a limited number of contractors. Therefore, from the perspective

Table 11.7 Construction and development (W4) concentration indexes

Contracting authority	Value of HHI	Level of concentration
All procurement authorities in the sample	203	Low
Ministry of Agriculture	160	Low
Central departments	1,715	High
Provincial departments	170	Low
PDA Agadir	978	Moderate
PDA Oujda	1,157	Moderate
Urban district of Casablanca	3,205	High

Source: Conseil de la Concurrence and Mazars (n.d.). The values refer to the HHI based on the number of suppliers competing for public procurements by each contracting authority. Data are lacking for the Ministry of Energy and the rural commune of SYZ.

Table 11.8 Office equipment (P3) concentration indexes

Contracting authority	Value of HHI	Level of concentration
All procurement authorities in the sample	1,043	Moderate
Ministry of Agriculture	831	Low
Central departments	854	Low
Ministry of energy	2,404	High
Rural commune of SYZ	1,600	Moderate

Source: Conseil de la Concurrence and Mazars (n.d.). The values refer to HHI based on the number of suppliers competing for public procurements by each contracting authority. Data are lacking for PDAs, as well as for the urban district of Casablanca.

of the contracting authority, the market seems less open to competition. In that regard, the scale of the analysis is important.

Table 11.7 indicates that for the sector of works (W4: Construction and development), market competition seems to prevail for the PDAs, when taken together. This is not the case when each of them is treated individually. The aggregate concentration index for PDAs measured by the HHI amounts to 170, indicating an absence of concentration. By contrast, indexes for individual provincial departments show the presence of moderate to high market concentration with values of HHI exceeding 1000. Tellingly, the large urban district of Casablanca is shown to face a highly concentrated market.[4]

Similarly, for the sector of 'office equipment and supplies' (P3), Table 11.8 reports a value of HHI of 1043 when tenders awarded by the public authorities in the sample are aggregated together. There is an absence of concentration for the Ministry of Agriculture, but a moderate level of concentration for the rural commune of SYZ and a high concentration for the Ministry of Energy.

'Computing equipment and supplies' (P5) seems much more concentrated in terms of awarded contracts both at the aggregate level and for individual contracting authority for which enough data is available. The HHI amounts to 2174 for all contracting authorities in the sample, 1923 for the Ministry of Agriculture and 3030 for the Ministry of Energy.

In 'Technical equipment and tools' (P6), the level of concentration seems moderate at the aggregate level, contrasting with the situation among individual contracting authorities for which data is available. The PDAs show absence of concentration with HHI of 280. On the other hand, the Ministry of Energy faces an extremely high concentration with inverse HHI of 7692. This is due to the purchase of highly specialized equipment that can be provided by a very limited number of suppliers.

As for the service sector of 'Studies and business analysis' (S2), the level of concentration seems low at the aggregate level but higher only for the PDAs.

IMPEDIMENTS TO COMPETITION IN PROCUREMENT

Market Access Barriers

Three categories of barriers to entry are examined in this chapter: regulatory, structural and strategic. The first category is driven by the regulatory framework. Structural barriers are sector-specific and relate to production costs and demand. By contrast, strategic barriers are created or deliberately strengthened by existing contractors to deter new entries in the market.

Tables 11.9, 11.10 and 11.11 set out a detailed picture of the strength of entry barriers by type of procurement (works, products and services) and by procedure (open tendering, restrictive tendering, two-stage tendering, negotiated tendering and call for quotation).

The tables show that overall barriers seem to be generally lower for 'products'. Strategic barriers, on the other hand, are the most significant and present in all types of procurements (works, products and services). Barriers of this type can, however, be strengthened or diminished by the contracting authority in the way that the specifications are drafted.

Strategic barriers are the outcome of a game of connections and appropriate price-setting, which is of critical importance because of the lowest-price rule that drives the award of public procurement contracts, once bids

Table 11.9 Works: barriers to entry by tender procedure

	Open tendering	Restricted tendering	Two-stage tendering	Negotiated procurement	Call for quotation
Regulatory barriers					
Complex procedure	2	2	2	1	1
Criteria for selecting bids	6	6	6	5	6
Guarantee of fair treatment	3	3	3	3	3
Deadlines	5	5	5	5	4
Structural barriers					
Infrastructure	3	3	3	3	3
Expertise	5	5	5	5	1
Economies of scale	3	3	3	3	3
Segmentation	1	1	1	1	1
Authority's capacity	5	5	5	4	4
Strategic barriers					
Price setting	6	6	6	5	6
Connections	5	6	5	6	6

Note: Barrier intensity takes scores ranging for one to six (6: highest intensity and 1: lowest intensity).

Source: Conseil de la Concurrence and Mazars (n.d.).

are through the selection filter. Thus, suppliers seek in the first instance to build connections with the contracting authority to better communicate their offer and influence the specification of the demand in a way that would benefit them, or to better understand the needs of the contracting authority and adjust their offers to fit those needs. When there is no connection with the contracting authority, suppliers would opt for reducing their prices in order to win the procurement. Those suppliers who win procurements based on connections can impose higher prices.

Connections created with a contracting authority play a substantial role in access to calls for quotations and negotiated tendering. These two procedures, which would otherwise seem to be relatively easier for a new entrant to overcome, become uncertain for a supplier with solid references but without any connection with the contracting authority.

For open and restricted (with pre-qualification) tenders, barriers related to 'selection criteria for bids' and 'expertise' are the most binding. These two barriers are related to the applicant's experience in similar conditions. The contracting authority tends to have a preference for the candidate that is familiar with the tendering process and has fulfilled a previous contract.

Some entry barriers tend to be similar across all types of procurements

Table 11.10 Products: barriers to entry by tender procedure

	Open tendering	Restricted tendering	Two-stage tendering	Negotiated procurement	Call for quotation
Regulatory barriers					
Complex procedure	1	1	1	1	1
Criteria for selecting bids	5	5	5	5	6
Guarantee of fair treatment	3	3	3	3	3
Deadlines	4	4	4	4	2
Structural barriers					
Infrastructure	2	2	2	2	2
Expertise	5	5	5	5	2
Economies of scale	3	3	3	3	3
Segmentation	1	1	1	1	1
Authority's capacity	4	4	4	2	2
Strategic barriers					
Price setting	6	6	6	5	6
Connections	5	6	5	6	6

Note: Barrier intensity takes scores ranging for one to six (6: highest intensity and 1: lowest intensity)

Source: Conseil de la Concurrence and Mazars (n.d.).

(works, products and services). This is mainly due to the fact that the intensity of barriers depends on other characteristics: the product line, the size of contracts and the capability of the contracting authority are more important causes of the level of competition. Some types of procurement tend to confer incumbent advantages on the contract holder because no market activity takes place except that financed by public expenditure, for instance, in provision of road signs, installation of concrete pipes, etc. Some suppliers don't participate in tenders that are too large or too small for them; and some suppliers restrict their bids to a geographical area, either voluntarily for objective reasons such as the high cost of moving production equipment or because of an agreement. Some suppliers expect competitors to respect the special relationship that they may have with specific contracting authorities and conversely are reluctant to intervene elsewhere and refrain from bidding in competitors' 'reserved' markets.

Market entry events have been identified through data from a sample of suppliers to the Ministry of Agriculture. Table 11.12 shows the reasons given by suppliers for non-attainment of a contract award in general compared to the reasons given in cases where they lost out to a new entrant.

Despite the difficulty of identifying a new entrant in public procurement – suppliers are here identified simplistically as new entrants as far as the

Table 11.11 Services: barriers to entry by tender procedure

	Open tendering	Restricted tendering	Two-stage tendering	Negotiated procurement	Call for quotation
Regulatory barriers					
Complex procedure	2	2	2	1	1
Criteria for selecting bids	6	6	6	5	6
Guarantee of fair treatment	4	4	4	4	3
Deadlines	5	5	5	5	4
Structural barriers					
Infrastructure	2	2	2	2	2
Expertise	5	5	5	5	2
Economies of scale	3	3	3	3	3
Segmentation	1	1	1	1	1
Authority's capacity	5	5	5	3	3
Strategic barriers					
Price setting	6	6	6	5	6
Connections	5	6	5	6	6

Note: Barrier intensity takes scores ranging for one to six (6: highest intensity and 1: lowest intensity).

Source: Conseil de la Concurrence and Mazars (n.d.).

Table 11.12 Reasons for non-award of procurements in general and in the case of a winning bid from a new entrant, Ministry of Agriculture procurements

	Reasons for non-award in general	Reasons for non-award where contract was awarded to a new entrant
Technical criteria	53	41
Price-related criteria	35	45
Administrative criteria	12	14

Source: Conseil de la Concurrence and Mazars (n.d.).

contracting authority is concerned – some key elements can be identified. When a contract is won by a newcomer, the likelihood that other bids have been rejected for price-related reasons increases 10 per cent. There is a very small increased probability of non-award of a contract on administrative grounds (2 per cent).

It appears therefore that price remains the key determinant of a supplier's ability to enter a new market. This suggests the importance of maintaining the lowest-price bid rule in the face of changes in regulation. However, it raises the possibility that quality may be compromised in the provision of the work or product. Currently, contracting authorities have limited capability to assess quality. The practice of relying exclusively on price without controlling for product quality is not optimal.

Concerted Submissions

Bids are said to be rigged when bidders, which are in principle competitors, reach an agreement in order to increase their margin (or secure it with minimal effort) above the level they could attain in a market open to competition. The margin is generally increased at the expense of the purchaser who will face higher prices and/or lower-quality services. Bid-rigging defeats open tendering procedures, reduces confidence in the system and costs money to the taxpayer.

The Organisation for Economic Co-operation and Development (OECD 2009b) describes four strategies frequently used in bid-rigging cases: fake bids that aim at providing an appearance of genuine competition through excessively high bids or bids that don't meet the buyer's requirements; elimination schemes that result in the withdrawal of accomplices' bids before the end of the process; rotating tenders, when accomplices participate in all (or most) bids but arrange that each of them will win in turn; and market-sharing, where suppliers divide markets and agree not to compete with each other for certain customers or on certain geographic areas.

No cases of collusion have as yet been investigated or brought to the courts in Morocco. The analysis here of bids for the Ministry of Agriculture has shown that suppliers frequently limit their bids to a single procurement authority, which suggests a high level of market-sharing. The procurement regulations can be scrutinized for the vulnerability of the procurement system in respect of other strategies of collusion.

Vulnerability to Bid-rigging

The OECD guidelines identify a set of characteristics that expose particular sectors and procurement markets to bid-rigging and recommends ways of overcoming the vulnerability. Table 11.13 assesses the regulations and actual procurement practices in relation to the OECD recommendations.

Based on Table 11.13, it appears that the system set up in Morocco is vulnerable to bid-rigging. One issue raised by the vulnerability analysis is the public bid opening procedure. This stems from a trade-off made when drafting the 1998 and 2007 decrees, which contained a commitment to

Table 11.13 Assessment of Moroccan procurement regulations and practices in relation to OECD guidelines

OECD recommendation	Morocco's regulation	Prevailing practice
Collect and share information on a market so as to better understand that market and be able to optimize spending. Develop in-house expertise.	No scheme to promote collection and sharing of information on different markets.	The qualification and classification system set by the Ministry of Equipment and Transport enables procurement officials to have some knowledge of sectors covered.
Design tendering procedures to ensure maximum participation of genuine competing suppliers by reducing bid costs, opening participation to suppliers from other regions, etc.	The Prime Ministerial Circular No. 7/2007 requires that tendering processes are moved online. It offers flexibility to all applicants (domestic and foreign).	The bid security deposit system is maintained, which limits participation. The launch of the public procurement portal has been subject to several delays. Rigidity of the tendering procedure generates a significant cost for small bidders.
The specifications must be clear and not drafted in a way that favours anyone. They must focus on functional performance or the outcome to be achieved, rather than on implementation rules. Predictability of procurements' outcomes should be avoided.	The regulations stipulate clear non-discriminatory rules and criteria (2007 decree (Articles 15 and 18), and Circular 3/2007 of the Prime Minister on 'Elaboration of Medium Expenditure Framework (MTEF)'.	The drafting of special requirements may sometimes ease the award of contracts to a particular bidder. Description of actions to be implemented regularly favours implementation rules at the expense of functional performance.
Design the tender procedure to reduce communication among competitors; support detection of factors facilitating	Procedures promote transparency, to the extent that competitors are informed of prices charged by all	Practices are consistent with regulations in this instance.

Table 11.13 (continued)

OECD recommendation	Morocco's regulation	Prevailing practice
collusion within a general framework of transparency.	bidders. This increases vulnerability to bid-rigging as it allows competitors to get to know each other better.	
Selection and allocation criteria must not deter credible bidders (especially small and medium-sized suppliers).	Section 18 of the 2007 decree aims to standardize and streamline the selection criteria.	Multiple criteria are used coupled with high (and sometimes unnecessary) requirements of expertise and resources. This limits competition and favours collusion.
Educate officers to suspect bid-rigging and facilitate detection (bid-rigging can often be detected by scrutinizing procurements over time).	Implementation provisions stipulate that staff in charge of public procurement must be trained.	The majority of officials in charge of public procurements have not taken part in any specific training. There is no systematic monitoring of public procurements.

Source: Conseil de la Concurrence and Mazars (n.d.).

transparency to fight corruption. It was decided to disseminate transparent financial information about bids at the risk of favouring the emergence of cartels.

The present system suffers from poor training of officials in charge of drafting consultation documents and conducting tenders. Procurement officials are almost entirely unaware of the risks of and harms caused by bid-rigging.

On the other hand, the shift to e-government has been slow. The public procurement portal needs to be improved to facilitate access to documents and improve search quality, and bandwidth provision needs to be enhanced. Delays in e-procurement penalize competition and increase vulnerability to harm from collusion.

The absence of an observatory of public procurement or similar institution with the powers of identifying bid-rigging is a key weakness in the system, especially since solid approaches for detecting and preventing bid-rigging have been greatly improved worldwide in recent years.

The OECD proposes a series of ways to facilitate the detection of cartels by an observatory, as follows:

- Search for warning signals and revealing patterns in the way suppliers undertake their bids and analyze the frequency at which contracts are awarded as well as their geographical distribution.
- Review and compare documents submitted by competitors to detect signs of bid-rigging. For instance, different bids may contain similar calculation errors or a large number of identical estimates for some items.
- In cases of requests for quotation, search for 'fake' bids. Signals of fake bidding are the existence of unduly large price differences between the winning bid and other bids and large price differences in the offers of a single supplier in different procurements.
- Be alert for statements suggesting that suppliers may have agreed or coordinated their prices or their sale practices. For instance, statements revealing the existence of non-viable, fictitious or symbolic tenders or use of the same words by several bidders to justify high prices.
- Examine behaviours that suggest that bidders may have had the opportunity to discuss prices, or that suggest that a supplier is behaving in a way that only benefits other suppliers.
- Examine indicators of potential bid-rigging closely, but do not automatically interpret them as evidence of bid-rigging. Suspicious behaviour repeated over time can often offer the best evidence. For this reason, it is crucial to carefully store all information in order to be able to establish bidders' pattern of behaviour over time.

Competition Distorting Practices in the Procurement Lifecycle

In general, competition mechanisms refer to the means and practices implemented by each competitor to strengthen its own position. These are mainly product positioning, brand development, price discrimination and promotions for different market segments, as well as advertising. In the context of public procurement, access to market by competitors depends broadly on two factors: experience in the preparation of proposals (technical and administrative) and lower offer prices.

Nevertheless, public procurement practitioners highlighted the existence of other procedures that distort, voluntarily or not, competition. Table 11.14 presents the main practices encountered in public procurements classified based on the steps of the procurement lifecycle.

These practices and behaviours differ in their frequency as well as their impact on competition. For instance, practices such as designation of fake competitors in two-stage tenders and false contradictory quotes seem frequent and detrimental to competition. Agreement to divide the market to ensure more profits compared to real competition is also a practice that strongly distorts competition but is much less frequent. Similarly, the practice of fragmenting public spending, which allows a competitive procurement to be transformed into a call for quotations, while of medium frequency, is highly detrimental to competition.

The analysis highlights the prevalence of situations characterized by poor enforcement of procurement regulations or implementation of contracts contradicting the spirit of the regulations. Nearly two-thirds of behaviours and practices distorting competition are due to a deliberate intention or serious negligence on the part of the actors. Even though these are usually unauthorized behaviours, weak controls and the absence of effective sanctions make them persist and flourish. Lack of technical skills of the key players does not in itself harm competition but it promotes the development of anticompetitive behaviour. The most frequent and harmful practices relate to call for quotations.

POLICY RECOMMENDATIONS

To improve competition in public procurement, actors need to change current practices that result from three elements: (1) existing regulations, (2) actors' competence with regard to those regulations and their market knowledge and (3) actors' degree of compliance with existing regulations. It is should be possible to reinforce competition in public procurement based on the pillars of regulations, actors' competence, and monitoring and control devices to increase compliance (see Table 11.15).

This chapter's recommendations have been developed around those pillars. They entail the following actions on the part of the legislative or executive branches of government:

Recommendations Related to Regulations

- Amend the regulations to strengthen provisions that support competition: regulations should guarantee transparency of procedures, limit officials' discretion to prevent abuses and reduce entry barriers to public procurement.
- Pursue implementation of the electronic submission system: electronic procedures structure exchanges among actors in public procurement

Table 11.14 Competition distorting procedures in the procurement lifecycle

Steps lifecycle	Description
Procurement preparation	1. Preparation of tender documents by simple copy of pre-existing documents.
	2. Preparation of tender documents by a bidder.
	3. Drafting of an undifferentiated tender although the procurement involves different elements.
	4. Fragmenting public expenditure in order to be able to use call for quotations and escape the tendering procedure.
Applicants' eligibility	1. Excessive weight given to reference certificates in bids' assessment.
	2. Fake or misleading reference certificates among suppliers of the same sector, or between a parent company and its subsidiary.
	3. Excessive requirements on profiles and requested experts.
	4. Inclusion of experts in the bid, which will not be mobilized in the procurement.
	5. Request an excessive bid security deposit.
Contract award	1. Designation of fake competitors in two-stage tenders.
	2. Agreement to divide market (territorial agreements) to ensure more profits compared to real competition.
	3. Complacent bids (false contradictory quotes, less competitive).
	4. Unspecified assessment criteria of technical proposals in tendering of works and supplies.
	5. Meeting of the commission despite the lack of quorum or absence of a mandatory member of the commission (representative of the contractor, the service manager or the Ministry of Finance).
	6. Favouritism linked to connections between the experts involved in technical commissions and some bidders.
	7. Cancelling of *a priori* valid tender.
	8. Rejection of competitors on formal grounds (missing signature of special requirements' document, etc.).
	9. Lack of complaints by harmed bidders.
Procurement contract implementation	1. Agreed change in quantity in the case of a procurement using unit prices, agreed change between technical services and the supplier (example: during construction, due changes in prices of building materials).
	2. Adjustment of implementation period through stop and resume orders.
	3. Excessive or insufficient time to witness service done.

Table 11.14 (continued)

Steps lifecycle	Description
	4. Intentional implementation of a lower-than-expected service in order to lower the price in the financial offer. 5. Use of non-authorized subcontractors by the regulations to implement part of works. Generally subcontractors without required qualifications or authorized subcontractor but implementing more than 50 per cent of the contract.

Source: Conseil de la Concurrence and Mazars (n.d.).

Table 11.15 Three pillars of influence on actors' behaviours

Pillar 1	What do actors have the right and/or duty to do?	Regulation: promote the three principles that support competition (transparency, equal treatment simplified procedures).
Pillar 2	What are actors good at?	Competence: ensure professionalization of public purchaser (train procuring staff, respect professional standards and code of ethics, have procedures and structures dedicated to foster competence).
Pillar 3	What do actors tend to do?	Monitoring and control: ensure compliance with regulations and requirements via effective control and sanction mechanisms and by better treatment of complains.

Source: Conseil de la Concurrence and Mazars (n.d.).

and reduce their physical interaction. They ease procedures and reduce opportunities for illicit agreements or favouritism.

- Strengthen the independence and effectiveness of the redress mechanism: appeal is a necessary mechanism to move towards healthier competition. It should allow unsatisfied bidders to check the honesty and rigour of the procuring authority's decisions and be a critical piece in changing actors' behaviour.

Recommendations Related to Staff Training

- Grant recognition and professional status to public purchasers: the public purchaser is the weakest link in the expenditure chain.

Strengthening their status and increasing their responsibilities make them less susceptible to bribes that distort competition.
- Upgrade public procurement documents (special requirements): procurement documents are important for avoiding distortion of competition, either through favouritism or through non-participation of suppliers who find it difficult to understand contracting authorities' requests.
- Ensure mastery of procedures at all levels: deep knowledge of public procurement procedures on the part of officials, alongside a broad vision of markets, are essential for detecting signs of bid-rigging.

Recommendations Related to Monitoring and Control

- Check the need for spending: an unjustified tender or tender with unnecessary items is the first step that could lead to fraud and to situations of non-competition. By controlling the opportunity of spending, it would be possible to detect these situations and restore fair competition.
- Strengthen post-tender performance-based control: the objective is to assess the quality of deliverables and prevent favouritism that distorts competition at the expense of the contracting authority needs. Post-tender controls can also highlight situations of collusion among suppliers.
- Ensure better governance in public management and enforce sanctions: changing actors' behaviour requires enforcing sanctions for non-compliance with regulations. Penalties should be effective regardless of the hierarchical position of those involved.

CONCLUSIONS

This chapter highlights the difficulty that new entrants have in accessing public procurements. Indeed, to be able to participate, any new supplier must justify substantial experience through certificates and references to avoid rejection. Facing procurement staff concerned with justifying their selection and sometimes without means to assess the substance of a proposal, the 'volume of experience' tends to become the criterion by default that is hard to contest.

Barriers to access stem from other factors: grey areas of the regulations may deter potential new entrants from bidding. Two particular phases are singled out: procurement preparation and procurement implementation. Currently, both phases are poorly regulated and officials have regularly to deal with complex technical requirements and subtle regulations with neither the right training nor detailed guidelines to support them. This situation (deliberately or not) nurtures practices unfavourable to competition by including poorly drafted tendering documents or those with specifications likely to favour a particular supplier, inaccurate cost and time estimates, and difficulties in monitoring and controlling contract implementation. Those deficiencies offer fertile grounds for unscrupulous suppliers to save on their costs by cheating on the quality of deliverables.

Although the overwhelming majority of contracts awarded by major contracting entities have taken the form of open tenders, the most intricate and large procurements are implemented under a negotiated procedure with no room for competition.

Such a competition environment has led suppliers to adapt their strategies as to maximize their chances of winning contracts by focusing on specific niches not only in terms of business sectors but also in terms of territories and contracting entities.

Overall, public procurements do not seem to face a market that lacks competition. Nevertheless, the chapter findings indicate that to succeed in public procurement it is better for suppliers to focus on a limited number of procuring entities. Due to their high risk-aversion, government buyers tend to prefer suppliers they know and trust. The absence of guarantees for complaints, systematic audits and controls of markets pushes suppliers to develop 'privileged' relationships with targeted procuring authorities. Such behaviour does not necessarily mean that agreements or corruption are present.

The overall market size allows new bidders to access markets and various competition situations to coexist. In practice, however, barriers to entry can be very significant in the form of references and past experience. Corruption and favouritism are two other barriers that limit competition. Potential agreements among suppliers in the same sector may be distorting competition and limiting opportunities for a large number of competitors. This finding justifies the need to strengthen the role of the competition authority in addressing public procurement competition concerns.

The chapter also emphasizes the difficulties for procuring officers in drafting technical specifications and the high frequency of problems of implementation. Bidders consider that the process of awarding contracts is mostly done fairly and provides room for competition but they also point to the presence of many remaining situations of favouritism that are difficult to challenge.

It will be vital to grant the status of law to the rules governing public procurement and strengthen the appeal system and protect bidders' rights. Equally important is to better define sanctions – either administrative or, if appropriate, criminal – to punish non-compliance. The government also needs to ensure that professionally trained procurement staff monitor supplier behaviour and detect cases of non-compliance. The government should also review the function of the public buyer and create a system for sharing information and experience among public buyers. Finally, it should consider the establishment of a public procurement observatory to be in charge of analyzing public expenditure and detecting cartels and other competition distorting behaviours.

NOTES

1. This chapter is based to a very large extent on the synthesis report of the study undertaken by the Morocco's Competition Council (Conseil de la Concurrence) and Mazars (n.d.) entitled, *Réalisation d'une étude sur la concurrentiabilité des marchés publics*. We would like to thank the president of the Competition Council Dr Abdelali Benamour and the council's secretary-general Dr Mohamed Merghadi for their unconditional support.
2. This is also known as purchase orders.
3. The largest value contracts are issued for strategic interventions such as the programme to mitigate the impact of climate change and the influenza vaccination campaign.
4. Data is insufficient to make this calculation for the Ministry of Energy and for the rural commune of SYZ.

REFERENCES

Conseil de la Concurrence and Mazars (n.d.) *Réalisation d'une étude sur la concurrentiabilité des marchés publics*, Maroc: Rapport de synthèse.
OECD (2009a) *Enhancing Integrity in Public Procurement: OECD Joint Learning Study on Morocco*, Paris: Organisation for Economic Co-operation and Development.
OECD (2009b) *Guidelines for the Fight Against Bid Rigging in Public Procurement*, Paris: Organisation for Economic Co-operation and Development.
Sánchez Graells, A. (2015), *Public Procurement and the EU Competition Rules*, 2nd edn, Oxford and Portland, OR: Hart Publishing.

Index

abuse of dominance
Argentinian TV distribution services 207–8, 216
Armenian consumer goods distribution sector 11, 56–8, 60–66, 67–8, 69, 72
Costa Rican supermarkets sector 11–12, 31, 32–3, 50
Indian public procurement 17–18, 231, 233, 240–46
Malian cereals market 83
Moroccan public procurement 17–18
Uzbekistani money transfers market 3, 178–9, 181, 185–6
and vertical arrangements 10
Vietnamese pharmaceuticals sector 142, 153–4, 155, 157
Zambian beef, poultry and milk sectors 12, 95, 98–9, 101, 113–18
AC Inversora (Argentina) 209, 213
'active' market power 124, 128, 138
advertising
Argentinian TV distribution services 194, 200–201, 203, 209, 214
Armenian consumer goods distribution sector 58, 68, 71
Indian public procurement 19, 225, 235, 236, 239, 242, 247
Jamaican pharmaceuticals sector 125
Vietnamese pharmaceuticals sector 147–8, 149, 155
AFA (Argentine Football Association) 202–3, 205
Afrodita (Argentina) 206
AFSCA (Federal Authority for Audiovisual Communication Services, Argentina) 202
'à la carte' programming 217
anticompetitive conduct
Argentinian TV distribution services 16, 192, 202–8, 211, 212–17
Armenian consumer goods distribution sector 55, 56–9, 60–73
Costa Rican supermarkets sector 30, 32–3, 34–5, 41, 52
and cross-cutting issues 24
and foodstuffs distribution 10–11, 12
Indian public procurement 17, 18–20, 232–46
Jamaican pharmaceuticals sector 13, 125, 128, 133, 134–8, 140
Malian cereals market 83–4, 91–2
Moroccan public procurement 17, 18–20, 257, 268–76, 277–8, 279–80
and state of competition 4–5
Uzbekistani money transfers market 164–5, 166, 178–80, 185–7, 189
Vietnamese pharmaceuticals sector 142–3, 148–55
Zambian beef, poultry and milk sectors 95–6, 113–17
see also under individual types of anticompetitive conduct
APIC (Antimonopoly Policy Improvement Center) 163, 170, 182, 185, 189
Argentinian TV distribution services
abuse of dominance 207–8, 216
advertising 194, 200–201, 203, 209, 214
anticompetitive conduct 192, 202–8, 211, 212–17
cable television 191, 194–6, 201, 202–8, 215, 217
codified television 192, 195, 198, 199, 215
collusion 16, 213

competition law 191, 192, 202, 207, 214–16
concerted practices 202–4
and cross-cutting issues 21, 22
economics of content production 201–2
entry barriers 209
evolution of TV industry 191–3
exclusionary practices 202, 204–7, 214–15
free-to-air television 191, 193–4, 198–9, 200, 208, 209–10, 216
horizontal integration 191, 192, 204, 205, 206–7, 208–10, 211, 212–14
major competition cases 202–11
and market power 213–16
merger cases 208–11, 212–15
monopolies/monopolistic practices 192, 197, 209, 211–17
pay-per-view television 192, 197, 198, 208, 215
pay-television 191, 194–202, 210
policy implications/changes 212–17
practical research problems 9
price-fixing 192, 193, 203–4, 212
and product market groupings 15–16
satellite television 191, 194, 195, 197, 200, 206, 208
and state of competition 6, 7
vertical integration 191, 192, 200, 201–2, 204–6, 208, 209, 210–11, 214–15
ARIL (Arshiya Rail Infrastructure Limited, India) 240
Armenian consumer goods distribution sector
abuse of dominance 11, 56–8, 60–66, 67–8, 69, 72
advertising 58, 68, 71
anticompetitive conduct 55, 56–9, 60–73
beer market 64–5
butter and vegetable oil market 63
coercive conduct in vertical agreements 67–71
competition authority (SCPEC) 55, 56–69, 70, 72
competition law 55, 56–7, 58, 62, 64, 66, 67–9, 72
context of study 55–9
and cross-cutting issues 21, 22, 24
eggs market 61–2
exclusivity deals 58, 60, 67, 68, 69
legal treatment of distribution arrangements 59–60
meat products market 65–6
monopolies/monopolistic practices 56, 60, 72
non-food consumer goods market 66–7
practical research problems 8–9
and product market groupings 9, 10, 11
scope and summary findings of study 54–5
selected product market decisions 60–67
and state of competition 6
state-owned enterprises 11, 55–6, 57
sugar market 63–4
under-reporting of economic activities 57, 60
unfair trade/competition 58, 60–61, 67–8
Artear (Argentina) 198–9, 210
Arzni Pedigree CPS (Armenia) 61–2
Association of Ukrainian Banks 185
ASUM (Asociación de Supermercados) 40–41, 49
ATC (Anatomical Therapeutic Classification) 157–8
Atlántica Comunicaciones (Argentina) 209, 213
Automercados (supermarket, Costa Rica) 36, 37
Azia Express (Russian–Uzbek money transfer system) 180, 182

banking system (Uzbekistan) 164, 165, 167–9, 170–72, 174–5, 188
beef, poultry and milk sectors (Zambia) *see* Zambian beef, poultry and milk sectors
beer market (Armenia) 64–5
benefits of negotiation (Costa Rican supermarkets sector) 47
Better Regulation Commission (Costa Rica) 34

BHEL (Bharat Heavy Electricals Limited) 224–5, 234–5, 239
bid-rigging
Indian public procurement sector 18, 19, 231–2, 233, 239, 241–2, 243–5, 247, 248, 251–2
Moroccan public procurement sector 19, 20, 254, 263, 272–5, 279
bioequivalence 128–9
Bokomo (Zambia) 107, 108, 117–18
broiler chickens market (Zambia) 103–7, 108, 116–17
butter and vegetable oil market (Armenia) 63

Cable Grande vs. EDEERSA (2003) 206
cable television (Argentina) 191, 194–6, 201, 202–8, 215, 217
Cablevisión (Argentina) 192, 195–6, 197, 203, 204–5, 207, 210, 215
CAG (Comptroller and Auditor General, India) 226, 229–30, 231, 234–5, 239, 244, 251
'call for quotations' 18–19, 264, 268–71, 276, 277
Canal 7 (Argentina) 193–4
cartels
in Indian public procurement 231–2, 235, 239, 241–2, 243–6, 248
in Moroccan public procurement 257, 274–5, 281
CCI (Competition Commission of India) 226, 231–2, 236, 240–41, 244–5, 250, 251–2
CDCE (State Committee of the Republic of Uzbekistan on Demonopolization, Support of Competition
and Entrepreneurship) 163, 179–80, 189
Central Bank of Uzbekistan 164, 168–70, 174–5, 188
central planning 11, 55–6
Central Vigilance Commission Act (India, 2003) 226
cereals market (Mali) *see* Malian cereals market
CIL (Coal India Ltd) 241
CIS (Commonwealth of Independent States) 163, 165, 185
CNDC (National Commission of Competition Defense, Argentina) 192, 202–11, 213, 215–16
CNDC vs. TRISA, TSC and others (2002) 213
Coca-Cola Company 70, 72–3
codified television (Argentina) 192, 195, 198, 199, 215
Cold Storage Board (Zambia) 96
collusion
Argentinian TV distribution services 16, 213
Armenian consumer goods distribution sector 67
Indian public procurement 231, 232, 233, 241–5, 246–52
Jamaican pharmaceuticals sector 125–6, 128, 131, 135–8
Moroccan public procurement 254, 257, 262, 263, 272, 274, 279
and public procurement 17, 20
and state of competition 4
Vietnamese pharmaceuticals sector 142, 143, 152, 156
COMFER (Federal Broadcasting Committee, Argentina) 193, 195
Competition Act (India, 2002) 231–2, 240, 245
'competition allies' 128
competition analysis 5, 7, 15–16, 17, 22–3
Competition and Commission Protection Act (Zambia, 2010) 115
Competition and Consumer Protection Commission (Zambia) 117–18
competition culture 23
Competition Directorate (European Commission) 117
Competition Enforcement Authority (Costa Rica) 34–5
Competition Law (Costa Rica, 1994) 33–4
concerted practices (Argentinian TV distribution services) 202–4
concerted submissions 272
CONCOR (Container Corporation of India Limited) 240–41

consensus (in collusive agreements) 125, 126
Constitution of India 223
consumer goods distribution sector (Armenia) *see* Armenian consumer goods distribution sector
consumer welfare standard 2
Contact (Russian money transfer system) 172–3, 175, 176, 181, 185, 186
COPROCOM (Commission of the Promotion of Competition, Costa Rica) 30, 34–5, 41–2, 48–9, 51, 52
Costa Rican supermarkets sector
  abuse of dominance 11–12, 31, 32–3, 50
  anticompetitive conduct 30, 32–3, 34–5, 41, 52
  benefits of negotiation 47
  changes in worldwide supermarket business 29–30
  Commission of the Promotion of Competition 30, 34–5, 41–2, 48–9, 51, 52
  Competition Enforcement Authority 34–5
  competition issues in retail distribution 31–2
  Competition Law 33–4
  consumers' shopping outlet choices 38–42, 50
  and cross-cutting issues 22
  degree of difficulty assessments 45
  household consumer survey 38–9
  information requests 46–7
  information sources and definitions of terms 30–31
  location preferences 39–40
  main market actors 35–8
  market concentration 11, 31, 32, 48–50
  market power 38
  market transparency 31, 41, 51
  monopolies/monopolistic practices 30, 33, 34, 41, 47, 51
  own-brand products 47–8, 51
  and product market groupings 9, 10, 11–12
  regulatory framework for competition promotion 33–5
  and state of competition 7
  summary findings of study 32–3
  supermarket–supplier relationships/transactions 42–8, 50–51
Crest Chickens (Zambia) 103, 105, 107
cross-cutting issues 21–4
cross-subsidization 9, 12, 109, 116–17
CSR Nanjing Puzhen Co Ltd vs. Kolkata Metro Rail Corporation Ltd (2010) 236
CSU (supermarket, Costa Rica) 35, 36, 37, 38, 39, 44
CVC (Central Vigilance Commission, India) 226, 229, 231, 235, 236–7, 238, 249, 251

Dangerous Drug Act (Jamaica, 1948) 126
DAV (Drug Administration of Vietnam) 145, 146, 149, 153, 154, 155, 157
day-old broiler chicks market (Zambia) 103, 107, 108
DBS (direct broadcast satellites) 195, 197
Decotevé vs. Pramer (2000) 215
Decotevé vs. TRISA and TSC (2003) 205
degree of difficulty assessments (Costa Rican supermarkets sector) 45
Department of National Defence (Morocco) 256
detection (in collusive agreements) 125
Dirección General de Comercio de Misiones vs. Posadas Cable and Televisión Misionera (2002) 207–8
DirecTV (Argentina) 197, 200, 205–6, 211
dissemination activities 8, 125–6, 128, 136–7, 139–40, 158, 274
DNCC (National Directorate for Trade and Competition, Mali) 84
DoJ (Department of Justice, USA) 187
drug certification 14, 140

EC (European Commission) 72–3, 117
economic regulation 5, 6
eggs market (Armenia) 61–2

EMC (Armenia) 67
entry barriers
Argentinian TV distribution services 209
Indian public procurement 19, 232, 233–40, 247, 248
Jamaican pharmaceuticals sector 125–6, 136
Moroccan public procurement 19, 256–7, 268–72, 276, 279–80
Vietnamese pharmaceuticals sector 14, 146
Zambian beef, poultry and milk sectors 118
e-procurement 20, 248, 274
EU (European Union) 10–11, 23, 256
Eureka Chickens (Zambia) 107
exclusionary practices 4, 16, 115, 134–5, 178, 186–7, 202, 204–7, 214–15, 231, 238
exclusivity deals
Armenian consumer goods distribution sector 58, 60, 67, 68, 69
Jamaican pharmaceuticals sector 134–5
Uzbekistani money transfers market 164, 166, 178–80, 185, 187, 188
Zambian beef, poultry and milk sectors 100–102, 105, 107, 112, 114–16
'experience and references' criterion 258
experience goods 14, 128
'extra-contractual' behaviour 70, 72

fake bids 272, 275
FCA (Fair Competition Act, Jamaica) 123–4, 135
FIEs (foreign invested enterprises) 150
Finta (Zambia) 111
'first-mover' company 3–4, 16, 172
Flamingo (Zambia) 109
Flesh (Armenia) 66
Food and Drug Act (Jamaica, 1975) 126
food security 6, 75, 76, 92
Food Security Commissariat (Mali) 92
foreign direct investment (FDI) 3, 29, 95, 109, 168
Fox Sports (TV channel) 204–5, 210–11
free-to-air television (Argentina) 191, 193–4, 198–9, 200, 208, 209–10, 216
FTC (Fair Trading Commission, Jamaica) 138, 139

Geghard Meat Factory (Armenia) 65–6
General Treasury (Morocco) 260–61
generic drugs 13–14, 123, 126, 128–9, 130–31, 133–4, 139–40
GFR (General Financial Rules, India) 223–5, 226, 227–9, 231, 234–5, 236–7, 238, 239, 243, 247
Gosbank (Uzbekistan) 168
Gossell-Williams, M. 126
gross margins (Malian cereals market) 84–6

Harriott, K.K. 125
Hart, O.D. 124
HBO (TV channel) 205–6
health insurance 13, 15, 123, 131, 143, 146
HHI (Herfindahl–Hirschman Index) 48–9, 98–9, 105–9, 177, 265–8
Hick Media 210–11, 215
horizontal agreements/integration
Argentinian TV distribution services 191, 192, 204, 205, 206–7, 208–10, 21, 212–14
Costa Rican supermarkets sector 31
and cross-cutting issues 21
Jamaican pharmaceuticals sector 131–2, 135–8
Vietnamese pharmaceuticals sector 148, 153
horizontal restraints 10, 205
household consumer survey (Costa Rica) 38–9
Hybrid Poultry (Zambia) 103, 105, 107, 108

IBOPE (television audience-measuring company, Argentina) 194, 195
IBs (innovator brand drugs) 152
Ideas del Sur (Argentina) 201

IDRC (International Development Research Centre) 8
Imagen Satelital (Argentina) 199, 200, 206, 209, 210
Imagen Satelital vs. Cablevisión (2004) 206
IMF (International Monetary Fund) 94
inclusion (in collusive agreements) 125–6
INDEC (National Institute of Statistics and the Census, Argentina) 195
Indian public procurement
  abuse of dominance 17–18, 231, 233, 240–46
  administrative oversight bodies 226, 229–30
  administrative regulation 223–5
  and advertising 19, 225, 235, 236, 239, 242, 247
  anticompetitive conduct 17, 18–20, 232–46
  assessment of regulatory framework 230–31
  bid-rigging 18, 19, 231–2, 233, 239, 241–2, 243–5, 247, 248, 251–2
  cartels 231–2, 235, 239, 241–2, 243–6, 248
  and collusion 231, 232, 233, 241–5, 246–52
  constitutional principles 223
  coordination and awareness-raising 251–2
  and cross-cutting issues 21, 22
  entry barriers 19, 232, 233–40, 247, 248
  e-procurement 248
  evaluation of bids 237–8
  facilitating factors in regulatory framework 242–3
  and Integrity Pact 20
  legislative and administrative rules 223–5
  limited tenders and pre-qualified suppliers 238–9, 247
  open tenders 18–19, 224–5, 234–5, 239, 247
  policy reform 246–52
  predatory pricing 239–40, 242, 243, 244
  and product market groupings 17–20
  recent reform efforts 249–50
  regulatory framework 223–32
  scale and economic importance of 221–2
  state-level and other relevant legislation 225–6
  and state of competition 6
  state-owned enterprises (PSUs) 221, 223–4, 227, 234–5, 236, 239, 240–41
  supply-side legislation 231–2
  transparency of processes 224, 226, 228, 231, 238–9, 243, 247–51
  unreasonable terms and conditions of tender invitations 236–7
  and value for money 221–2
Indian Contract Act (India, 1872) 226
Industry Canada 126
information asymmetry 14, 15, 124, 125–6, 130–31, 136, 138, 140
'information democracy' 214
information requests (Costa Rican supermarkets sector) 46–7
innovation 2, 7, 10, 13, 21, 109, 136, 146, 222, 233
International Competition Network 8
IP (Integrity Pact, India) 20, 249
IPRs (intellectual property rights) 146, 148, 149, 153, 154
IR (Indian Railways) 238–9, 243, 244–6
IRP (international reference price) 152

Jamaican pharmaceuticals sector
  affordability of drugs 123–4, 140
  anticompetitive conduct 13, 125, 128, 133, 134–8, 140
  and collusion 125–6, 128, 131, 135–8
  competition law 123–4, 125, 132, 135
  competition related issues 128–38
  entry barriers 125–6, 136
  exclusivity deals 134–5
  and generic drugs 13–14, 123, 126, 128–9, 130–31, 133–4, 139–40
  horizontal agreements 131–2, 135–8

information and competition 128–31, 139
and information asymmetry 14, 15, 124, 125–6, 130–31, 136, 138, 140
localized competition 132–4
market players' connections 131–2
market power 123, 124–5, 128, 132–4, 135, 138
market segmentation 132, 133, 135
market transparency 14, 136–7
and product market groupings 13–15
public pre-announcements 137–8
rationale and background of study 124–6
resale price maintenance 128, 135, 138, 140
and state of competition 6
study findings and policy issues 138–40
study methodology 126–8
tied-selling 128, 134, 135, 138
vertical integration 131–2, 137–8
Jamaica Gazette 126, 127
JCC (Jamaica Chamber of Commerce) 136

Kachema Meat Company (Zambia) 97
Kagh Petrol Service (Armenia) 66
Kaplow, L. 125
KIA Motors 67
Kitzmuller, M. 2
KMA (Kingstown Metropolitan Area) 127, 129
Kotayk Brewery (Armenia) 64

Lande, R.H. 125
last-minute purchases 40, 41, 50
Law of the Republic of Armenia on Protection of Economic Competition (2000) 55, 56–7, 58, 62, 64, 66, 67–9, 72
Law of the Republic of Armenia on Trade and Services (2011) 59
Liberty Media 210–11, 215
Licetti, M.M. 2
localized competition 132–4
'lowest bidder' rule 18, 245, 255, 258–9, 272
LPG (liquid petroleum gas) 236, 240
LPG (lowest-priced generic) drugs 152
Lusakert Pedigree Poultry Plant (Armenia) 61–2

major operators (Malian cereals market) 82
Majoru Investments Limited (Zambia) 97
Malian cereals market
anticompetitive conduct 83–4, 91–2
assembly market 84
cereal consumption 78–80
cereal production 77–8
collecting market 84–6
cross-border trade flows 80, 83
and cross-cutting issues 24
and food security 6, 75, 76, 92
gross margins 84–6
intermediaries 77, 84, 87, 92
international market price transmission 86–91
liberalization of 75–6
major operators 82
market competition 82–4
market dynamics 77–82
market information system 86, 92
and market power 91
methodology of study 76–7
price-setting 80, 82–4
price transmission 80, 84–91
and product market groupings 9, 12
production market 84–5
retail market 84–5, 86
small-scale operators 82
and state of competition 6, 7
subsidized imports 75, 81, 83, 85, 92
supply and distribution channels 80–82
wholesale/semi-wholesale market 77, 81–2, 84–7, 90–91
Mar del Plata (Argentina) 209, 213
market concentration
Costa Rican supermarkets sector 11, 31, 32, 48–50
Jamaican pharmaceuticals sector 123, 132
Moroccan public procurement 258, 264, 265–8

Uzbekistani money transfers market 177, 189
Vietnamese pharmaceuticals sector 143, 144–5, 148, 150, 154, 155, 157
Zambian beef, poultry and milk sectors 98–9, 105–9, 117
market division 148, 152, 192, 212, 272, 276, 277
market failures 5, 6, 23, 126
market information system (Malian cereals market) 86, 92
market infrastructure 7, 23–4, 110, 154, 188
'market making' institutions 5, 12, 23–4
market niches 5–6, 255, 280
market power 2, 4, 10–14
Argentinian TV distribution services 213–16
Costa Rican supermarket sector 38
Jamaican pharmaceuticals sector 123, 124–5, 128, 132–4, 135, 138
Malian cereals market 91
Vietnamese pharmaceuticals sector 145, 146, 148, 150, 152, 152, 155–6
Uzbekistani money transfers market 186–7
market segmentation 132, 133, 135, 255
market transparency
Costa Rican supermarkets sector 31, 41, 51
Indian public procurement 224, 226, 228, 231, 238–9, 243, 247–51
Jamaican pharmaceuticals sector 14, 136–7
Moroccan public procurement 256–7, 273–4, 276, 278
Uzbekistani international money transfer market 165, 189
Vietnamese pharmaceuticals sector 14, 155, 158
market/trade liberalization
and Costa Rican supermarkets sector 29
and cross-cutting issues 23
and foodstuffs distribution 10
and Malian cereals market 75–6
and Zambian beef, poultry and milk sectors 94–5, 96, 109, 113
marketing approach (to tariff-setting) 181
Marvel, H.P. 125
meat products market (Armenia) 65–6
'meeting of minds' 58, 67
Mega Eggs (Zambia) 117–18
Mega Super (supermarket, Costa Rica) 35–6, 37, 38
MEIC (Ministry of Economy, Industry and Trade, Costa Rica) 34, 35
Ministry of Agriculture and Fisheries (Morocco) 261–3, 264, 265–8, 270, 271, 272
Ministry of Energy, Mining, Water and Environment (Morocco) 261–3, 264, 265–8
Ministry of Equipment and Transport (Morocco) 261–3, 273
Ministry of Health (Morocco) 261–3
MoneyGram 171, 172–3, 175, 176, 182, 185
money transfer market (Uzbekistan) *see* Uzbekistani international money transfer market
monopolies/monopolistic practices 9
Argentinian TV distribution services 192, 197, 209, 211–17
Armenian consumer goods distribution sector 56, 60, 72
Costa Rican supermarkets sector 30, 33, 34, 41, 47, 51
Indian public procurement 232–3
Jamaican pharmaceuticals sector 124, 125
and pharmaceuticals distribution 13
Uzbekistani money transfers market 163, 166, 175, 179, 181, 185–8
Zambian beef, poultry and milk sectors 94–5, 96, 99, 101, 103, 105, 111, 113–15
MoR (Ministry of Railways, India) 240–41
Moroccan public procurement
abuse of dominance 17–18
admissibility and pre-qualification regulations 257–8

anticompetitive conduct 17, 18–20, 257, 268–76, 277–8, 279–80
bidding conditions 258–9
bid-rigging 19, 20, 254, 263, 272–5, 279
business sectors 265–6, 280
call for quotations 264, 268–71, 276, 277
cartels 257, 274–5, 281
and collusion 254, 257, 262, 263, 272, 274, 279
competition distorting practices 275–6, 277–8
complaints and litigation procedures 259–60
concerted submissions 272
entry barriers 19, 256–7, 268–72, 276, 279–80
'lowest bidder' rule 245, 255, 258–9, 272
market concentration 258, 264, 265–8
market division 272, 276, 277
market niches 255, 280
market size 260–65, 280
monitoring and control 255, 276, 278, 279, 280–81
negotiated procurement 269–71
open tenders 18–19, 255, 256, 261–2, 268–72, 280
policy recommendations 276–9
procurement preparation 277, 279–80
and product market groupings 17–20
regulatory framework 256–60
restricted tendering 256, 269–71
scope of study 254–5
and state of competition 6, 7
training of officials 255, 274, 278–9, 280, 281
transparency of processes 256–7, 273–4, 276, 278
two-stage tendering 256, 268–71, 276

Moscow Arbitration Court 186–7
M/S Pankaj Gas Cylinders Ltd vs. Indian Oil Corporation Ltd (2011) 236, 240
Multicanal (Argentina) 192, 195–6, 197, 200, 201, 203, 204–5, 207
Multicanal vs. Fox Sports and others (2004) 204–5
Mwaiseni Stores (Zambia) 96
'mystery shoppers' 41

National Bank of Ukraine 185
national champions 23
National Consumer Commission (Costa Rica) 34
National Court of Appeals on Criminal Economic Matters (Argentina) 204
National University of Córdoba vs. Durford (1997) 208, 216
nature of investigations 2, 8–9
'negative clearance' 117
negotiated procurement 269–71
NIC (National Informatics Centre, India) 235
NIEC (National Import and Export Corporation, Zambia) 94, 96
non-food consumer goods market (Armenia) 66–7

OECD (Organisation for Economic Co-operation and Development) 8, 23, 34, 221, 244, 247, 272–5
OMA (Observatoire du Marché Agricole, Mali) 86
OMI (organizations and methods instructions) 224
OPAM (Agency for Agricultural Produce) 75, 81, 83
open tenders
in Indian public procurement 18–19, 224–5, 234–5, 239, 247
in Moroccan public procurement 18–19, 255, 256, 261–2, 268–72, 280
own-brand products (Costa Rican supermarkets sector) 47–8, 51

PAC (Public Accounts Committee, India) 229–30
Parmalat (Zambia) 111, 112–13
'passive' market power 124, 125, 138
patents 13–14, 123, 124, 140, 142, 146, 156
pay-per-view television (Argentina) 192, 197, 198, 208, 215

pay-television (Argentina) 191, 194–202, 210
PCJ (Pharmacy Council of Jamaica) 126, 127, 136
PDAs (Provincial Departments of Agriculture, Morocco) 264, 266–8
Perimercados (supermarket, Costa Rica) 35, 36, 37, 38
Pharmaceutical Council of Jamaica 126
pharmaceuticals sector (Jamaica) *see* Jamaican pharmaceuticals sector
pharmaceuticals sector (Vietnam) *see* Vietnamese pharmaceuticals sector
Pharmacy Act (Jamaica, 1975) 126
PIOJ (Planning Institute of Jamaica) 127
Pol-Ka (Argentina) 201
Post Office network (Uzbekistan) 164, 165, 171, 189
powdered milk market (Zambia) 111–12
PPT (Pensado Para Televisión, Argentina) 201
practical research problems 8–9
Pramer (Argentina) 198–9, 200, 210, 215
predatory pricing 239–40, 242, 243, 244
Prevention of Corruption Act (India, 1988) 226
price controls 6, 34, 94, 142, 148
price-fixing
  Argentinian TV distribution services 192, 193, 203–4, 212, 216
  and horizontal restraints 10
  Indian public procurement 245
  Malian cereals market 91–2
  Vietnamese pharmaceuticals sector 142, 148, 150, 152, 154, 157
  Zambian beef, poultry and milk sectors 115
price-setting 56, 66, 72, 80, 82–4
Price Smart (supermarket, Costa Rica) 36, 37
price transmission 80, 84–91
PRMC (Programme to Restructure the Cereal Market) 75
procedural regulation 5–6, 7, 14
processed fresh milk market (Zambia) 111
Proconsumer vs. DirecTV and HBO (2003) 205–6
producer effects 1–2
product market groupings 1
  foodstuffs distribution 9–12
  pharmaceuticals distribution 13–15
  public procurement 17–20
  selected services 15–16
production efficiency 2, 97
PSJ (Pharmaceutical Society of Jamaica) 136
PSUs (public sector undertakings, India) 221, 223–4, 227, 234–5, 236, 239, 240–41
public pre-announcements 137–8
public procurement (India) *see* Indian public procurement
public procurement (Morocco) *see* Moroccan public procurement
Public Procurement Law of India (proposed) 223, 249–50, 252
punishment (in collusive agreements) 125
purchasing power 76, 90–91, 222

'quality checkers' 128

Rainbow Chicken Limited (Zambia) 118
RB (Railway Board, India) 240, 244–5
R.D. Shifty vs. International Airport Authority 28 (1979) 223
RDSO (Research Design and Standards Organization) 238–9
Real Meat Company (Zambia) 97
reconstituted milk market (Zambia) 111
Red Intercable (Argentina) 196
'refusal to stock' 68, 71
regulatory market barriers 268–71
restricted tendering 256, 269–71
Right to Information Act (India, 2005) 226
R. Lloveras vs. Cablevisión (2002) 207
Robinson, Joan 125
Ross Breeders (Zambia) 107
RPM (resale price maintenance) 128, 135, 138

Sale of Goods Act (India, 1930) 226
Salex Group (Armenia) 63–4
satellite television (Argentina) 191, 194, 195, 197, 200, 206, 208
SCPEC (State Commission for Protection of Economic Competition of Republic of Armenia) 55, 56–69, 70, 72
search goods 14, 128
Shapiro, C. 125
Shirak Gyumri Beer-Malt Factory (Armenia) 64, 65
Shoprite (supermarket, Zambia) 100–102, 105, 107, 112, 114–16
small-scale operators (Malian cereals market) 82
SmartPay technology 169
SMEs (small and medium-sized enterprises) 81, 92, 102, 149–50, 238, 274
social approach (to tariff-setting) 181
social regulation 5, 23
Standards and Regulation Division of the Ministry of Health (Jamaica, 1999) 126
state of competition 2, 3–7
 and anticompetitive conduct 4–5
 beef, poultry and milk sector (Zambia) 4, 7
 and cereals market (Mali) 6, 7
 and consumer goods distribution sector (Armenia) 6
 international money transfers (Uzbekistan) 3–4, 7
 and market infrastructure 7
 and market niches 5–6
 and pharmaceuticals sector 6
 and public procurement 6, 7
 and sector regulation 5–6
 and supermarkets sector (Costa Rica) 7
 and TV distribution services (Argentina) 6, 7
state-owned enterprises
 Armenian consumer goods distribution sector 11, 55–6, 57
 and Indian public procurement 221, 223–4, 227, 234–5, 236, 239, 240–41
 Vietnamese pharmaceuticals sector 147, 149
 Zambian beef, poultry and milk sectors 94–5, 96
STATIN (Statistical Institute of Jamaica) 127
Stigler, G. 124
strategic market barriers 268–71
'strategic partners' 132
structural market barriers 268–71
subsidies
 cross-subsidization 9, 12, 109, 116–17
 Malian cereals market 75, 81, 83, 85, 92
 and state of competition 6
 Zambian beef, poultry and milk sectors 109, 116–17
Supercanal (Argentina) 196, 205
Supercanal vs. Tevefé (2003) 205
sugar market (Armenia) 63–4
supermarkets sector (Costa Rica) *see* Costa Rican supermarkets sector
Surcor TV (Argentina) 207
Surcor TV vs. Cablevisión and Multicanal (2002) 207
Survey of Living Conditions (Jamaica, 2002) 127

table eggs market (Zambia) 107–9, 114, 117–18
'tacit collusion' 152
Tamil Nadu Act (India, 1998) 226, 227–9, 242
TC (Tender Committee) 237–8
technical approach (to tariff-setting) 181
Technical Support Unit (of COPROCOM) 35
Telecentro (Argentina) 196
Telecor (Argentina) 210
Teledifusora Bahiense (Argentina) 210
Teledifusora vs. TSC (2002) 205
Teledigital (Argentina) 196, 200, 209, 213
Telefónica (Argentina) 209, 213
Tevefé (Argentina) 198–9, 205
therapeutic equivalence 129–30, 146
tied-selling 128, 134, 135, 138, 142

Torneos y Competencias group (Argentina) 200, 211
total welfare standard 2
transaction costs 84, 86, 91
Transparency International 249
TRIPS (Trade-Related Aspects of Intellectual Property Rights) 154
TRISA (Argentina) 199, 200, 202–4, 205, 213, 215
TSC (Argentina) 199, 200, 202–4, 205, 213, 215
TV distribution services (Argentina) *see* Argentinian TV distribution services
two-stage tendering 247, 256, 268–71, 276
TyC Max/Sports (Argentina) 199, 200, 205, 209, 211

UNCITRAL (United Nations Commission on International Trade Law) 249–50, 256
UNCTAD (United Nations Conference on Trade and Development) 23, 72
unfair trade/competition 22, 34, 58, 60–61, 67–8, 143, 147, 148, 154–5
United Nations 8, 249–50
unprocessed (raw) fresh milk market (Zambia) 111
Uzbekistani international money transfer market
  abuse of dominance 3, 178–9, 181, 185–6
  anticompetitive conduct 164–5, 166, 178–80, 185–7, 189
  background of study 165–70
  banking system 164, 165, 167–9, 170–72, 174–5, 188
  competition investigations 182, 185–7
  and cross-cutting issues 22
  exclusivity deals 164, 166, 178–80, 185, 187, 188
  market concentration 177, 189
  market definition 170–72
  market participants/market share 172–7, 185
  market power 186–7
  market transparency 165, 189
  migration flows 163, 165, 166–8, 189
  monopolies 163, 166, 175, 179, 181, 185–8
  pricing behaviour 181–2
  production costs of payments 180–81
  and product market groupings 15–16
  recommendations 188–9
  regulatory framework for transfers 168–70
  remittance payments technology 170–71
  scope and summary findings of study 163–5, 188
  state of competition 3–4, 7
  tariff rates 164, 165, 181–2, 183–4, 188

value for money 18, 221–2, 257
VAT (value-added tax) 62, 90–91
VCA (Vietnam Competition Authority) 155, 157–8
VCC (Argentina) 202, 203, 204, 207
Venado Tuerto (Argentina) 209
Venus (Argentina) 206
Verino (Zambia) 103
vertical agreements/integration
  Argentinian TV distribution services 191, 192, 200, 201–2, 204–6, 208, 209, 210–11, 214–15
  Armenian consumer goods distribution sector 56, 67–71
  Costa Rican supermarkets sector 31–2
  and cross-cutting issues 21
  and foodstuffs distribution 10–11
  Jamaican pharmaceuticals sector 131–2, 137–8
  Uzbekistani money transfers market 163
  Vietnamese pharmaceuticals sector 147, 148–52, 155, 156–7
  Zambian beef, poultry and milk sectors 95, 103, 107, 114, 115, 118
Vietnamese pharmaceuticals sector
  abuse of dominance 142, 153–4, 155, 157

advertising 147–8, 149, 155
anticompetitive conduct 142–3, 148–55
collusion 142, 143, 152, 156
competition law 143, 144, 147–8, 150, 152, 153–6, 158
and cross-cutting issues 22
entry barriers 14, 146
healthcare policy objectives 142
horizontal agreements 148, 153
legal framework for drug distribution and competition 147–8
market concentration 143, 144–5, 148, 150, 154, 155, 157
market division 148, 152
market power 145, 146, 148, 150, 152, 152, 155–6
market structure 143–7
market transparency 14, 155, 158
policy recommendations 155–8
price-fixing 142, 148, 152
and product market groupings 13–15
and state of competition 6
unfair competition 143, 147, 148, 154–5
vertical integration 147, 148–52, 155, 156–7
Vietnam Competition Authority 143

Walmart Stores, Inc. (USA) 38
Western Union 164, 165, 170–71, 172–3, 174–5, 176–7, 178–82, 185–7, 188
WHO (World Health Organization) 123, 153, 157
Wolinsky, A. 124
World Bank 2, 13, 23, 87–90, 94, 256
WTO (World Trade Organization) 143, 148, 154, 250, 256

Yerevan Beer (Armenia) 64
Yerevan Poultry Plant (Armenia) 62

Zambeef (Zambia) 95–7, 98–9, 100–102, 105, 107, 112, 113–17
Zambian beef, poultry and milk sectors
abuse of dominance 12, 95, 98–9, 101, 113–18
anticompetitive conduct 95–6, 113–17
beef distribution channels 99–102
beef market structure 98–9
beef production 96–8
beef quality grades 98, 100, 101–2
and cross-cutting issues 22
and cross-subsidization 109, 116–17
day-old broiler chicks 103, 107, 108
entry barriers 118
exclusivity deals 100–102, 105, 107, 112, 114–16
foreign direct investment 95, 109
formal dairy sector 109–10
market concentration 98–9, 105–9, 117
market reforms and liberalization 94–5, 96, 109, 113
milk distribution 112–13
milk product markets 111–12
milk production system 110
monopolies/monopolistic practices 94–5, 96, 99, 101, 103, 105, 111, 113–15
nationalization programmes 94
poultry meat (broilers) 103–7, 108, 116–17
practical research problems 9
and product market groupings 9, 10, 12
restrictions on movement of livestock 97–8, 99, 104
and state of competition 4, 7
study background 94–6
subsidies 109, 116–17
table eggs market 107–9, 114, 117–18
and vertical integration 95, 103, 107, 114, 115, 118
Zambia Dairy Processors Association 111
Zambian Competition Commission 117
Zamchick (Zambia) 103, 104, 107, 108, 109, 118
Zammilk (Zambia) 111, 112–13
ZCBC (Zambia Consumer Buying Corporation) 94, 96